The Precip

Ivan Aleksandrovich Goncharov

Alpha Editions

This edition published in 2024

ISBN 9789361472404

Design and Setting By

Alpha Editions
www.alphaedis.com

Email - info@alphaedis.com

As per information held with us this book is in Public Domain.
This book is a reproduction of an important historical work.
Alpha Editions uses the best technology to reproduce historical work
in the same manner it was first published to preserve its original nature.
Any marks or number seen are left intentionally to preserve.

Contents

PREFACE	- 1 -
CHAPTER I	- 3 -
CHAPTER II	- 11 -
CHAPTER III	- 16 -
CHAPTER IV	- 21 -
CHAPTER V	- 26 -
CHAPTER VI	- 30 -
CHAPTER VII	- 42 -
CHAPTER VIII	- 51 -
CHAPTER IX	- 57 -
CHAPTER X	- 70 -
CHAPTER XI	- 81 -
CHAPTER XII	- 92 -
CHAPTER XIII	- 101 -
CHAPTER XIV	- 113 -
CHAPTER XV	- 116 -
CHAPTER XVI	- 124 -
CHAPTER XVII	- 132 -
CHAPTER XVIII	- 139 -
CHAPTER XIX	- 145 -
CHAPTER XX	- 153 -
CHAPTER XXI	- 164 -
CHAPTER XXII	- 174 -
CHAPTER XXIII	- 177 -
CHAPTER XXIV	- 190 -

CHAPTER XXV	- 196 -
CHAPTER XXVI	- 201 -
CHAPTER XXVII	- 207 -
CHAPTER XXVIII	- 214 -
CHAPTER XXIX	- 219 -
CHAPTER XXX	- 227 -
CHAPTER XXXI	- 233 -
CHAPTER XXXII	- 239 -
CHAPTER XXXIII	- 247 -
CHAPTER XXXIV	- 253 -
CHAPTER XXXV	- 260 -
CHAPTER XXXVI	- 265 -
CHAPTER XXXVII	- 271 -

PREFACE

Ivan Alexandrovich Goncharov (1812-1891) was one of the leading members of the great circle of Russian writers who, in the middle of the nineteenth century, gathered around the *Sovremmenik* (Contemporary) under Nekrasov's editorship—a circle including Turgenev, Dostoyevsky, Tolstoy, Byelinsky, and Herzen. He had not the marked genius of the first three of these; but that he is so much less known to the western reader is perhaps also due to the fact that there was nothing sensational either in his life or his literary method. His strength was in the steady delineation of character, conscious of, but not deeply disturbed by, the problems which were obsessing and distracting smaller and greater minds.

Tolstoy has a characteristically prejudiced reminiscence: "I remember how Goncharov, the author, a very sensible and educated man but a thorough townsman and an aesthete, said to me that, after Turgenev, there was nothing left to write about in the life of the lower classes. It was all used up. The life of our wealthy people, with their amorousness and dissatisfaction with their lives, seemed to him full of inexhaustible subject-matter. One hero kissed his lady on her palm, and another on her elbow, and a third somewhere else. One man is discontented through idleness, another because people don't love him. And Goncharov thought that in this sphere there is no end of variety."

In fact, his greatest success was the portrait of Oblomov in the novel of that name, which was at once recognised as a peculiarly national character—a man of thirty-two years, careless, bored, untidy, lazy, but gentle and good-natured. In the present work, now translated for the first time into English, the type reappears with some differences. Raisky seems to have been "born tired." He has plenty of intelligence, some artistic gifts, charm, and an abundant kindliness, yet he achieves nothing, either in work or in love, and in the end fades ineffectually out of the story. "He knew he would do better to begin a big piece of work instead of these trifles; but he told himself that Russians did not understand hard work, or that real work demanded rude strength, the use of the hands, the shoulders, and the back." "He is only half a man," says Mark Volokov, the wolfish outlaw who quotes Proudhon and talks about "the new knowledge, the new life." This rascal, whose violent pursuit of the heroine produces the tragedy of the book, is a much less convincing figure, though he also represents a reality of Russian life then, and even now.

The true contrast to Raisky of which Goncharov had deep and sympathetic knowledge is shown in the splendid picture of the two women—Vera, the infatuated beauty, and Aunt Tatiana, whose agony of motherly concern and shamed remembrance is depicted with great power. The book is remarkable as a study in the psychology of passionate emotion; for the western reader, it is also delightful for the glimpses it gives of the old Russian country life which is slowly passing away. The scene lies beside one of the small towns on the Volga—"like other towns, a cemetery ... the tranquillity of the grave. What a frame for a novel, if only he knew what to put in the novel.... If the image of passion should float over this motionless, sleepy little world, the picture would glow into the enchanting colour of life." The storm of passion does break over the edge of the hill overlooking the mighty river, and, amid the wreckage, the two victims rise into a nobility that the reckless reformer and the pleasant dilettante have never conceived.

Goncharov had passed many years in Governmental service and had, in fact, reached the age of thirty-five when his first work, *"A Common Story,"* was published. *"The Frigate Pallada,"* which followed, is a lengthy descriptive account of an official expedition to Japan and Siberia in which Goncharov took part. After the publication of *"The Precipice,"* its author was moved to write an essay, *"Better Late Than Never,"* in which he attempted to explain that the purpose of his three novels was to present the eternal struggle between East and West—the lethargy of the Russian and the ferment of foreign influences. Thus he ranged himself more closely with the great figures among his contemporaries. Two other volumes consist of critical study and reminiscence.

CHAPTER I

Boris Pavlovich Raisky had a vivacious, unusually mobile face. At first sight he appeared younger than his years. The high, white forehead gave an impression of freshness and vigour; the eyes blazed one moment with intelligence, emotion or gaiety, a moment later they wore a meditative, dreamy expression, then again they looked young, even childlike. At other times they evidenced knowledge of life, or looked so weary, so bored that they betrayed their owner's age; at these times there appeared between them three furrows, certain indications of time and knowledge of life. Smooth black hair fell on his neck and half covered the ears, with here and there silver threads about the temples. His complexion had kept the tints of youth except on the temples and the chin, which were a brownish-yellow colour.

It was easy to guess from his physiognomy that the conflict between youth and maturity was past, that he had passed the early stages of life's journey and that sorrow and sickness had left their marks on him. Only the mouth, with its delicate lines, with the fresh, almost childlike smile remained unchanged by age.

He had been left an orphan in childhood, and for some time his indifferent, bachelor guardian had left his education to a relative, Boris's aunt.

This lady was endowed with a rich temperament, but her horizon did not stretch far beyond her own home, where in the tranquil atmosphere of woods and gardens, in the environment of the family and the estate, Boris had passed several years. When he grew older his guardian sent him to the High School, where the family traditions of former wealth and of the connexion with other old noble families faded.

His further development, occupations and inclinations led him still further from the traditions of his childhood. Raisky had lived for about ten years in St. Petersburg; that is to say he rented three pleasant rooms from a German landlord, which he retained, although after he had left the civil service he rarely spent two successive half-years in the capital.

He had left the civil service as casually as he had entered it, because, when he had had time to consider his position, he came to the conclusion that the service is not an aim in itself, but merely a means to bring together a number of men who would otherwise have had no justification for their existence. If these men had not existed, the posts which they filled need never have been created.

Now, he had already passed his thirtieth year, and had neither sowed nor reaped. He did not follow the same path as the other ordinary arrival from the interior of Russia, for he was neither an officer nor an official, nor did he seek a career for himself by hard work or by influence. He was inscribed in the registers of his police district as a civil servant.

It would have been hard for the expert in physiognomy to decipher Raisky's characteristics, inclinations and character from his face because of its extraordinary mobility. Still less could his mental physiognomy be defined. He had moments when, to use his own expression, he embraced the whole world, so that many people declared that there was no kinder, more amiable man in existence. Others, on the contrary, who came across him at an unfortunate moment, when the yellow patches on his face were most marked, when his lips were drawn in a sinister, nervous quiver, and he returned kindness and sympathy with cold looks and sharp words, were repelled by him and even pursued him with their dislike. Some called him egotistic and proud, while others declared themselves enchanted with him; some again maintained that he was theatrical, others that he was not to be trusted. Two or three friends judged otherwise. "A noble nature," they said, "most honourable, but with all its virtues, nervous, passionate, excitable, fiery tempered...." So there had never been any unanimous opinion of him.

Even in early childhood while he lived with his aunt, and later, after his school-days had begun, he showed the same enigmatic and contradictory traits.

It might be expected that the first effort of a new boy would be to listen to the teacher's questions and the pupils' answers. But Raisky stared at the teacher, as if seeking to impress on his memory the details of his appearance, his speech, how he took snuff; he looked at his eyebrows, his beard, then at his clothes, at the cornelian seal suspended across his waistcoat, and so on. Then he would observe each of the other boys and note their peculiarities, or he would study his own person, and wonder what his own face was like, what the others thought of him....

"What did I say just now?" interrupted the master, noticing Boris's wandering glance.

To the teacher's amazement Boris replied word for word, "And what is the meaning of this?" He had listened mechanically, and had caught the actual syllables.

The master repeated his explanation, and again Boris caught the sound of his voice, noticing that sometimes he spoke shortly, staccato—

sometimes drawled as if he were singing, and then rapped out his words smartly like nuts.

"Well?"

Raisky blushed, perspired with anxiety, and was silent.

It was the mathematical master. He went to the blackboard, wrote up the problem, and again began the explanation. Raisky only noticed with what rapidity and certainty he wrote the figures, how the waistcoat with the cornelian seal and then the snuff-spattered shirt front came nearer—nothing, except the solution of the problem, escaped him.

Now and then a notion penetrated to his brain, but when it came to equations he grew weary with the effort required. Sometimes the teacher lost patience with him, and generally concluded: "Go back to your place, you are a blockhead."

But if a whiff of originality passed over the master himself, if he taught as if it were a game, and had recourse neither to his book nor to the blackboard, then the solution flashed on Raisky, and he found the answer quicker than any of the others.

He consumed passionately history, novels and tales; wherever he could he begged for books. But he did not like facts or theories or anything that drew him from the world of fancy towards the world of reality. In the geography lesson he could not understand how any boy could answer in class, but once out of class he could talk about foreign countries and cities, or about the sea, to the amazement of his classmates. He had not learnt it from the teacher or from a book, but he gave a picture of the place as if he had actually been there.

"You are inventing," a sceptical listener would say. "Vassili Nikitich never said that."

His companions did not know what to make of him, for his sympathies changed so often that he had neither constant friends nor constant enemies. One week he would attach himself to one boy, seek his society, sit with him, read to him, talk to him and give him his confidence. Then, for no reason, he would leave him, enter into close relations with another boy, and then as speedily forget him.

If one of his companions annoyed him he became angry with him and pursued hostilities obstinately long after the original cause was forgotten. Then suddenly he would have a friendly, magnanimous impulse, would carefully arrange a scene of reconciliation, which interested everyone, himself most of all.

When he was out of school, everyday life attracted him very little; he cared neither for its gayer side nor its sterner activities. If his guardian asked him how the corn should be threshed, the cloth milled or linen bleached, he turned away and went out on to the verandah to look out on the woods, or made his way along the river to the thicket to watch the insects at work, or to observe the birds, to see how they alighted, how they sharpened their beaks. He caught a hedgehog and made a playmate of it, went out fishing all day long with the village boys, or listened to the tales about Pugachev told by a half-witted old woman living in a mud hut, greedily drinking in the most singular of the horrible incidents she related, while he looked into the old woman's toothless mouth and into the caverns of her fading eyes.

For hours he would listen with morbid curiosity to the babble of the idiot Feklusha. At home he read in the most desultory way. He deemed the secrets of Eastern magic, Russian tales and folk-lore, skimmed Ossian, Tasso, Homer, or wandered with Cook in strange lands. If he found nothing to read he lay motionless all day long, as if he were exhausted with hard work; his fancy carried him beyond Ossian and Homer, beyond the tales of Cook, until fevered with his imaginings he rose tired, exhausted, and unable for a long time to resume normal life.

People called him an idler. He feared this accusation, and wept over it in secret, though he was convinced that he was no idler, but something different, that no one but himself comprehended.

Unfortunately, there was no one to guide him in a definite direction. On the one hand, his guardian merely saw to it that his masters came at stated times and that Boris did not avoid school; on the other, his aunt contented herself with seeing that he was in good health, ate and slept well, was decently dressed, and as a well-brought-up boy should, did not consort with every village lout.

Nobody cared to see what he read; his aunt gave him the keys of his father's library in the old house, where he shut himself in, now to read Spinoza, now a novel, and another day Voltaire or Boccaccio.

He made better progress in the arts than in the sciences. Here too he had his tricks. One day the teacher set the pupils to draw eyes, but Raisky grew tired of that, and proceeded to add a nose and a moustache. The master surprised him, and seized him by the hair. When he looked closer at the drawing, however, he asked: "Where did you learn to do that?"

"Nowhere," was the reply.

"But it is well done, my lad. See yourself what this hurry to get on leads to; the forehead and nose are good enough, but the ear you have put in the wrong place, and the hair looks like tow."

Raisky was triumphant. The words, "But it is well done; the forehead and nose are good enough," were for him a crown of laurel.

He walked round the school yard proud in the consciousness that he was the best in the drawing class; this mood lasted to the next day, when he came to grief in the ordinary lessons. But he conceived a passion for drawing, and during the month that followed drew a curly-headed boy, then the head of Fingal. His fancy was caught by a woman's head which hung in the master's room; it leaned a little towards one shoulder, and looked away into the distance with melancholy, meditative eyes. "Allow me to make a copy," he begged with a gentle, tremulous voice, and with a nervous quiver of the upper lip.

"Don't break the glass," the master warned him, and gave him the picture. Boris was happy. For a whole week his masters did not secure a single intelligent answer from him. He sat silently in his corner and drew. At night he took the drawing to his bedroom, and as he looked into its gracious eyes, followed the lines of the delicately bent neck, he shivered, his heart stood still, there was a catch in his breath, and he closed his eyes; with a faint sigh he pressed the picture to his breast where the breath came so painfully—and then there was a crash and the glass fell clattering on the floor.

When he had drawn the head his pride knew no bounds. His work was exhibited with the drawings of pupils of the top class, the teacher had made few corrections, had only here and there put broad strokes in the shading, had drawn three or four more decided lines, had put a point in each eye—and the eyes were now like life.

"How lifelike and bold it is!" thought Raisky, as he looked at the strokes inserted by his master, and more especially at the points in the eyes, which had so suddenly given them the look of life. This step forward intoxicated him. "Talent! Talent!" sang in his ears.

He sketched the maids, the coachman, the peasants of the countryside. He was particularly successful with the idiot Feklusha, seated in a cavern with her bust in the shade, and the light on her wild hair; he had not the patience nor the skill to finish bust, hands and feet. How could anybody be expected to sit still all the morning, when the sun was shedding its rays so gaily and so generously on stream and meadow?

Within three days the picture had faded in his imagination, and new images were thronging his brain. He would like to have drawn a round dance, a drunken old man, the rapid passage of a troïka. For two days he was taken up with this picture, which stood before his mind's eye in every detail; the peasants and the women were finished, but not the waggon with its three fleet horses.

In a week he had forgotten this picture also.

He loved music to distraction. At school he had an enduring affection for the dull Vassyvkov, who was the laughing stock of the other boys. A boy would seize Vassyvkov by the ear, crying, "Get out, stupid, blockhead," but Raisky stood by him, because Vassyvkov, inattentive, sleepy, idle, who never did his work even for the universally beloved Russian master, would every afternoon after dinner take his violin, and as he played, forget the school, the masters and the nose-pullings. His eyes as they gazed into the distance, apparently seeking something strange, enticing, and mysterious, became wild and gloomy, and often filled with tears.

He was no longer Vassyvkov, but another creature. His pupils dilated, his eyes ceased to blink, becoming clearer and deeper; his glance was proud and intelligent; his breath came long and deep. Over his face stole an expression of happiness, of gentleness; his eyes became darker and seemed to radiate light. In a word he became beautiful.

Raisky began to think the thoughts of Vassyvkov, to see what he saw. His surroundings vanished, and boys and benches were lost in a mist. More notes ... and a wide space opened before him. A world in motion arose. He heard the murmur of running streams, saw ships, men, woods, and drifting clouds; everywhere was light, motion, and gaiety. He had the sensation that he himself was growing taller, he caught his breath....

The dream continued just so long as the notes were heard. Suddenly he heard a noise, he was awakened with a start, Vassyvkov had ceased to play; the moving, musical waves vanished, and there were only the boys, benches and tables. Vassyvkov laid aside his violin, and somebody tweaked his ear. Raisky threw himself in a rage on the offender, struck him—all the while possessed by the magic notes.

Every nerve in his body sang. Life, thought, emotion broke in waves in the seething sea of his consciousness. The notes strike a chord of memory. A cloud of recollection hovers before him, shaping the figure of a woman who holds him to her breast. He gropes in his consciousness—it was thus that his mother's arms cradled him, his face pressed to her breast ... her figure grows in distinctness, as if she had risen from the grave....

He had begun to take lessons from Vassyvkov. For a whole week he had been moving the bow up and down, but its scratching set his teeth on edge. He caught two strings at once, and his hand trembled with weakness. It was clearly no use. When Vassyvkov played his hand seemed to play of itself.

Tired of the torment, Raisky begged his guardian to allow him to take piano lessons.

"It will be easier on the pianoforte," he thought.

His guardian engaged a German master, but took the opportunity of saying a few words to his nephew.

"Boris," he said, "for what are you preparing yourself? I have been intending to ask you for a long time."

Boris did not understand the question, and made no answer.

"You are nearly sixteen years old, and it is time you began to think of serious things. It is plain that you have not yet considered what faculty you will follow in the University, and to which branch of the service you will devote yourself. You cannot well go into the army, because you have no great fortune, and yet, for the sake of your family, could hardly serve elsewhere than in the Guards."

Boris was silent, and watched through the window how the hens strutted about, how the pigs wallowed in the mire, how the cat was stalking a pigeon....

"I am speaking to you seriously, and you stare out of the window. For what future are you preparing yourself?"

"I want to be an artist."

"Wha-at?"

"An artist."

"The devil only knows what notions you have got into your head. Who would agree to that? Do you even know what an artist is?"

Raisky made no answer.

"An artist ... is a man who borrows money from you, or chatters foolish nonsense, and drives you to distraction.... Artist! ... These people lead a wild gipsy life, are destitute of money, clothes, shoes, and all the time they dream of wealth. Artists live on this earth like the birds of heaven. I have seen enough of them in St. Petersburg: bold rascals who meet one another in the evening dressed in fantastic costumes, lie upon divans, smoke pipes, talk about trifles, read poetry, drink brandy and declare that they are artists. Uncombed, unwashed...."

"I have heard, Uncle, that artists are now held in high esteem. You are thinking of the past. Now, the Academy produces many famous people."

"I am not very old, and I have seen the world. You have heard the bells ring, but do not know in what tower. Famous people! There are famous artists as there are famous doctors. But when do they achieve fame? When do they enter the service and reach the rank of Councillor? If a man builds a cathedral or erects a monument in a public place, then people begin to seek him out. But artists begin in poverty, with a crust of bread. You will find they are for the most part freed serfs, small tradespeople or foreigners, or Jews. Poverty drives them to art. But you—a Raisky! You have land of your own, and bread to eat. It's pleasant enough to have graceful talents in society, to play the piano, to sketch in an album, and to sing a song, and I have therefore engaged a German professor for you. But what an abominable idea to be an artist by profession! Have you ever heard of a prince or a count who has painted a picture, or a nobleman who has chiselled a statue? No, and why?"

"What about Rubens? He was a courtier, an ambassador...."

"Where have you dug that out? Two hundred years ago.... Among the Germans ... but you are going to the University, to enter the faculty of law, then you will study for the service in St. Petersburg, try to get a position as advocate, and your connexions will help you to a place at court. And if you keep your eyes open, with your name and your connexions, you will be a Governor in thirty years' time. That is the career for you. But there seem to be no serious ideas in your head; you catch fish with the village boors, have sketched a swamp and a drunken beggar, but you have not the remotest idea of when this or that crop should be sown, or at what price it is sold."

Raisky trembled. His guardian's lecture affected his nerves.

Like Vassyvkov, the music master began to bend his fingers. If Raisky had not been ashamed before his guardian he would not have endured the torture. As it was he succeeded in a few months, after much trouble, in completing the first stages of his instruction. Very soon he surpassed and surprised the local young ladies by the strength and boldness of his playing. His master saw his abilities were remarkable, his indolence still more remarkable.

That, he thought, was no misfortune. Indolence and negligence are native to artists. He had been told too that a man who has talent should not work too hard. Hard work is only for those with moderate abilities.

CHAPTER II

Raisky entered the University, and spent the summer vacation with his aunt, Tatiana Markovna Berezhkov.

His aunt lived in a family estate which Boris had inherited from his mother—a piece of land on the Volga, close by a little town, with fifty souls and two residences, one built of stone and now neglected, the other a wooden building built by Boris's father. In this newer house Tatiana Markovna lived with two orphan girls of six and five years old respectively, who had been left in her care by a niece whom she had loved as a daughter.

Tatiana Markovna had an estate and a village of her own, but after the death of Raisky's parents she had established herself on their little estate, which she ruled like a miniature kingdom, wisely, economically, carefully and despotically. She never permitted Boris's guardian to interfere in her business, took no heed of documents, papers, or deeds, but carried on the affairs of the estate according to the practice of its former owners. She told Boris's guardian that all the documents, papers and deeds were inscribed in her memory, and that she would render account to Boris when he came of age; until that day came she, according to the verbal instructions of his parents, was mistress of the estate. Boris's guardian was content. It was an excellent estate, and could not be better administered than by the old lady.

What a Paradise Raisky evolved for himself in this corner of the earth, from which he had been taken away in his childhood and where he had spent many a summer visit in his schooldays. What views in the neighbourhood! Every window in the house framed a lovely landscape. From one side could be seen the Volga with its steep banks; from the others wide meadows and gorges, and the whole seemed to melt into the distant blue hills. From the third side could be seen fields, villages, and part of the town. The air was cool and invigorating, and as refreshing as a bathe on a summer day.

In the immediate neighbourhood of the two houses the great park, with its dark alleys, arbours and seats, was kept in good order, but beyond these limits it was left wild. There were broad stretching elms, cherry and apple trees, service trees, and there were lime trees intended to form an avenue, which lost itself in a wood in the friendly neighbourhood of pines and birches. Suddenly the whole ended in a precipice, thickly overgrown with bushes, which overhung a plain about one and a-half versts in breadth along the banks of the Volga.

Nearer the wooden house lay the vegetable garden, and just in front of its windows lay the flower garden. Tatiana Markovna liked to have a space clear of trees in front of the house, so that the place was flooded with sunshine and the scent of flowers. From the other side of the house one could watch all that was going on in the courtyard and could see the servants' quarters, the kitchens, the hayricks, and the stable. In the depths of the courtyard stood the old house, gloomy, always in shadow, stained with age, with here and there a cracked window pane, with heavy doors fastened by heavy bolts, and the path leading up to it overgrown with grass. But on the new house the sun streamed from morning to night; the flower garden, full of roses and dahlias, surrounded it like a garland, and the gay flowers seemed to be trying to force their way in through the windows. Swallows nesting under the eaves flew hither and thither; in the garden and the trees there were hedge-sparrows, siskins and goldfinches, and when darkness fell the nightingale began to sing. Around the flowers there were swarms of bees, humble-bees, dragon-flies, and glittering butterflies; and in the corners cats and kittens stretched themselves comfortably in the sunshine.

In the house itself peace and joy reigned. The rooms were small, but cosy. Antique pieces of furniture had been brought over from the great house, as had the portraits of Raisky's parents and grandparents. The floors were painted, waxed and polished; the stoves were adorned with old-fashioned tiles, also brought over from the other house; the cupboards were full of plate and silver; there were old Dresden cups and figures, Chinese ornaments, tea-pots, sugar-basins, heavy old spoons. Round stools bound with brass, and inlaid tables stood in pleasant corners.

In Tatiana Markovna's sitting-room stood an old-fashioned carved bureau with a mirror, urns, lyres, and genii. But she had hung up the mirror, because she said it was a hindrance to writing when you stared at your own stupid face. The room also contained a round table where she lunched and drank her tea and coffee, and a rather hard leather-covered armchair with a high back. Grandmother {1} was old-fashioned; she did not approve of lounging, but held herself upright and was simple and reserved in her manners.

How beautiful Boris thought her! And indeed she was beautiful.

Tall, neither stout nor thin, a vivacious old lady ... not indeed an old lady, but a woman of fifty, with quick black eyes, and so kind and gracious a smile that even when she was angry, and the storm-light flickered in her eyes, the blue sky could be observed behind the clouds. She had a slight moustache, and, on her left cheek, near the chin, a birth-mark with a little bunch of hairs, details which gave her face a remarkable expression of kindness.

She cut her grey hair short, and went about in house, yard, garden with her head uncovered, but on feast days, or when guests were expected she put on a cap. The cap could not be kept in its place, and did not suit her at all, so that after about five minutes she would with apologies remove the tiresome headdress.

In the mornings she wore a wide white blouse with a girdle and big pockets; in the afternoon she put on a brown dress, and on feast days a heavy rustling silk dress that gleamed like silver, and over it a valuable shawl which only Vassilissa, her housekeeper, was allowed to take out of the press.

"Uncle Ivan Kusmich brought it from the East," she used to boast. "It cost three hundred gold roubles, and now no money would buy it."

At her girdle hung a bunch of keys, so that Grandmother could be heard from afar like a rattlesnake when she crossed the yard or the garden. At the sound the coachmen hid their pipes in their boots, because the mistress feared nothing so much as fire, and for that reason counted smoking as the greatest of crimes. The cooks seized the knife, the spoon or the broom; Kirusha, who had been joking with Matrona, hurried to the door, while Matrona hurried to the byre.

If the approaching clatter gave warning that the mistress was returning to the house Mashutka quickly took off her dirty apron and wiped her hands on a towel or a bit of rag, as the case might be. Spitting on her hands she smoothed down her dry, rebellious hair, and covered the round table with the finest of clean tablecloths. Vassilissa, silent, serious, of the same age as her mistress, buxom, but faded with much confinement indoors, would bring in the silver service with the steaming coffee.

Mashutka effaced herself as far as possible in a corner. The mistress insisted on cleanliness in her servants, but Mashutka had no gift for keeping herself spotless. When her hands were clean she could do nothing, but felt as if everything would slip through her fingers. If she was told to do her hair on Sunday, to wash and to put on tidy clothes, she felt the whole day as if she had been sewn into a sack. She only seemed to be happy when, smeared and wet with washing the boards, the windows, the silver, or the doors, she had become almost unrecognisable, and had, if she wanted to rub her nose or her eyebrows, to use her elbow.

Vassilissa, on the contrary, respected herself, and was the only tidy woman among all the servants. She had been in the service of her mistress since her earliest days as her personal maid, had never been separated from her, knew every detail of her life, and now lived with her as housekeeper and confidential servant. The two women communicated with one another in monosyllables. Tatiana Markovna hardly needed to give instructions to Vassilissa, who knew herself what had to be done. If something unusual was required, her mistress did not give orders, but suggested that this or that should be done.

Vassilissa was the only one of her subjects whom Tatiana Markovna addressed by her full name. If she did address them by their baptismal names they were names that could not be compressed nor clipped, as for example Ferapont or Panteleimon. The village elder she did indeed address as Stepan Vassilich, but the others were to her Matroshka, Mashutka, Egorka and so on. The unlucky individual whom she addressed with his Christian name and patronymic knew that a storm was impending. "Here, Egor Prokhorich! where were you all day yesterday?" Or "Simeon Vassilich, you smoked a pipe yesterday in the hayrick. Take care!"

She would get up in the middle of the night to convince herself that a spark from a pipe had not set fire to anything, or that there was not someone walking about the yard or the coachhouse with a lantern.

Under no consideration could the gulf between the "people" and the family be bridged. She was moderately strict and moderately considerate, kindly, but always within the limits of her ideas of government. If Irene, Matrona or another of the maids gave birth to a child, she listened to the report of the event with an air of injured dignity, but gave Vassilissa to understand that the necessaries should be provided; and would add, "Only don't let me see the good-for-nothing." After Matrona or Irene had recovered she would keep out of her mistress's sight for a month or so; then it was as if nothing had happened, and the child was put out in the village.

If any of her people fell sick, Tatiana got up in the night, sent him spirits and embrocation, but next day she would send him either to the infirmary or oftener to the "wise woman," but she did not send for a doctor. But if one of her own relatives, her "grandchildren" showed a bad tongue, or a swollen face, Kirusha or Vlass must immediately ride post haste to the town for the doctor.

The "wise woman" was a woman in the suburbs who treated the "people" with simple remedies, and rapidly relieved them of their maladies. It did, indeed, happen that many a man remained crippled for life after her treatment. One lost his voice and could only crow, another lost an eye, or a piece of his jawbone, but the pain was gone and he went back to work. That seemed satisfactory to the patient as well as the proprietor of the estate. And as the "wise woman" only concerned herself with humble people, with serfs and the poorer classes, the medical profession did not interfere with her.

Tatiana Markovna fed her servants decently with cabbage soup and groats, on feast-days with rye and mutton; at Christmas geese and pigs were roasted. She allowed nothing out of the common on the servants' table or in their dress, but she gave the surplus from her own table now to one woman, now to another.

Vassilissa drank tea immediately after her mistress; after her came the maids in the house, and last old Yakob. On feast days, on account of the hardness of their work, a glass of brandy was handed to the coachman, the menservants and the Starost.

As soon as the tea was cleared away in the morning a stout, chubby-faced woman pushed her way into the room, always smiling. She was maid to the grandchildren, Veroshka and Marfinka. Close at her heels the twelve-year-old assistant, and together they brought the children to breakfast.

Never knowing which of the two to kiss first, Tatiana Markovna would begin: "Well, my birdies, how are you? Veroshka, darling, you have brushed your hair?"

"And me, Granny, me," Marfinka would cry.

"Why are Marfinka's eyes red? Has she been crying?" Tatiana Markovna inquired anxiously of the maid. "The sun has dazzled her. Are her curtains well drawn, you careless girl? I must see."

In the maid's room sat three or four young girls who sat all day long sewing, or making bobbin lace, without once stretching their limbs all day, because the mistress did not like to see idle hands. In the ante-room there sat idly the melancholy Yakob, Egorka, who was sixteen and always laughing, with two or three lackeys. Yakob did nothing but wait at table, where he idly flicked away the flies, and as idly changed the plates. He was almost too idle to speak, and when the visitors addressed him he answered in a tone indicating excessive boredom or a guilty conscience. Because he was quiet, never seriously drunk, and did not smoke, his master had made him butler; he was also very zealous at church.

{1} Tatiana Markovna was addressed by her grand-nieces and her grand-nephew as Grandmother.

CHAPTER III

Boris came in on his aunt during the children's breakfast. Tatiana Markovna clapped her hands and all but jumped from her chair; the plates were nearly shaken off the table.

"Borushka, tiresome boy! You have not even written, but descend like a thunderclap. How you frightened me!"

She took his head in her hands, looked for a full minute into his face, and would have wept, but she glanced away at his mother's portrait, and sighed.

"Well, well!" she seemed to say, but in fact said nothing, but smiled and wiped away her tears with her handkerchief. "Your mother's boy," she cried, "her very image! See how lovely she was, look, Vassilissa! Do you remember? Isn't he like her?"

With youthful appetite Boris devoured coffee, tea, cakes and bread, his aunt watching all the while.

"Call the people, tell the Starost and everybody that the Master is here, the real Master, the owner. Welcome, little father, welcome home!" she said, with an ironic air of humility, laughing and mimicking the pleasant speech. "Forsake us not with your favour. Tatiana Markovna insults us, ruins us, take us over into your charge.... Ha! Ha! Here are the keys, the accounts, at your service, demand a reckoning from the old lady. Ask her what she has done with the estate money, why the peasants' huts are in ruins. See how the Malinovka peasants beg in the streets of the town. Ha! Ha! Under your guardian and uncle in the new estate, I believe, the peasants wear polished boots and red shirts, and live in two-storied houses. Well, Sir, why this silence? Why do you not ask for the accounts? Have your breakfast, and then I will show you everything."

After breakfast Tatiana Markovna took her sunshade, put on her thick-soled shoes, covered her head with a light hood, and went to show Boris the garden.

"Now, Sir, keep your eyes wide open, and if there is anything wrong, don't spare your Grandmother. You will see I have just planted out the beds in front of the house. Veroshka and Marfinka play here under my eyes, in the sand. One cannot trust any nurse."

They reached the yard.

"Kirusha, Eromka, Matroshka, where have you all hidden yourselves? One of you come here."

Matroshka appeared, and announced that Kirusha and Eromka had gone into the village to fetch the peasants.

"Here is Matroshka. Do you remember her? What are you staring there for, fool. Kiss your Master's hand."

Matroshka came nearer. "I dare not," she said.

Boris shyly embraced the girl.

"You have built a new wing to the buildings, Grandmother," he said.

"You noticed that. Do you remember the old one? It was quite rotten, had holes in the floors as broad as my hand, and the dirt and the soot! And now look!"

They went into the new wing. His aunt showed Boris the alterations in the stables, the horses and the separate space for fowls, the laundry and byres.

"Here is the new kitchen which I built detached so that the kitchen range is outside the house, and the servants have more room. Now each has his own corner. Here is the pantry, there the new ice-cellar. What are you standing there for?" she said, turning to Matrona. "Go and tell Egorka to run into the village and say to the Starost that we are going over there."

In the garden his aunt showed him every tree and every bush, led him through the alleys, looked down from the top of the precipice into the brushwood, and went with him into the village. It was a warm day, and the winter corn waved gently in the pleasant breeze.

"Here is my nephew, Boris Pavlovich," she said to the Starost. "Are you getting in the hay while the warm weather lasts? We are sure to have rain before long after this heat. Here is the Master, the real Master, my nephew," she said, turning to the peasants. "Have you seen him before, Garashka? Take a good look at him. Is that your calf in the rye, Iliusha?" she said in passing to a peasant, while her attention already wandered to the pond.

"There they are again, hanging out the clothes on the trees," she remarked angrily to the village elder. "I have given orders for a line to be fixed. Tell blind Agasha so. It is she that likes to hang her things out on the willows. The branches will break...."

"We haven't a line long enough," answered the Starost sleepily. "We shall have to buy one in the town."

"Why did you not tell Vassilissa? She would have let me know. I go into the town every week, and would have brought a line long ago."

"I have told her, but she forgets, or says it is not worth while to bother the Mistress about it."

Tatiana Markovna made a knot in her handkerchief. She liked it to be said that nothing could be done without her; a clothes-line, for instance, could be bought by anybody, but God forbid that she should trust anybody with money. Although by no means avaricious, she was sparing with money. Before she brought herself to part with it she was thoughtful, sometimes angry, but the money once spent, she forgot all about it and did not like keeping account of it.

Besides the more important arrangements, her life was full of small matters of business. The maids had to be put to cutting out and sewing, or to cooking and cleaning. She arranged so that everything was carried out before her own eyes. She herself did not touch the actual work, but with the dignity of age she stood with one hand on her hip and the other pointing out exactly where and how everything was to be done. The clattering keys opened cupboards, chests, strong boxes, which contained a profusion of household linen, costly lace yellow with age, diamonds, destined for the dowry of her nieces, and money. The cupboards where tea, sugar, coffee and other provisions were kept were in Vassilissa's charge.

In the morning, after coffee, when she had given her orders for the farm, Tatiana Markovna sat down at her bureau to her accounts, then sat by the window and looked out into the field, watched the labourers, saw what was going on in the yard, and sent Yakob or Vassilissa when there was anything of which she disapproved.

When necessary she drove into the town to the market hall, or to make visits, but never was long away, returning always in time for the midday meal. She herself received many guests; she liked to be dispensing hospitality from morning to night.

When in winter afternoons she sat by the stove, she was silent and thoughtful, and liked everything around her quiet. Summer afternoons she spent in the garden, when she put on her gardening gloves and took a spade, a rake, or a watering can, by way of obtaining a little exercise. Then she spent the evening at the tea-table in the company of Tiet Nikonich Vatutin, her oldest and best friend and adviser.

Tiet Nikonich was a gentleman of birth and breeding. He owned in the province two or three hundred "souls"—he did not exactly know how many, and never attended to his estate, but left his peasants to do as they liked, and to pay him what dues they pleased. Shyly, and without counting it, he took the money they brought him, put it in his bureau, and signed to them to go where they pleased. He had been in the army, and old people remembered him as a handsome young officer, a modest, frank young man. In his youth he often visited his mother on the estate, and spent his leave with her. Eventually he took his discharge, and then built himself a little grey house in the town with three windows on to the street, and there established himself.

Although he had only received a moderate education in the cadet school, he liked to read, occupying himself chiefly with politics and natural science. In his speech, his manners and his gait he betrayed a gentle shyness, never obtruded his dignity, but was ready to show it if necessity arose. However intimate he might be with anyone, he always maintained a certain courtesy and reserve in word and gesture. He bowed to the Governor or a friend or a new acquaintance with the same old-fashioned politeness, drawing back one foot as he did so. In the street he addressed ladies with uncovered head, was the first to pick up a handkerchief or bring a footstool. If there were young girls in a house he visited he came armed with a pound of bonbons, a bunch of flowers, and tried to suit his conversation to their age, their tastes and their occupations. He always maintained his delicate politeness, tinged with the respectful manner of a courtier of the old school. When ladies were present he always wore his frock-coat. He neither smoked, nor used perfume, nor tried to make himself look younger, but was always spotless, and distinguished in his dress. His clothes were simple but dazzlingly neat. His nankeen trousers were freshly pressed, and his blue frock-coat looked as if it had come straight from the tailor. In spite of his fifty years, he had, with his perruque and his shaven chin, the air of a fresh, rosy-cheeked young man. With all his narrow means he gave the impression of wealth and good breeding, and put down his hundred roubles as if he had thousands to throw about.

For Tatiana Markovna he showed a respectful friendship, but one so devoted and ardent that it was evident from his manner that he loved her beyond all others. But although he was her daily guest he gave no sign of intimacy before strangers.

She showed great friendship for him, but there was more vivacity in her tone. Those who remembered them when they were young, said she had been a very beautiful girl. When she had thrown on her shawl and sat looking meditatively before her, she resembled a family portrait in the gallery of the old house. Occasionally there came over her moods which betrayed pride and a desire for domination; when this happened her face wore an earnest, dreamy expression, as if she were leading another life far from the small details of her actual existence.

Hardly a day went by that Tiet Nikonich did not bring some present for Grandmother or the little girls, a basket of strawberries, oranges, peaches, always the earliest on the market.

At one time it had been rumoured in the town—a rumour long since stilled—that Tiet Nikonich had loved Tatiana Markovna and Tatiana Markovna him, but that her parents had chosen another husband for her. She refused to assent, and remained unmarried. What truth there was in this, none knew but herself. But every day he came to her, either at midday or in the evening.

He liked to talk over with her what was going on in the world, who was at war, and with whom, and why. He knew why bread was cheap in Russia; the names of all the noble houses; he knew by heart the names of all the ministers and the men in high commands and their past history; he could tell why one sea lay at a higher tide than another; he was the first to know what the English or the French had invented, and whether the inventions were useful or not. If there was any business to be arranged in the law courts, Tiet Nikonich arranged it, and sometimes concealed the sums that he spent in so doing. If he was found out, she scolded him; he could not conceal his confusion, begged her pardon, kissed her hand, and took his leave.

Tatiana Markovna was always at loggerheads with the bureaucracy of the neighbourhood. If soldiers were to be billeted on her, the roads to be improved, or the taxes collected, she complained of outrage, argued and refused to pay. She would hear nothing about the public interest. In her opinion everyone had his own business to mind. She strongly objected to the police, and especially to the Superintendent, who was in her view a robber. More than once Tiet Nikonich tried, without success, to reconcile her to the doctrine of the public interest; he had to be content if she was reconciled with the officials and the police.

This was the patriarchal, peaceful atmosphere which young Raisky absorbed. Grandmother and the little girls were mother and sisters to him, and Tiet Nikonich the ideal uncle.

CHAPTER IV

Boris's aunt had only just begun to give him an idea of her methods of conducting the estate when he began to yawn.

"Listen, these are all your affairs; I am only your Starost," she said. But he could not suppress a yawn, watched the birds, the dragon-flies, picked the cornflowers, looked curiously at the peasants, and gazed up at the sky over-arching the wide horizon. Then his aunt began to talk to one of the peasants, and he hurried off to the garden, ran down to the edge of the precipice, and made his way through the undergrowth to the steep bank of the Volga.

"He is still too young, only a child, does not understand serious matters," thought his aunt, as she followed him with her eyes. "What will become of him?"

The Volga glided quietly between its overgrown banks, with here and there a sandbank or an island thickly covered with bushes. In the distance lay the sandhills and the darkening forest. Here and there shimmered a sail; gulls, with an even balancing of their wings, skimmed the water, and then rose with a more strenuous movement, while over the gardens, high in the air, the goshawks hovered.

Boris stood still for a long time, recalling his childhood. He remembered that he had sat on this spot with his mother, looking thoughtfully out at this same landscape. Then he went slowly back to the house, and climbed the precipice, with the picture of her vividly before his mind's eye.

In Malinovka and the neighbourhood there were tragic memories connected with this precipice. In the lifetime of Boris's parents a man wild with jealousy, a tailor from the town, had killed his wife and her lover there in the midst of the thicket, and had then cut his own throat. The suicide had been buried on the spot where he had committed the crime. Among the common people, as always happens in cases of this sort, there were rumours that the murderer, all dressed in white, wandered about the wood, climbed the precipice, and looked down on town and village before he vanished into air. And for superstitious reasons this part of the grounds had been left neglected. None of the servants went down the precipice, and the peasants from the outskirts of the town and from Malinovka made a détour to avoid it. The fence that divided the Raiskys' park from the woods had long since fallen into disrepair. Pines and bushes of hawthorn and dwarf-cherry had woven themselves together into a dense growth in the midst of which was concealed a neglected arbour.

Boris vividly imagined the scene, how the jealous husband, trembling with agitation, stole through the bushes, threw himself on his rival, and struck him with his knife; how the woman flung herself at his feet and begged his forgiveness. But he, with the foam of madness on his lips, struck her again and again, and then, in the presence of the two corpses, cut his own throat. Boris shuddered. Agitated and gloomy he turned from the accursed spot. Yet he was attracted by the mysterious darkness of the tangled wood to the precipice, to the lovely view over the Volga and its banks.

He closed his eyes, abandoning himself to the contemplation of the picture; his thoughts swept over him like the waves of the Volga; the lovely landscape was ever before his eyes, mirrored in his consciousness.

Veroshka and Marfinka provided him with amusement.

Veroshka was a little girl of six, with dark, brilliant eyes and dark complexion, who was beginning to be serious and to be ashamed of her baby ways. She would hop, skip and jump, then stand still, look shyly round and walk sedately along; then she would dart on again like a bird, pick a handful of currants and stuff them into her mouth. If Boris patted her hair, she smoothed it rapidly; if he gave her a kiss, she wiped it away. She was self-willed too. When she was sent on an errand she would shake her head, then run off to do it. She never asked Boris to draw for her, but if Marfinka asked him she watched silently and more intently than her sister. She did not, like Marfinka, beg either drawings or pencils.

Marfinka, a rosy little girl of four, was often self-willed, and often cried, but before the tears were dry she was laughing and shouting again. Veroshka rarely wept, and then quietly. She soon recovered, but she did not like to be told to beg pardon.

Boris's aunt wondered, as she saw him gay and serious by turns, what occupied his mind; she wondered what he did all day long. In answer Boris showed his sketching folio; then he would play her quadrilles, mazurkas, excerpts from opera, and finally his own improvisations.

Tatiana Markovna's astonishment remained. "Just like your mother," she said. "She was just as restless, always sighing as if she expected something to happen. Then she would begin to play and was gay again. See, Vassilissa, he has sketched you and me, like life! When Tiet Nikonich comes, hide yourself and make a sketch of him, and next day we will send it him, and it can hang on the study wall. What a boy you are! And you play as well as the

French emigré who used to live with your Aunt. Only it is impossible to talk to you about the farm; you are still too young."

She always wished to go through the accounts with him. "The accounts for Veroshka and Marfinka are separate, you see," she said. "You need not think that a penny of your money goes to them. See...."

But he never listened. He merely watched how his aunt wrote, how she looked at him over her spectacles, observed the wrinkles in her face, her birthmark, her eyes, her smile, and then burst out laughing, and, throwing himself into her arms, kissed her, and begged to go and look at the old house. She could refuse him nothing; so she unwillingly gave him the keys and he went to look at the rooms where he was born and had spent his childhood, of which he retained only a confused memory.

"I am going with Cousin Boris," said Marfinka.

"Where, my darling? It is uncanny over there," said Tatiana Markovna.

Marfinka was frightened. Veroshka said nothing, but when Boris reached the old house, she was already standing at the door, with her hand on the latch, as if she feared she might be driven away.

Boris shuddered as he entered the ante-room, and cast an anxious glance into the neighbouring hall, supported by pillars. Veroshka had run on in front.

"Where are you off to, Veroshka?"

She stood still a moment, her hand on the latch of the nearest door, and he had only just time to follow her before she vanished. Dark, smoke-stained reception rooms adjoined the hall. In one were two ghostly figures of shrouded statues and shrouded candelabra; by the walls were ranged dark stained oak pieces of furniture with brass decorations and inlaid work; there were huge Chinese vases, a clock representing Bacchus with a barrel, and great oval mirrors in elaborate gilded frames. In the bedroom stood an enormous bed, like a magnificent bier, with a brocade cover. Boris could not imagine how any human being could sleep in such a catafalque. Under the baldachin hovered a gilded Cupid, spotted and faded, with his arrow aimed at the bed. In the corners stood carved cupboards, damascened with ebony and mother-of-pearl. Veroshka opened a press and put her little face inside, and a musty, dusty smell came from the shelves, laden with old-fashioned caftans and embroidered uniforms with big buttons.

Raisky shivered. "Granny was right!" he laughed. "It is uncanny here."

"But everything here is so beautiful!" cried Vera, "the great pictures and the books!"

"Pictures? Books? Where? I don't remember. Bravo, little Veroshka."

He kissed her. She wiped her lips, and ran on in front to show him the books. He found some two thousand volumes, and was soon absorbed in reading the titles; many of the books were still uncut.

From this time he was not often to be seen in the wooden house. He did not even go down to the Volga, but devoured one volume after another. Then he wrote verses, read them aloud, and intoxicated himself with the sound of them; then gave all his time to drawing. He expected something, he knew not what, from the future. He was filled with passion, with the foretaste of pleasure; there rose before him a world of wonderful music, marvellous pictures, and the murmur of enchanting life.

"I have been wanting to ask you," said Tatiana Markovna, "why you have entered yourself for school again."

"Not the school, the University!"

"It's the same thing. You studied at your guardian's, and at the High School, you can draw, play the piano. What more do you want to learn? The students will only teach you to smoke a pipe, and in the end—which God forbid—to drink wine. You should go into the Guards."

"Uncle says my means are not sufficient...."

"Not sufficient! What next?" She pointed to the fields and the village. She counted out his resources in hundreds and thousands of roubles. She had had no experience of army circles, had never lived in the capital, and did not know how much money was needed.

"Your means insufficient! Why, I can send provision alone for a whole regiment. No means! What does your Uncle do with the revenues?"

"I intend to be an artist, Granny."

"What! An artist!"

"When I leave the University, I intend to enter the Academy."

"What's the matter with you, Borushka? Make the sign of the cross! Do you want to be a teacher!"

"All artists are not teachers. Among artists there are great geniuses, who are famous and receive large sums for pictures or music."

"And do you intend to sell your pictures for money, or to play the piano for money in the evenings? What a disgrace!"

"No, Grandmother, an artist...."

"No, Borushka, don't anger your Grandmother; let her have the joy of seeing you in your Guard's uniform."

"Uncle says I ought to go into the Civil Service."

"A clerk! Good heavens! To stoop over a desk all day, bathed in ink, run in and out of the courts! Who would marry you then? No, no; come home to me as an officer, and marry a rich woman!"

Although Boris shared neither his uncle's nor his aunt's views, yet for a moment there shimmered before his eyes a vision of his own figure in a hussar's or a court uniform. He saw how well he sat his horse, how well he danced. That day he made a sketch of himself, negligently seated in the saddle, with a cloak over his shoulders.

CHAPTER V

In Moscow Raisky spent his time partly in the University, partly in the Kremlin gardens. In the evening he sat in the club with his friends, hot-headed, good-hearted individuals. Every one of them made a great to-do, and confidently expected a great future.

At the University, as at school, Raisky paid little attention to the rules of grammar, but observed intently the professor and the students. But as soon as the lecture touched actual life and brought living men, Romans, Germans or Russians on the scene, whether in history or literature, he involuntarily gave the lecturer his attention, and the personages and their doings became real to him.

In his second year he made friends with a poor student named Koslov, the son of a deacon, who had been sent first of all to a seminary, but had taught himself Latin and Greek at home, and thus gained admission to the Gymnasium. He zealously studied the life of antiquity, but understood nothing of the life going on around him. Raisky felt himself drawn to this young man, at first because of his loneliness, his reserve, simplicity and kindness; later he discovered in him passion, the sacred fire, profundity of comprehension and austerity of thought and delicacy of perception—in all that pertained to antiquity. Koslov on his side was devoted to Raisky, whose vivacious temperament could not be permanently bound by anything. The outcome was the great gift of an intimate friendship.

In summer Raisky liked to explore the neighbourhood of Moscow. He explored old convents, examined their dark recesses, the blackened pictures of the saints and martyrs; his imagination interpreted old Russia for him better than the lectures of his professors.

The tsars, monks, warriors and statesmen of the past filed before him as they lived and moved. Moscow seemed to him to be a miniature tsardom. Here was conflict, here the death punishment was carried out; he saw Tatars, Cossacks of the Don. The varied life attracted him.

In spite of obstacles he passed from one course to another at the University. He was helped by the reputation for talent he had won by certain poems and essays, the subjects of which were drawn from Russian history.

"Which service do you mean to enter?" the Dean asked him one day. "In a week's time you will be leaving the University. What are you going to do?"

Raisky was silent.

"What profession have you selected?"

Raisky almost answered that he meant to be an artist, but he remembered in time the reception that this proposition had received from his guardian and his aunt. "I shall write verses," he answered in a low tone.

"But that is not a profession. You may write verses and yet...."

"Stories too."

"Naturally, you can write stories as well. You have talent and means to develop it. But what profession—profession, I asked."

"For the moment I shall enter the Guards, later on the Civil Service—I mean to be a barrister, a governor...."

The Dean smiled. "You begin by being an ensign, that is comprehensible. You and Leonid Koslov are exceptions; every other man has made his decision."

When Koslov was asked his intentions he replied that he would like to be a schoolmaster somewhere in the interior, and from this intention he refused to be turned aside.

Raisky moved among the golden youth of St. Petersburg society, first as young officer, then as bureaucrat, fulfilled his duties in devotion to the beauty of many an Armide, suffering to some degree, and gaining some experience in the process. After a time his dreams and his artistic consciousness revived. He seemed to see the Volga flowing between its steep banks, the shady garden, and the wooded precipice. He abandoned the Civil Service in its turn to enter the Academy of Arts. His education would never be finished, but he was determined to be a creative artist. His aunt scolded him by letter for having left the Guards; his guardian advised him to seek a position in the Senate, and sent him letters of recommendation.

But Raisky did not enter the Senate, but indolently pursued his artistic studies, read a great deal, wrote poems and prose, danced, went into society and to the theatre, indulged in wild dissipation, and at the same time did some musical composition, and drew a portrait of a lady. He would spend one week in dissipation and the next in diligent study at the Academy. Life knocked at the door and tore him from his artist's dreams to a dissolute existence of alternating pleasure and boredom.

The universal summer exodus from the capital had driven him abroad. But one day when he came home he found two letters awaiting him, one from Tatiana Markovna, the other from his comrade at the University,

Leonid Koslov, who had been installed in Raisky's native place as a master in the Gymnasium.

During all these years his aunt had often written to him, and sent him statements of accounts. His answers were short but affectionate; the accounts he tore up without having even looked at them.

"Is it not a sin," she wrote, "to forget an old woman like me, when I am all the family you have? But in these days it seems that old people have, in the judgment of youth, become superfluous. But I have not even leisure to die; I have two grown-up nieces, and until their future is settled to my satisfaction, I shall pray God to spare my life—and then His will be done. I do not complain that you forget me. But if I were not here my little girls, your sisters, would be alone. You are their next of kin and their natural protector. Think, too, of the estate. I am old, and can no longer be your bailiff. To whom do you intend to entrust the estate? The place will be ruined and the estate dissipated. It breaks my heart to think that your family silver, bronzes, pictures, diamonds, lace, china and glass will come into the hands of the servants, or the Jews, or the usurers. So long as your Grandmother lives, you may be sure that not a thread goes astray, but after that I can give no guarantee. And my two nieces, what is to become of them? Vera is a good, sensible, but retiring girl, and does not concern herself with domestic matters at all. Marfinka will be a splendid manager, but she is still young; although she ought to have been married before now, she is still such a child in her ideas, thank God! She will mature with experience, and meantime I shelter her. She appreciates this and does nothing against her Grandmother's will, for which may God reward her. In the house she is a great help, but I do not let her do anything on the estate; that is no work for a young girl.

"Do not defer your coming, but gladden your Grandmother's heart. She is devoted to you, not merely because of the relationship, but from her heart. You were conscious of the sympathy between us when you were a child. I don't know what you are in manhood, but you were then a good nephew. Come, if only to see your sisters, and perhaps happiness will reward your coming. If God grants me the joy of seeing you married and laying the estate in your hands I shall die happy. Marry, Borushka; you are long since of an age to do so. Then my little girls will still have a home. So long as you remain unmarried they cannot live in your house. Marry, please your Grandmother, and God will not forsake you. I wait your coming; let me know when to expect you.

"Tiet Nikonich desires to be remembered to you. He has aged, but is still hale and hearty, he has the same smile, still talks well and has such pleasant manners that none of the young dandies can hold a candle to him. Bring him, please, a vest and hose of Samian leather; it is worn now, I hear, as a specific against rheumatism. It will be a surprise for him. I enclose the account for the last two years. Accept my blessing."

CHAPTER VI

In a *kibitka* covered with bast, drawn by three lean and sleepy nags, Raisky drove slowly to his estate. It was not without agitation that he saw the smoke curling up from the chimneys of his own roof, the fresh, delicate green of the birches and the limes which overshadowed this place of refuge, the gables of the old house and the pale line of the Volga now gleaming between the trees and now hidden from view. He approached nearer and nearer; now he could see the shimmer of the flowers in the garden, the avenues of lime and acacia became visible, the old elm emerged, and there, more to the left, lay the orchard. There were dogs in the yard, cats sunning themselves, on the roof of the new house flocked the pigeon and the swallows flitted around the eaves. Behind the house, on the side towards the village, linen lay out to bleach. One woman was rolling a cask, the coachman was chopping wood, a peasant got into the *telega* and gathered up the reins—Boris saw only unfamiliar faces. But Yakob was there and looked sleepily round. One familiar face, but how aged!

Raisky observed the scene intently. He alighted from the *kibitka*, and walked along the fence which divided house, yard, garden and park from the road, feasting his eyes on the well-remembered prospect, when suddenly his eye was caught by an unexpected apparition.

On the verandah, which led down to the garden and was decorated by lemon and pomegranate trees in tubs, and with cactus and aloe and flowering plants, stood a young girl of about twenty, scattering millet from two plates held by a barefooted child of twelve. At her feet were assembled hens, turkeys, ducks, pigeons, sparrows and daws. She called to the birds to come to breakfast, and cocks, hens and pigeons fell to, looking round every moment as if they feared treason, and then again falling to. As the morning sun shed a fierce light on the busy group of birds and on the young girl herself, Raisky saw her large, dark grey eyes, her round, healthy cheeks, her narrow white teeth, her long light-brown tresses wound twice round her head, and the strong young breasts rising and sinking underneath her white blouse. Her white, slightly tanned neck was innocent of collar or scarf. A hasty movement loosened one plait of hair over her head and back, but she took no notice, but continued to scatter the corn, taking care that all received their share and that sparrows and daws did not obtrude too much, and looking as fresh and happy as the morning itself.

"Didn't you see the goose?" she asked the little girl in a loud clear voice.

"No," answered the child, "it is the cat's fault. Afimua says it will die."

"I shall look after it myself. Afimua has no pity." Motionless, Raisky watched the scene without his presence being suspected. This must be his cousin, and how charming! But which one, Veroshka or Marfinka? Without waiting for the *kibitka* to turn in through the gate, he ran forward, and stood before the young girl.

"Cousin," he cried, extending his arms.

In a moment both girls had vanished as if by magic, the sparrows were away on the roof, and the pigeons in flight. The servants in the yard stopped their work. Raisky looked in amazement on the emptiness and at the corn scattered at his feet.

Then he heard in the house bustle, murmurs, movement, the clatter of keys, and his aunt's voice, "Where is he?" Her face lighted up when she saw Raisky and she opened her arms, to press him to her breast. She had aged, but in so even, so healthy a fashion, that there were no unwholesome patches, no deep hanging pockets about the eyes and mouth, no sadness or gloom in her eyes. Life had not conquered her; she conquered life, and only slowly laid down her weapons in the combat. Her voice was not so clear as of old, and she leaned on a stick, but she made no complaint. She still wore no cap on her short hair. Health and kindliness shone from her eyes, and not only from her eyes, from her whole figure.

"Borushka, my friend!" Three times she embraced him. Tears stood in her eyes. In her embrace, her voice, in the sudden grip of joy, there was tenderness, affection, and ardour.

He felt that he was almost a criminal, that he had been playing with his emotions and seeking forbidden fruit, wandering homelessly in the world, while Nature himself had been preparing for him a nest where sympathy and happiness awaited him.

"Marfinka, where are you, come here," cried her grandmother. "She was so terrified when she saw you, and terrified me too. Let me look at you, Borushka."

She led him to the light and looked at him long and earnestly.

"How ill you look," she said. "But no, you are sunburnt. The moustache suits you, why do you grow a beard? Shave it off, Borushka, I can't endure it. Ah! grey hairs here and there already. You are beginning to age too soon."

"It's not with age, Granny."

"Why then? Are you in good health?"

"I'm well enough. Let us talk of something else. You, thank God, are always the same."

"What do you mean?"

"You don't alter a bit, are still as beautiful as ever. I never saw an old lady whose age adorned her so."

"Thanks for the compliment, my child. It would be better for you to spend your admiration on your sisters. I will whisper the truth to you. Two such beauties you will not find in the town, especially the other...."

"Where is my other sister?"

"On a visit to the pope's wife on the other side of the Volga. It is a pity. The pope's wife has been ill and sent for her, of course just now. A messenger shall go."

"No! No! Why should anyone be disturbed on my account?"

"And you have come on your Grandmother so suddenly. We waited, waited, in vain. The peasants sat up for you at night, I have just sent Egorka on to the highway to look for you and Savili into the town. Now you must have your breakfast. Why is it so long in coming? The master has come, and there is nothing ready, just as if the house was nothing better than a station. Serve what is ready."

"I need nothing, Granny. I am stuffed with food. At one station I drank tea, milk at another, and at the third there was a wedding, and I was treated to wine, meat and gingerbread."

"You are on your way home to your Grandmother, and are not ashamed to eat and drink all sorts of things. Gingerbread in the morning! Marfinka ought to have been there; she loves weddings and gingerbread. Come in. Marfinka, don't be so shy. She is ashamed because you caught her in her morning gown. Come here, darling; he is your brother."

Tea and coffee appeared, and finally breakfast. However much he protested Raisky had to eat, for otherwise his aunt's morning would have been spoiled.

"Marfinka, come here and entertain us."

After about five minutes the door opened slowly and quietly, and Marfinka entered, blushing with confusion and with downcast eyes. At her heels followed Vassilissa with a tea-tray full of sweets, preserves, cakes, etc. Marfinka stood still, betraying in her confusion a certain curiosity. She wore lace at her neck and wrists; her hair was plaited firmly around her head and the waist of her barège dress encircled by a blue ribbon.

Raisky threw down his napkin, and jumped up, to stand before her in admiration. "How lovely," he cried. "This is my little sister, Marfa Vassilievna. And is the goose still alive?"

Marfinka became still more embarrassed, returned his greeting awkwardly, and retired to a corner.

"You have both gone mad," interrupted their aunt. "Is that the way to greet one another?"

"Marfa Vassilievna," said Raisky, as he sought to kiss Marfinka's hand.

"Vassilievna!" cried Tatiana Markovna. "Don't you love her any more? Marfinka, not Marfa Vassilievna! You will be addressing me as Tatiana Markovna next! Kiss one another. Are you not brother and sister?"

"I won't, Grandmama. He is teasing me about the goose. It is not polite to spy on people," she said severely.

Everybody laughed. Raisky kissed her on both cheeks, embraced her, and overcame her confusion. She kissed him in return, and her shyness vanished.

"Do you remember, Marfinka, how we used to run about and draw, and how you cried?"

"No ... but yes. I do remember as if in a dream."

"How should she remember, when she was only five?" interrupted her aunt.

"But I do, Grandmama, as in a dream."

Raisky had hardly captured his old memories when Marfinka disappeared. Soon she returned with sketch books, drawings and toys, and sitting down by Raisky in friendly fashion began, "Granny says that I don't remember. I remember how you used to draw, and how I sat on your knee. Granny has all your drawings, portraits and sketch books. She has kept them all in the dark room where the silver, the diamonds and the lace are. She got them out, and gave them to me a little time ago, when she heard you were coming. Here is my portrait. How funny I looked! And here is Veroshka, and Granny, and Vassilissa. Do you remember how you held me, and Veroshka sat on your shoulder, and you carried us over the water?"

"Do you remember that too?" asked her aunt. "Boastful child! Veroshka said the other day...."

"This is how I draw now," said Marfinka, handing him a drawing of a bunch of flowers.

"Splendid, little sister! Is it done from nature?"

"Yes, from nature. I can make wax-flowers, too."

"And do you play or sing?"

"I play the piano."

"And does Veroshka draw and play?"

Marfinka shook her head.

"Does she like needlework? No? Then is she fond of reading?"

"Yes, she reads a great deal. But she does not tell us what she reads, nor show us the book, nor even say where she got it."

"She hides herself from everybody, does my strange child," sighed Tatiana Markovna. "God only knows what will become of her. Now, Marfinka, don't waste your brother's time any longer with your chatter about trifles. We will talk about serious matters, about the estate."

The old lady had worn a serious expression while she watched Boris as he talked to Marfinka. She recognised his mother's features, but the changes in his face did not escape her—the indications of vanishing youth, the premature furrows; and she was baffled by the original expression of his eyes. Formerly she had always been able to read his face, but now there was much inscribed on it that was undecipherable for her. Yet his temperament was open and affectionate and his words frankly interpreted his thoughts.

Now his aunt stood before him wearing a most business-like expression; in her hand were accounts and a ledger.

"Are you not weary with your journey?" she said. "You are yawning and perhaps you would like a little sleep. Business can wait till to-morrow."

"I slept a good deal on the journey. But you are giving yourself useless trouble, Grandmother, for I am not going to look at your accounts."

"What? You have surely come to take over the estate and to ask for an account of my stewardship. The accounts and statements that I sent you—"

"I have never even read, Grandmother."

"You haven't read them. I have sent you precise information about your income and you don't even know how your money is spent."

"And I don't want to know," answered Raisky, looking out of the window away towards the banks of the Volga.

"Imagine, Marfinka," he said, "I remember a verse I learnt as a child—

"'Oh Volga, proudest of rivers,

Stem thy hurrying flood;

Oh Volga, hearken, hearken,

To the ringing song of the poet,

The unknown, whose life thou hast spared.'"

"Don't be vexed with me, Borushka," cried Tatiana Markovna, "but I think you are mad. What have you done with the papers I sent you? Have you brought them?"

"Where are they?" she continued, as he shook his head.

"Granny, I tore up all the accounts, and I swear I will do the same with these if you worry me with them."

He seized the paper, but she snatched them away, exclaiming, "You dare to tear up my accounts."

He laughed, suddenly embraced her, and kissed her lips as he had done when he was a child. She shook herself free and wiped her mouth.

"I toil till midnight, adding up and writing down every kopek, and he tears up my work. That is why you never wrote about money matters, gave any orders, made any preparations, or did anything of the kind. Did you never think of your estate?"

"Not at all, Granny. I forgot all about it. If I thought at all I thought of these rooms in which lives the only woman who loves me and is loved by me, you alone in the whole world. And now," he said, turning to Marfinka, "I want to win my sisters too."

His aunt took off her spectacles and gazed at him.

"In all my days I have never seen anything like it," she said. "Here the only person with no roots like that is Markushka."

"What sort of person is this Markushka. Leonti Koslov writes about him. How is Leonti, Granny? I must look him up."

"How should he be? He crouches in one spot with a book, and his wife in another. But he does not even see what goes on under his nose, and can any good come from his friendship with this Markushka. Only the other day your friend came here to complain that that Markushka was destroying books from your library. You know, don't you, that the library from the old house has been installed in Koslov's house?"

Raisky hummed an air from *"Il Barbiere."*

"You are an extraordinary man," cried his aunt angrily. "Why did you come at all? Do talk sensibly."

"I came to see you, Granny, to live here for a little while, to breathe freely, to look out over the Volga, to write, to draw...."

"But the estate? If you are not tired we will drive out into the field, to look at the sowing of the winter-corn."

"Later on, Granny."

"Will you take over the management of the estate?"

"No, Granny, I will not." "Who then is to look after it? I am old and can no longer do all the work. Do you wish me to put the estate into strange hands?"

"Farm it yourself, Granny, so long as you take any pleasure in it."

"And if I die?"

"Then leave everything as it is."

Tatiana Markovna looked at the portrait of Raisky's mother, for a long time she looked at the languishing eyes, the melancholy smile.

"Yes," she whispered. "I honour the memory of the departed, but hers is the fault. She kept you by her side, talked to you, played the piano, read out of books and wept as she did so. And this is the result. Singing and painting. Now tell me, Borushka," she went on in her ordinary tone, "what is to become of the house, of the linen, the silver, the diamonds? Shall you order them to be given to the peasants?"

"Do I possess diamonds and silver?"

"How often have I told you so? From your mother you have inherited all these things; what is to be done with them. I will show you the inventory of them."

"Don't do that, for Heaven's sake. I can believe they are mine. And so I can dispose of them as I please?"

"Of course; you are the proprietor. We live here as your guests, though we do not eat your bread. See here are my receipts and expenditure," she said, thrusting towards another big ledger which he waved away.

"But I believe all you say, Granny," he said. "Send for a clerk and tell him to make out a deed, by which I give the house, the land, and all that belongs to it to my dear cousins, Veroshka and Marfinka, as dowry." The old lady wrinkled her brow, and waited impatiently till he should finish speaking. "So long as you live, dear Granny," he continued, "the estate naturally remains under your control; the peasants must have their freedom...."

"Never," interrupted his aunt, "Veroshka and Marfinka are not beggars—each of them has her fifty thousand roubles—and after my death three times that sum, perhaps more. All I have is for my little girls, and, thank God, I am not a pauper. I have a corner of my own, a bit of land, and a roof to cover them. One would think you were a millionaire. You make gifts; you will have this, and you won't have that. Here, Marfinka! where have you hidden yourself?"

"Directly!" cried Marfinka's clear voice from a neighbouring room. Happy, gay, smiling and frank, she fluttered into the room, looked hesitatingly, first at Raisky, then at her aunt, who was nearly beside herself.

"Your cousin, Marfinka, is pleased to present you with a house, silver, and lace. You are, he thinks, a beggared, dowerless girl. Make a curtsey, thank your benefactor, kiss his hand—Well?"

Marfinka, who did not know what to say, squeezed herself flat against the stove and looked at her two relatives. Her aunt pushed papers and books on one side, crossed her hands over her breast, and looked out of the window, while Raisky sat down beside Marfinka, and took her hand.

"Would you like to go away from here, Marfinka, into a strange house, perhaps in an altogether different district?"

"God forbid! How could such a thing happen. Who ever imagined such nonsense?"

"Granny," laughed Raisky.

Happily "Granny" had not heard the words. Marfinka was embarrassed, and looked out of the window.

"Here I have everything I want, the lovely flowers in the garden, the birds. Who would look after the birds? I will never go away from here, never!"

"But Granny wants to go and take you with her."

"Granny! Where? Why?" she asked her aunt in her caressing, coaxing way.

"Don't tease me," said Tatiana Markovna.

"Marfinka, you don't want to leave home?" asked Boris.

"Not for anything in the world. How could such a thing be?"

"What would Veroshka say about it?"

"She would never be separated from the old house."

"She loves the old house?"

"Yes. She is only happy when she is here. If she were taken away from it she would die. We both should."

"That matter is settled then, little sister. You two, Veroshka and you, will accept the gift from me, won't you?"

"I will if Veroshka agrees."

"Agreed, dear sister. You are not so proud as Granny," he said, as he kissed her forehead.

"What is agreed?" suddenly grumbled Tatiana Markovna. "You have accepted? Who told you you might accept? Grandmother will never permit you to live at a stranger's expense. Be so kind, Boris Pavlovich, as to take over books, accounts, inventories and sales. I am not your paid servant." She pushed papers and books towards him.

"Granny!"

"Granny! My name is Tatiana Markovna Berezhkov." She stood up, and opened the door into the servants' room. "Send Savili here."

A quarter of an hour later, a peasant of almost forty-five years of age opened the door with a casual greeting. He was strongly-built, big boned, and was robust, without being fat. His eyes with their overhanging brows and wide heavy lids, wasted no idle glances; he neither spoke an unnecessary word, nor made a superfluous gesture.

"The proprietor is here," said Tatiana Markovna, indicating Raisky. "You must now make your reports to him. He intends to administer the estate himself."

Savili looked askance at Raisky.

"At your orders," he said stiffly, slowly raising his eyes. "What orders are you pleased to give?" he asked, lowering his eyes again. Raisky thought for a moment before he replied:

"Do you know an official who could draw up a document for the transfer of the estate?"

"Gavril Ivanov Meshetshnikov draws up the papers we require," he said.

"Send for him."

As Savili bowed, and slowly retired, Raisky followed him with his eyes.

"An anxious rascal," was his comment.

"How should he be other than anxious," said his aunt, "when he is tied to a wife like Marina Antipovna? Do you remember Antip? Well, she is his daughter. But for his marriage he is a treasure. He does my important business, sells the corn, and collects the money. He is honest and practical, but fate deals her blows where she will, and every man must bear his own burden. But what idea have you in your head now? Are you beside yourself?"

"Something must be done. I am going away, and you will not administer the estate, so some arrangement must be made."

"And is that your reason for going? I thought you were now going to take over the management of your estate. You have done enough gadding about. Why not marry and settle here?"

She was visibly struggling with herself. It had never entered her head to give up the administration; she would not have known what to do with herself. Her idea had been to alarm Raisky, and he was taking her seriously.

"What is to be done?" she said. "I will see after the estate as long as I have the strength to do so. How else should you live, you strange creature?"

"I receive two thousand roubles from my other estate, and that is a sufficient income. I want to work, to draw, to write, to travel for a little; and for that purpose I might mortgage or sell the other estate."

"God bless you, Borushka, what next? Are you so near beggary? You talk of drawing, writing, alienating your land; next it will be giving lessons or school teaching. Instead of arriving with four horses and a travelling carriage you sneak in, without a servant, in a miserable *kibitka*, you, a Raisky. Look at the old house, at the portraits of your ancestors, and take shame to yourself. Shame, Borushka! How splendid it would have been if you had come epauletted like Sergei Ivanovich, and had married a wife with a dowry of three thousand souls."

Raisky burst out laughing.

"Why laugh? I am speaking seriously when I tell you what a joy it would have been for your Grandmother. Then you would have wanted the lace and the silver, and not be flinging it away."

"But as I am not marrying, I don't need these things. Therefore it is settled that Veroshka and Marfinka shall have them."

"Your decision is final?"

"It is final. And it is further settled that if you do not like this arrangement, everything passes into the hands of strangers. You have my word for it."

"Your word for it," cried his aunt. "You are a lost man. Where have you lived, and what have you done. Tell me, for Heaven's sake, what your purpose in life is, and what you really are?"

"What I am, Grandmother? The unhappiest of men!" He leaned his head back on the cushion as he spoke.

"Never say such a thing," she interrupted. "Fate hears and exacts the penalty, and you will one day be unhappy. Either be content or feign content."

She looked anxiously round, as if Fate were already standing at her shoulder.

Raisky rose from the divan.

"Let us be reconciled," he said. "Agree to keep this little corner of God's earth under your protection."

"It is an estate, not a 'corner.'"

"Resign yourself to my gift of this old stuff to the dear girls. A lonely man like me has no use for it, but they will be mistresses of a house. If you don't agree, I will present it to the school...."

"The school-children! Those rascals who steal our apples, shall not have it."

"Come to the point, Granny! You don't really want to leave this nest in your old age."

"We'll see, we'll see. Give them the lace on their wedding-day. I can do nothing with you; talk to Tiet Nikonich who is coming to dinner." And she wondered what would come of such strangeness.

Raisky took his cap to go out, and Marfinka went with him. She showed him the park, her own garden, the vegetable and flower gardens, and the arbours. When they came to the precipice she looked anxiously over the edge, and drew back with a shudder. Raisky looked down on the Volga, which was in flood, and had overflowed into the meadows. In the distance were ships which appeared to be motionless, and above hung heaped banks of cloud. Marfinka drew closer to Raisky, and looked down indifferently on the familiar picture.

"Come down!" he said suddenly, and seized her hand.

"No, I am afraid," she answered trembling, and drew back.

"I won't let you fall. Do you think I can't take care of you?"

"Not at all, but I am afraid. Veroshka has no fear, but goes down alone, even in the dusk. Although a murderer lies buried there, she is not afraid."

"Try, shut your eyes, and give me your hand. You will see how carefully I take you down."

Marfinka half closed her eyes, but she had hardly taken his hand and made one step, when she found herself standing on the edge of the precipice. Shuddering she withdrew her hand.

"I would not go down for anything in the world," she cried as she ran back. "Where are you going to!"

No answer reached her. She approached the edge and looked timidly over. She saw how the bushes were bent noisily aside, as Raisky sprang down, step by step. How horrible! she thought as she returned to the house.

CHAPTER VII

Raisky went nearly all round the town, and when he climbed the cliffs once more, he was on the extreme boundary of his estate. A steep path led down to the suburbs, and the town lay before him as in the palm of a hand. Stirred with the passion aroused by his memories of childhood, he looked at the rows of houses, cottages and huts. It was not a town, but, like other towns, a cemetery. Going from street to street, Raisky saw through the windows, how in one house the family sat at dinner, and in another the amovar had already been brought in. In the empty streets, every conversation could be heard a *verst* away; voices and footsteps re-echoed on the wooden pavement. It seemed to Raisky a picture of dreamy peace, the tranquillity of the grave. What a frame for a novel, if only he knew what to put in the novel. The houses fell into their places in the picture that filled his mind, he drew in the faces of the towns-people, grouped the servants with his aunt, the whole composition centring in Marfinka. The figures stood sharply outlined in his mind; they lived and breathed. If the image of passion should float over this motionless sleeping little world, the picture would glow with the enchanting colour of life. Where was he to find the passion, the colour?

"Passion!" he repeated to himself. If her burning fire could but be poured out upon him, and engulf the artist in her destroying waves.

As he moved forward he remembered that his stroll had an aim. He wondered how Leonid Koslov was, whether he had changed, or whether he had remained what he had been before, a child for all his learning. He too was a good subject for an artist. Raisky thought of Leonti's beautiful wife, whose acquaintance he had made during his student days in Moscow, when she was a young girl. She used to call Leonti her fiancé, without any denial on his part, and five years after he had left the University he made the journey to Moscow, and married her. He loved his wife as a man loves air and warmth; absorbed in the life and art of the ancients, his lover's eyes saw in her the antique ideal of beauty. The lines of her neck and bosom charmed him, and her head recalled to him Roman heads seen on bas-reliefs and cameos.

Leonti did not recognise Raisky, when his friend suddenly entered his study.

"I have not the honour," he began.

But when Boris Pavlovich opened his lips he embraced him.

"Wife! Ulinka!" he cried into the garden. "Come quickly, and see who has come to see us."

She came hastily, and kissed Raisky.

"What a man you have grown, and how much more handsome you are!" she said, her eyes flashing.

Her eyes, her mien, her whole figure betrayed audacity. Just over thirty years old, she gave the impression of a splendidly developed specimen of blooming womanhood.

"Have you forgotten me?" she asked.

"How should he forget you?" broke in Leonti. "But Ulinka is right. You have altered, and are hardly recognisable with your beard. How delighted your Aunt must have been to see you."

"Ah! his Aunt!" remarked Juliana Andreevna in a tone of displeasure. "I don't like her."

"Why not?"

"She is despotic and censorious."

"Yes, she is a despot," answered Raisky. "That comes from intercourse with serfs. Old customs!"

"According to Tatiana Markovna," continued Juliana Andreevna, "everybody should stay on one spot, turn his head neither to right nor left, and never exchange a word with his neighbours. She is a past mistress in fault-finding; nevertheless she and Tiet Nikonich are inseparable, he spends his days and nights with her."

Raisky laughed and said, "She is a saint nevertheless, whatever you may find to say about her."

"A saint perhaps, but nothing is right for her. Her world is in her two nieces, and who knows how they will turn out? Marfinka plays with her canaries and her flowers, and the other sits in the corner like the family ghost, and not a word can be got from her. We shall see what will become of her."

"Veroshka? I haven't seen her yet. She is away on a visit on the other side of the Volga."

"And who knows what her business is there?"

"I love my Aunt as if she were my Mother," said Raisky emphatically. "She is wise, honourable, just! She has strength and individuality, and there is nothing commonplace about her."

"You will believe everything she says?" asked Juliana Andreevna, drawing him away to the window, while Leonti collected the scattered papers, laid them in cupboards and put the books on the shelves.

"Yes, everything," she said.

"Don't believe her. I know she will tell you all sorts of nonsense—about Monsieur Charles."

"Who is he?"

"A Frenchman, a teacher, and a colleague of my husband's. They sit there reading till all hours. How can I help it? Yet God knows what they make out of it in the town, as if I.... Don't believe it," she went on, as she saw Raisky was silent. "It is idle talk, there is nothing," she concluded, with a false smile intended to be allowing.

"What business is it of mine?" returned Raisky, turning away from her. "Shall we go into the garden?"

"Yes, we will have dinner outside," said Leonti. "Serve what there is, Ulinka. Come, Boris, now we can talk." Then as an idea struck him, he added, "What shall you have to say to me about the library?"

"About what library? You wrote to me about it, but I did not understand what you were talking about. I think you said some person called Mark, had been tearing the books."

"You cannot imagine, Boris, how vexed I was about it," he said as he took down some books with torn backs from the shelves.

Raisky pushed the books away. "What does it matter to me?" he said. "You are like my grandmother; she bothers me about accounts, you about books."

"But Boris, I don't know what accounts she bothered you about, but these books are your most precious possession. Look!" he said, pointing with pride to the rows of books which filled the study to the ceiling.

"Only on this shelf nearly everything is ruined by that accursed Mark! The other books are all right. See, I drew up a catalogue, which took a whole year to do," and he pointed self-consciously to a thick bound volume of manuscript. "I wrote it all with my own hand," he continued. "Sit down, Boris, and read out the names. I will get on the ladder, and show you the books; they are arranged according to their numbers."

"What an idea!"

"Or better wait till after dinner; we shall not be able to finish before."

"Listen, should you like to have a library like that?" asked Raisky.

"I!—a library like that?"

Sunshine blazed from Leonti's eyes, he smiled so broadly that even the hair on his brow stirred with the dislocation caused. "A library like that?" He shook his head. "You must be mad."

"Tell me, do you love me as you used to do?"

"Why do you ask? Of course."

"Then the books shall be yours for good and all, under one condition."

"I—take these books!"

Leonti looked now at the books, now at Raisky, then made a gesture of refusal, and sighed.

"Do not laugh at me, Boris! Don't tempt me."

"I am not joking."

Here Juliana Andreevna, who had heard the last words, chimed in with, "Take what is given you."

"She is always like that," sighed Leonti. "On feast days the tradesmen come with presents, and on the eve of the examinations the parents. I send them away, but my wife receives them at the side door. She looks like Lucretia, but she has a sweet tooth, a dainty one."

Raisky laughed, but Juliana Andreevna was annoyed.

"Go to your Lucretia," she said indifferently. "He compares me with everybody. One day I am Cleopatra, then Lavinia, then Cornelia. Better take the books when they are offered you. Boris Pavlovich will give them to me."

"Don't take it on yourself to ask him for gifts," commanded Leonti. "And what can we give him? Shall I hand you over to him, for instance?" he added as he embraced her.

"Splendid! Take me, Boris Pavlovich," she cried, throwing a sparkling glance at him.

"If you don't take the books, Leonti," said Raisky, "I will make them over to the Gymnasium. Give me the catalogue, and I'll send it to the Director to-morrow."

He put his hand out for the catalogue, of which Leonti kept a tight hold.

"The Gymnasium shall never get one of them," he cried. "You don't know the Director, who cares for books just about as much as I do for perfume and pomade. They will be destroyed, torn, and worse handled than by Mark."

"Then take them."

"To give away such treasures all in a minute. It would be comprehensible if you were selling them to responsible hands. I have never wanted so much to be rich. I would give five thousand. I cannot accept, I cannot. You are a spendthrift, or rather a blind, ignorant child—"

"Many thanks."

"I didn't mean that," cried Leonti in confusion. "You are an artist; you need pictures, statues, music; and books are nothing to you. Besides, you don't know what treasures you possess; after dinner I will show you."

"Well, in the afternoon, instead of drinking coffee, you will go over with the books to the Gymnasium for me."

"Wait, Boris, what was the condition on which you would give me the books. Will you take instalments from my salary for them? I would sell all I have, pledge myself and my wife."

"No, thank you," broke in Juliana Andreevna, "I can pledge or sell myself if I want to."

Leonti and Raisky looked at one another.

"She does not think before she speaks," said Leonti. "But tell me what the condition is."

"That you never mention these books to me again, even if Mark tears them to pieces."

"Do you mean I am not to let him have access to them?"

"He is not likely to ask you," put in Juliana Andreevna. "As if that monster cared for what you may say."

"How Ulinka loves me," said Leonti to Raisky. "Would that every woman loved her husband like that."

He embraced her. She dropped her eyes, and the smile died from her face.

"But for her you would not see a single button on my clothes," continued Leonti. "I eat and sleep comfortably, and our household goes on evenly and placidly. However small my means are she knows how to make them provide for everything." She raised her eyes, and looked at them, for the last statement was true. "It's a pity," continued Leonti, "that she does not care about books. She can chatter French fast enough, but if you give her a book, she does not understand half of it. She still writes Russian incorrectly. If she sees Greek characters, she says they would make a good pattern for cotton printing, and sets the book upside down. And she cannot even read a Latin title."

"That will do. Not another word about the books. Only on that condition, I don't send them to the Gymnasium. Now let us sit down to table, or I shall go to my Grandmother's, for I am famished."

"Do you intend to spend your whole life like this?" asked Raisky as he was sitting after dinner alone with Leonti in the study.

"Yes, what more do I need?"

"Have you no desires, does nothing call you away from this place, have you no longings for freedom and space, and don't you feel cramped in this narrow frame of hedge, church spire and house, under your very nose?"

"Have I so little to look at under my nose?" asked Leonti, pointing to the books. "I have books, pupils, and in addition a wife and peace of heart, isn't that enough?"

"Are books life? This old trash has a great deal to answer for. Men strive forwards, seek to improve themselves, to cleanse their conceptions, to drive away the mist, to meet the problems of society by justice, civilisation, orderly administration, while you instead of looking at life, study books."

"What is not to be found in books is not to be found in life either, or if there is anything it is of no importance," said Leonti firmly. "The whole programme of public and private life lies behind us; we can find an example for everything."

"You are still the same old student, Leonti, always worrying about what has been experienced in the past, and never thinking of what you yourself are."

"What I am! I am a teacher of the classics. I am as deeply concerned with the life of the past, as you with ideals and figures. You are an artist. Why should you wonder that certain figures are dear to me? Since when have artists ceased to draw water from the wells of the ancients?"

"Yes, an artist," said Raisky, with a sigh. He pointed to his head and breast. "Here are figures, notes, forms, enthusiasm, the creative passion, and as yet I have done almost nothing."

"What restrains you? You are now painting, you wrote me, a great picture, which you mean to exhibit."

"The devil take the great pictures. I shall hardly be able to devote my whole energy to painting now. One must put one's whole being into a great picture, and then to give effect to one hundredth part of what one has put in a representation of a fleeting, irrecoverable impression. Sometimes I paint portraits...."

"What art are you following now?"

"There is but one Art that can satisfy the artist of to-day, the art of words, of poetry, which is limitless in its possibilities."

"You write verses then?"

"Verses are children's food. In verse you celebrate a love affair, a festival, flowers, a nightingale."

"And satire. Remember the use made of it by the Romans."

With these words he would have gone to the bookshelf, but Raisky held him back. "You may," he said, "be able now and then to hit a diseased spot with satire. Satire is a rod, whose stroke stings but has no further consequences; but she does not show you figures brimming with life, she does not reveal the depths of life with its secret mainsprings of action, she holds no mirror before your eyes. It is only the novel that comprehends and mirrors the life of man."

"So you are writing a novel? On what subject?"

"I have not yet quite decided."

"Don't at all events describe this pettifogging, miserable existence which stares us in the face without the medium of art. Our contemporary literature squeezes every worm, every peasant-girl, and I don't know what else, into the novel. Choose a historical subject, worthy of your vivacious imagination and your clean-cut style. Do you remember how you used to write of old Russia? Now it is the fashion to choose material from the ant-heap, the talking shop of everyday life. This is to be the stuff of which literature is made. Bah! it is the merest journalism."

"There we are again on the old controversy. If you once mount that horse, there will be no calling you back. Let us leave this question for the moment, and go back to my question. Are you satisfied to spend your life here, as you are now doing, with no desires for anything further?"

Leonti looked at him in astonishment, with wide opened eyes.

"You do nothing for your generation," Raisky went on, "but creep backwards like a crab. Why are you for ever talking of the Greeks and

Romans? Their work is done, and ours is to bring life into these cemeteries, to shake the slumbering ghosts out of their twilight dreams."

"And how is the task to be begun?"

"I mean to draw a picture of this existence, to reflect it as in a mirror. And you...."

"I too accomplish something. I have prepared several boys for the University," remarked Leonti with hesitation, for he was not sure whether this was meritorious or not. "You imagine that I go into my class, then home, and forget about everything. That is not the case. Young people gather round me, attach themselves to me, and I show them drawings of old buildings, utensils, make sketches and give explanations, as I once did for you. What I know myself I communicate to others, explain the ancient ideals of virtue, expound classical life, just as our own classics are explained. Is that no longer essential?"

"Certainly it has its advantage. But it has nothing to do with real life. One cannot live like that to-day. So much has disappeared, so many things have arisen that the Greeks and Romans never knew. But we need models from contemporary life, we must educate ourselves and others to be men. That is our task."

"No, I do not take that upon my shoulders; it is sufficient for one to take the models of ancient virtue from books. I myself live for and through myself. You see I live quietly and modestly, eat my vermicelli soup...."

"Life for and through yourself is not life at all, it is a passive condition, and man is a fighting animal."

"I have already told you that I do my duty and do not interfere in anybody else's business; and no one interferes with mine."

"Life's arm is long, and will not spare even you. And how will you meet her blows—unprepared."

"What has Life to do with a humble man like me? I shall pass unnoticed. I have books, although they are not mine," he said glancing hesitatingly at Raisky, "but you give me free use of them. My needs are small, I feel no boredom. I have a wife who loves me...."

Raisky looked away.

"And," he added in a whisper, "I love her."

It was plain that as his mind nourished itself on the books, so his heart had found a warm refuge; he himself did not even know what bound him to life and books, and did not guess that he might keep his books and lose his life, and that his life would be maimed if his "Roman head" was stolen from him.

Happy child, thought Raisky. In his learned sleep he does not notice the darkness that is hidden in that dear Roman head, nor how empty the woman's heart is. He is helpless as far as she is concerned, and will never convince her of the virtues of the ancient ideals.

CHAPTER VIII

The sun was setting when Raisky returned home, and was received at the door by Marfinka.

"Where did you get lost, Cousin?" she asked him. "Grandmother is very angry, and is grumbling...."

"I was with Leonti," returned Raisky indifferently.

"I thought so, and told Grandmother so, but she won't listen and will hardly speak even to Tiet Nikonich. He is with her now and Paulina Karpovna too. Go to Grandmother, and it will be all right. Are you afraid. Does your heart beat fast?"

Raisky had to laugh.

"She is very angry. We had prepared so many dishes."

"We will eat them up for supper."

"Will you? Grandmother, Grandmother," she cried happily, "Cousin has come and wants his supper."

His aunt sat severely there, and did not look up when Raisky entered. Tiet Nikonich embraced him. He received an elegant bow from Paulina Karpovna, an elaborately got-up person of forty-five in a low cut muslin gown, with a fine lace handkerchief and a fan, which she kept constantly in motion although there was no heat.

"What a man you have grown! I should hardly have known you," said Tiet Nikonich, beaming with kindness and pleasure.

"He has grown very, very handsome," said Paulina Karpovna Kritzki.

"You have not altered, Tiet Nikonich," remarked Raisky. "You have hardly aged at all, and are as gay, as fresh, as kind and amiable...."

"Thank God! there is nothing worse than rheumatism the matter with me, and my digestion is no longer quite as good as it was. That is age, age. But how glad I am that you, our guest, have arrived in such good spirits. Tatiana Markovna was anxious about you. You will be staying here for some time?"

"Of course you will spend the summer with us," said Paulina Karpovna. "Here is nature, and fine air, and so many people are interested in you."

He looked at her askance, and said nothing.

"Do you remember me?" she asked. Boris's aunt noticed with displeasure that Paulina Karpovna was ogling her nephew.

"No, I must confess I forgot."

"Yes, impressions are quickly forgotten in the capital," she said in a languishing tone. She looked him up and down and then added, "What an admirable travelling suit."

"That reminds me I am still in my travelling clothes. Egor must be sent for and must take my clothes and linen out of the trunk. For you, Granny, and for you, my dear sisters, I have brought some small things for remembrance."

Marfinka grew crimson with pleasure.

"Granny, where are you going to put me up?"

"The house belongs to you. Where you will," she returned coldly.

"Don't be angry, Granny," he laughed. "It won't happen twice."

"You may laugh, you may laugh, Boris Pavlovich. Here, in the presence of our guests, I tell you you have behaved badly. You have hardly put your nose inside the house, and straightway vanish. That is an insult to your Grandmother."

"Surely, Granny, we shall be together every day. I have been visiting an old friend, and we forgot ourselves in talking."

"Cousin Boris did not do it on purpose, Granny," said Marfinka. "Leonti Ivanovich is so good."

"Please be silent when you are not addressed. You are too young to contradict your Grandmother, who knows what she is saying."

Smilingly Marfinka drew back into her corner.

"No doubt Juliana Andreevna was able to entertain you better, and knows better than I how to entertain a Petersburger. What friccassee did she give you?" asked his aunt, not without a little real curiosity.

"Vermicelli soup, pastry with cabbage, then beef and potatoes."

Tatiana Markovna laughed ironically, "Vermicelli soup and beef!"

"And groats in the pan...."

"It's a long time since you tasted such delicacies."

"Excellent dishes," said Tiet Nikonich kindly, "but heavy for the digestion."

"To-morrow, Marfinka," said the old lady, "we will entertain our guest with a gosling, pickled pork, carrots, and perhaps with a goose."

"A goose, stuffed with groats, would be acceptable," put in Raisky.

"Indigestible!" protested Tiet Nikonich. "The best is a light soup, with pearl barley, a cutlet, pastries and jelly; that is the proper midday meal."

"But I should like groats."

"Do you like mushrooms too, Cousin?" asked Marfinka. "Because we have so many."

"Rather! Can't we have them for supper tonight?"

In spite of Tiet Nikonich's caution against this heavy food, Tatiana Markovna sent Marfinka to Peter and to the cook to order mushrooms for supper.

"If there is any champagne in the cellar, Granny, let us have a bottle up. Tiet Nikonich and I would like to drink your health. Isn't that so, Tiet Nikonich?"

"Yes, to celebrate your arrival, though mushrooms and champagne are indigestible."

"Tell the cook to bring champagne on ice, Marfinka," said the old lady.

"*Ce que femme veut,*" said Tiet Nikonich amiably, with a slight bow.

"Supper is a special occasion, but one ought to dine at home too. You have vexed your Grandmother by going out on the very day of your return."

"Ah, Tatiana Markovna," sighed Paulina Karpovna, "our ways here are so bourgeois, but in the capital...."

The old lady's eyes blazed, as she pointed to the wall where hung the portraits of Raisky's and the young girls' parents, and exclaimed: "There was nothing bourgeois about those, Paulina Karpovna."

"Granny," said Raisky, "let us allow one another absolute freedom. I am now making up for my absence at midday, and shall be here all night. But I can't tell where I shall dine to-morrow, or where I shall sleep."

Paulina Karpovna could not refrain from applauding, but his aunt looked at him with amazement, and inquired if he were really a gipsy.

"Monsieur Raisky is a poet, and poets are as free as air," remarked Paulina Karpovna. Again she made play with her eyes, shifted the pointed toes of her shoes in an effort to arouse Raisky's attention. The more she twisted and turned, the more icy was his indifference, for her presence made an uncomfortable impression on him. Marfinka observed the by-play and smiled to herself.

"You have two houses, land, peasants, silver and glass, and talk of wandering about from one shelter to another like a beggar, like Markushka, the vagrant."

"Markushka again! I must certainly make his acquaintance."

"No, don't do that and add to your Grandmother's anxieties. If you see him, make your escape."

"But why?"

"He will lead you astray."

"That's of no consequence, Grandmother. It looks as if he were an interesting individual, doesn't it, Tiet Nikonich?"

"He is a riddle to everybody," Tiet Nikonich answered with a smile. "He must have gone astray very early in life, but he has apparently good brains and considerable knowledge, and might have been a useful member of society."

Paulina Karpovna turned her head away, and dismissed Mark with the criticism, "No manners."

"Brains! You bought his brains for three hundred roubles. Has he repaid them?" asked Tatiana Markovna.

"I did not remind him of his debt. But to me he is, for the matter of that, almost polite."

"That is to say he does not strike you, or shoot in your direction. Just imagine, Boris, that he nearly shot Niel Andreevich."

"His dogs tore my train," complained Paulina Karpovna.

"Did he never visit you unceremoniously at dinner again?" Tatiana Markovna asked Tiet Nikonich.

"No, you don't like me to receive him, so I refuse him admission. He once came to me at night," he went on, addressing Raisky. "He had been out hunting, and had eaten nothing for twenty-four hours. I gave him food, and we passed the time very pleasantly."

"Pleasantly!" exclaimed Tatiana Markovna. "How can you say such things? If he came to me at that hour, I would settle him. No, Boris Pavlovich, live like other decent people. Stay with us, have dinner with us, go out with us, keep suspicious people at a distance, see how I administer your estate, and find fault if I do anything wrong."

"That is so monotonous, Grandmother. Let us rather live each one after his own ideas and inclinations."

"You are an exception," sighed his aunt.

"No, Grandmother, it is you who are an exceptional woman. Why should we bother about one another."

"To please your Grandmother."

"Why don't you want to please your Grandson? You are a despot, Grandmother."

"A despot! Boris Pavlovich, I have waited anxiously for you, I have hardly slept, have tried to have everything as you liked it."

"But you did all that because activity is a pleasure to you. All this care and trouble is a pleasant stimulant, keeps you busy. If Markushka came to you, you would receive him in the same fashion."

"You are right, Cousin," broke in Marfinka. "Grandmother is kindness itself, but she tries to disguise it."

"Don't give your opinion when it is not asked. She contradicts her Grandmother only when you are here, Boris Pavlovich; at other times she is modest enough. And now the ideas she suddenly takes into her head. I? entertain Markushka!"

"You did as you pleased," continued Raisky. "And then when it entered my head too to do as I pleased, I disturbed your arrangements and made a breach in your despotism. Isn't that so, Granny? And now kiss me, and we will give one another full liberty."

"What a strange boy? Do you hear, Tiet Nikonich, what nonsense he talks."

On that evening Tatiana Markovna and Raisky concluded, if not peace, at least a truce. She was assured that Boris loved and esteemed her; she was, in truth, easily convinced. After supper Raisky unpacked his trunk, and brought down his gifts; for his aunt, a few pounds of excellent tea, of which she was a connoisseur, a coffee machine of a new kind, with a coffee-pot, and a dark brown silk dress; bracelets with monograms for his cousins; and for Tiet Nikonich vest and hose of Samian leather, as his aunt had desired.

Tatiana Markovna, with tears in her eyes, sat down beside him, and putting her hand on his shoulder said, "And you remembered me?"

"Whom else should I remember? You are my nearest and dearest, Grandmother."

When Tiet Nikonich and Paulina Karpovna took leave, the lady said that she had left orders with no one to fetch her, and that she hoped someone would accompany her, looking towards Raisky as she spoke. Tiet Nikonich expressed himself ready to see her home.

"Egorka could have taken her," whispered Tatiana Markovna. "Why didn't she stay at home; she was not invited."

"Thank you, thank you," said Paulina Karpovna to Raisky as she passed him.

"What for?" asked Raisky in amazement.

"For the pleasant, witty conversation, although it was not directed to me. What pleasure it gave me!"

"A practical conversation about groats, a goose, and a quarrel with Grandmother."

"Ah, I understand," she continued, "but I caught two glances, which were intended for me, confess they were. I am filled with hope and expectation."

As she went out Raisky asked Marfinka what she was talking about.

"She's always like that," laughed Marfinka.

Tatiana Markovna followed Raisky to his room, smoothed the sheets of his bed once more, drew the curtains so that the sun should not awaken him in the morning, felt the feather bed to test its softness, and had a jug of water placed on the table beside him. She came back three times to see if he were asleep or wanted anything. Touched by so much kindly thought he recognised that his grandmother's activity was not only exerted to gratify herself.

CHAPTER IX

The days passed quietly by. Every morning the sun climbed up through the blue air, and lighted up the Volga and its banks. At midday the snowy clouds crept up, often piled one on another until the blue sky was hidden, and the cooling rain fell on woods and fields; then once more the clouds stole away before the approach of the warm, pleasant evening.

Life at Malinovka passed just as peacefully. The naiveté of the surroundings had not yet lost its charm for Raisky. The sunshine insinuating itself everywhere, his aunt's kind face, Marfinka's friendliness, and the willing attention of the servants made up a pleasant, friendly environment. He even felt pleasure in the watchful guardianship that his aunt exercised over him; he smiled when she preached order to him, warned him of crime and temptation, reproached him for his gipsy tendencies and tried to lead him to a definite plan of life.

He liked Tiet Nikonich, and saw in his courtesy and his extreme good manners, his care for his health, and the universal esteem and affection in which he was held, a survival from the last century. When he felt very good tempered he found even Paulina Karpovna's eccentricities amusing. She had induced him to lunch with her one day, when she assured him that she was not indifferent to him, and that he himself was on the eve of returning her sentiments!

The even, monotonous life lulled him like a cradle song. He wrote idly at his novel, strengthened a situation here, grouped a scene there, or accentuated a character. He watched his aunt, Leonti and his wife, and Marfinka, or looked at the villages and fields lying in an enchanted sleep along the banks of the Volga. In this ocean of silence he caught notes which he could interpret in terms of music, and determined, in his abundant leisure, to pursue the subject.

One day, after a lonely walk along the shore, he climbed the cliff, and passed Koslov's house. Seeing that the windows were lighted, he was going up to the door, when suddenly he heard someone climb over the fence and jump down into the garden. Standing in the shadow of the fence, Raisky hesitated. He was afraid to sound the alarm until he knew whether it was a thief or an admirer of Juliana Andreevna's, some Monsieur Charles or other. However, he decided to pursue the intruder, and promptly climbed the fence and followed him. The man stopped before a window and hammered on the pane.

"That is no thief, possibly Mark," thought Raisky. He was right.

"Philosopher, open! Quick!" cried the intruder.

"Go round to the entrance," said Leonti's voice dully through the glass.

"To the entrance, to wake the dog! Open!"

"Wait!" said Leonti, and as he opened the window Mark swung himself into the room.

"Who is that behind you. Whom have you brought with you?" asked Leonti in terror.

"No one. Do you imagine there's a ghost. Ah! there is someone scrambling up."

"Boris, you? How did you happen to arrive together," he exclaimed as Raisky sprang into the room.

Mark cast a hasty glance on Boris and turned to Leonti. "Give me another pair of trousers. Have you any wine in the house?

"What's the matter, and where have you been?" asked Leonti suddenly, who had just noticed that Mark was covered up to the waist with wet and slime.

"Give me another pair of trousers quick," said Mark impatiently. "What is the good of chattering?"

"I have no wine, because we drank it all at dinner, when Monsieur Charles was our guest."

"Where do you keep your clothes?"

"My wife is asleep and I don't know; you must ask Avdotya."

"Fool! I will find them myself!"

He took a light, and went into the next room.

"You see what he is like," sighed Leonti, addressing Raisky.

After about ten minutes, Mark returned with the trousers and Leonti questioned him as to how he had got wet through.

"I was crossing the Volga in a fishing-boat. The ass of a fisherman fell asleep, and brought us right up into the reeds by the island, and we had to get out among the reeds to extricate the boat."

Without taking any heed of Raisky, he changed his trousers and sat down with his feet drawn up under him in the great armchair, so that his knees were on a level with his face, and he supported his bearded chin upon them.

Raisky observed him silently. Mark was twenty-seven, built as if his muscles were iron, and well proportioned; a thick mane of light brown hair framed his pale face with its high arched forehead, and fell in long locks on his neck. The full beard was paler in colour. His open, bold, irregular, rather thin face was illuminated every now and then by a smile—of which it was hard to read the meaning; one could not tell whether it spelt vexation, mockery or pleasure. His grey eyes could be bold and commanding, but for the most part wore a cold expression of contempt. Tied up in a knot as he was, he now sat motionless with staring eyes, stirring neither hand nor foot.

There was something restless and watchful in the motionless attitude, as in that of a dog apparently at rest, but ready to spring.

Suddenly his eyes gleamed, and he turned to Raisky. "You will have brought some good cigars from St. Petersburg," he began without ceremony. "Give me one."

Raisky offered his cigar case, and reminded Leonti that he had not introduced them.

"What need is there of introduction! You came in by the same way, and both know who the other is."

"Words of wisdom from the scholar!" ejaculated Mark.

"That same Mark of whom I wrote to you, don't you remember!" said Leonti.

"Wait, I will introduce myself," cried Mark, springing from the easy chair. He posed ceremoniously, and bowed.

"I have the honour to present myself, Mark Volokov, under police surveillance, involuntary citizen of this town."

He puffed away at his cigar, and again rolled himself up in a ball.

"What do you do with yourself here?" asked Raisky.

"I think, as you do."

"You love art, are perhaps an artist?"

"And are you an artist?"

"Painter and musician," broke in Leonti, "and now he is writing a novel. Take care, brother, he may put you in too."

Raisky signed to him to be silent.

"Yes, I am an artist," Mark went on, "but of a different kind. Your Aunt will have acquainted you with my works."

"She won't hear your name mentioned."

"There you have it. But it was only a matter of a hundred apples or so that I plucked from over the fence."

"The apples are mine; you may take as many as you like."

"Many thanks. But why should I need your permission? I am accustomed to do everything in this life without permission. Therefore I will take the apples without your permission, they taste better."

"I was curious to make your acquaintance. I hear so many tales about you."

"What do they say?"

"Little that is good."

"Probably they tell you I am a thief, a monster, the terror of the neighbourhood."

"That's about it."

"But if this reputation precedes me, why should you seek my acquaintance. I have torn your books, as no doubt our friend there has informed you."

"There he is to the point," cried Leonti. "I am glad he began the subject himself. He is a good sort at the bottom. If one is ill, he waits on one like a nurse, runs to the chemist, and takes any amount of trouble. But the rascal wanders round and gives no one any peace."

"Don't chatter so," interrupted Mark.

"For that matter," said Raisky, "everybody does not abuse you. Tiet Nikonich Vatutin, for instance, goes out of his way to speak well of you."

"Is it possible! The sugar marquis! I left him some souvenirs of my presence. More than once I have waked him in the night by opening his bedroom window. He is always fussing about his health, but in all the forty years since he came here no one remembers him to have been ill. I shall never return the money he lent me. What more provocation would he have? And yet he praises me."

"So that is your department of art," said Raisky gaily.

"What kind of an artist are you? It is your turn to tell me."

"I love and adore beauty. I love art, draw, and make music, and just now I am trying to write a great work, a novel."

"Yes, yes, I see. You are an artist of the kind we all are."

"All?"

"With us Russians everybody is an artist. They use the chisel, paint, strum, write poetry, as you and your like do. Others drive in the mornings to the courts or the government offices, others sit before their stalls playing draughts, and still others stick on their estates—Art is everywhere."

"Do you feel no desire to enter any of these categories."

"I have tried, but don't know how to. What brought you here?"

"I don't know myself. It is all the same to me where I go. I had a letter summoning me here from my Aunt, and I came."

Mark busied himself in his thoughts, and took no further interest in Raisky. Raisky on the other hand examined the extraordinary person before him attentively, studied the expression of his face, followed his movements, and tried to grasp the outline of a strong character. "Thank God," he said to himself, "that I am not the only idle, aimless person here. In this man there is something similar; he wanders about, reconciles himself to his fate, and does nothing. I at least draw and try to write my novel, while he does nothing. Is he the victim of secret discord like myself? Is he always struggling between two fires? Imagination striving upward to the ideal lures him on on the one hand—man, nature and life in all its manifestations; on the other he is attracted by a cold, destructive analysis which allows nothing to live, and will forget nothing, an analysis that leads to eternal discontent and blighting cold. Is that his secret?" He glanced at Mark, who was already drowsing.

"Good-bye, Leonti," he said, "it's time I was going home."

"What am I to do with him?"

"He can stay here all right."

"Think of the books. It's leaving the goat loose in the vegetable garden."

"I might wheel him in the armchair into that dark little room, and lock him in," thought Leonti, "but if he woke, he might pull the roof down."

Mark helped him out of his dilemma by jumping to his feet.

"I am going with you," he said to Raisky. "It is time for you to go to bed, philosopher," he said to Leonti. "Don't sit up at nights. You have already got a yellow patch in your face, and your eyes are hollow."

He put out the light, stuffed on his cap, and leapt out of the window. Raisky followed his example, and they went down the garden once more, climbed the fence, and came out in the street.

"Listen," said Mark. "I am hungry, and Leonti has nothing to give me. Can you help me to storm an inn?"

"As far as I am concerned. But the thing can be managed without the application of force."

"It is late, and the inns are shut. No one will open willingly, especially when it is known that I am in the case; consequently we must enter by storm. We will call 'Fire!' and then they will open at once, and we can get in."

"And be hurled out into the street again."

"There you are wrong. It is possible that I might be refused entrance, but once in, I remain."

"A siege, a row at night...."

"Ah, you are afraid of the police," laughed Mark. "You are thinking of what the Governor would decide on in such a serious case, what Niel Andreevich would say, how the company would take it. Now good-bye, I will go and storm my entrance alone."

"Wait, I have another, more delightful plan," said Raisky. "My Aunt cannot, you say, bear to hear your name; only the other day she declared she would in no circumstances give you hospitality."

"Well, what then?"

"Come home with me to supper, and stay the night with me."

"That's not a bad plan. Let us go."

They walked in silence, almost feeling their way through the darkness. When they came to the fence of the Malinovka estate, which bounded the vegetable garden, Raisky proposed to climb it.

"It would be better," said Mark, "to go by way of the orchard or from the precipice. Here we shall wake the house and must make a circuit in addition. I always go the other way."

"You—come—here—into the garden? What to do?"

"To get apples."

"You have my permission, so long as Tatiana Markovna does not catch you."

"I shan't be caught so easily. Look, someone has just leaped over the fence, like us. Hi! Stop! Don't try to hide. Who's there? Halt! Raisky, come and help me!"

He ran forward a few paces, and seized someone.

Raisky hurried to the point from which voices were audible, remarking, "What cat's eyes you have!" The man who was held fast by Mark's strong arms twisted round to free himself, and in the end fell to the ground and made for the fence.

"Catch him, hold fast! There is another sneaking round in the vegetable garden," cried Raisky.

Raisky saw dimly a figure about to spring down from the fence, and demanded who it was.

"Sir, let me go, do not ruin me!" whispered a woman's voice.

"Is it you, Marina, what are you doing here?"

"Gently, Sir. Don't call me by name. Savili will hear, and will beat me."

"Off with you! No, stop. I have found you at the right moment. Can you bring some supper to my room?"

"Anything, Sir. Only, for God's sake, don't betray me."

"I won't betray you. Tell me what there is in the kitchen."

"The whole supper is there. As you did not come, no one ate anything. There is sturgeon in jelly, turkey, all on ice."

"Bring it, and what about wine?"

"There is a bottle in the sideboard, and the fruit liqueurs are in Marfa Vassilievna's room."

"Be careful not to wake her."

"She sleeps soundly. Let me go now, Sir, for my husband may hear us."

"Run, but take care you don't run into him."

"He dare not do anything if he does meet me now. I shall tell him that you have given me orders...."

Meanwhile, Mark had dragged his man from hiding. "Savili Ilivich," the unknown murmured, "don't strike me."

"I ought to know the voice," said Raisky.

"Ah! You are not Savili Ilivich, thank God. I Sir, I am the gardener from over there."

"What are you doing here?"

"I came on a real errand, Sir. Our clock has stopped, and I came here to wait for the church-clock to strike."

"Devil take you," cried Mark, and gave the man a push that sent him reeling.

The man sprang over the ditch, and vanished in the darkness.

Raisky, meantime, returned to the main entrance. He tried to open the door, not wishing to knock for fear of awaking his aunt. "Marina," he called in a low voice, "Marina, open!"

The bolt was pushed back. Raisky pushed open the door with his foot. Before him stood—he recognised the voice—Savili, who flung himself upon him and held him.

"Wait, my little dove, I will make my reckoning with you, not with Marina."

"Take your hands off, Savili, it is I."

"Who, not the Master?" exclaimed Savili, loosening his prisoner. "You were so good as to call Marina? But," after a pause, "have you not seen her."

"I had already asked her to leave some supper for me and to open the door," he said untruthfully, by way of protecting the unfaithful wife. "She had already heard that I am here. Now let my guest pass, shut the door, and go to bed."

"Yes, Sir," said Savili, and went slowly to his quarters, meeting Marina on the way.

"Why aren't you in bed, you demon?" she cried, dashing past him. "You sneak around at night, you might be twisting the manes of the horses like a goblin, and put me to shame before the gentry."

Marina sped past light-footed as a sylph, skilfully balancing dishes and plates in her hands, and vanished into the dark night. Savili's answer was a threatening gesture with his whip.

Mark was indeed hungry, and as Raisky showed no hesitation either, the sturgeon soon disappeared, and when Marina came to clear away there was not much to take.

"Now we should like something sweet," suggested Raisky.

"No sweets are left," Marina assured them, "but I could get some preserves, of which Vassilissa has the keys."

"Better still punch," said Mark. "Have you any rum?"

"Probably," she said, in answer to an inquiring glance from Raisky. "The cook was given a bottle this morning for a pudding. I will see."

Marina returned with a bottle of rum, a lemon and sugar, and then left the room. The bowl was soon in flames, which lighted up the darkened room with their pale blue light. Mark stirred it with the spoon, while the sugar held between two spoons dripped slowly into the bowl. From time to time he tasted it.

"How long have you been in our town?" asked Raisky after a short silence.

"About two years."

"You must assuredly be bored?"

"I try to amuse myself," he said, pouring out a glass for himself and emptying it. "Drink," he said, pushing a glass towards Raisky.

Raisky drank slowly, not from inclination, but out of politeness to his guest. "It must be essential for you to do something, and yet you appear to do nothing?"

"And what do you do?"

"I told you I am an artist."

"Show me proof of your art."

"At the moment I have nothing except a trifling thing, and even that is not complete."

He rose from the divan and uncovered Marfinka's portrait.

"H'm, it's like her, and good," declared Mark. He told himself that Raisky had talent. "And it would be excellent, but the head is too large in proportion and the shoulders a trifle broad."

"He has a straight eye," thought Raisky.

"I like best the lightly-observed background and accessories, from which the figure detaches itself light, gay, and transparent. You have found the secret of Marfinka's figure. The tone suits her hair and her complexion."

Raisky recognised that he had taste and comprehension, and wondered if he were really an artist in a disguise.

"Do you know Marfinka?" he asked.

"Yes."

"And Vera?"

"Vera too."

"Where have you met my cousins? You do not come to the house."

"At church."

"At church? But they say you never look inside a church."

"I don't exactly remember where I have seen them, in the village, in the field."

Raisky concluded his guest was a drunkard, as he drunk down glass after glass of punch. Mark guessed his thoughts.

"You think it extraordinary that I should drink. I do it out of sheer boredom, because I am idle and have no occupation. But don't be afraid that I shall set the house on fire or murder anybody. To-day I am drinking more than usual because I am tired and cold. But I am not a drunkard."

"It depends on ourselves whether we are idle or not."

"When you climbed over Leonti's fence, I thought you were a sensible individual, but now I see that you belong to the same kind of preaching person as Niel Andreevich...."

"Is it true that you fired on him?" asked Raisky curiously.

"What nonsense! I fired a shot among the pigeons to empty the barrel of my gun, as I was returning from hunting. He came up and shouted that I should stop, because it was sinful. If he had been content with protesting I should merely have called him a fool, and there it would have ended. But he began to stamp and to threaten, 'I will have you put in prison, you ruffian, and will have you locked up where not even the raven will bring you a bone.' I allowed him to run through the whole gamut of polite remarks, and listened calmly—and then I 'took aim at him.'"

"And he?"

"Ducked, lost his stick and goloshes, finally squatted on the ground and whimpered for forgiveness. I shot into the air. That's all."

"A pretty distraction," commented Raisky ironically.

"No distraction," said Mark seriously. "There was more in it, a badly-needed lesson for the old boy."

"And then what?"

"Nothing. He lied to the Governor, saying that I had aimed at him, but missed. If I had been a peaceful citizen of the town I should have been thrust into gaol without delay; but as I am an outlaw, the Governor inquired into the matter and advised Niel Andreevich to say nothing. So that no enquiry should be instituted from St. Petersburg; they fear that like fire."

"When I spoke of idleness," said Raisky, "I did not mean to read a moral. Yet when I see what your mind, your abilities and your education are...."

"What have you seen? That I can climb a hedge, shoot at a fool, eat and drink heavily?" he asked as he drained his glass.

Raisky watched him, and wondered uneasily how it would all end.

"We were speaking of the art you love so much," said Mark.

"I have been snatched from Art as if from my mother's breast," sighed Raisky, "but I shall return and shall reach my goal."

"No, you will not," laughed Mark.

"Why not, don't you believe in firm intentions?"

"How should I do otherwise, since they say the way to Hell is paved with them. No, you will do little more than you have accomplished already—that is very little. We, and many like us, simply rot and die. The only wonder is that you don't drink. That is how our artists, half men, usually end their careers."

Smiling he thrust a glass towards his host, but emptied it himself. Raisky concluded that he was cold, malicious and heartless. But the last remark had disturbed him. Was he really only half a man? Had he not a firm determination to reach the goal he had set before himself? He was only making fun of him.

"You see that I don't drink away my talents," he remarked.

"Yes, that is an improvement, a step forward. You haven't succumbed to society, to perfumes, gloves and dancing. Drinking is a different thing. It goes to one man's head, another is susceptible to passion. Tell me, do you easily take fire? Ah! I have touched the spot," he went on as Raisky coloured. "That belongs to the artistic temperament, to which nothing is foreign—*Nihil humanum*, etc. One loves wine, another women, a third cards. The artists have usurped all these things for themselves. Now kindly explain what I am."

"What you are. Why, an artist, without doubt, who on a first acquaintance will drink, storm public houses, shoot, borrow money—"

"And not repay it. Bravo! an admirable description. To justify your last remark and prove its truth beyond doubt, lend me a hundred roubles. I will never pay them back unless you and I should have exchanged our respective situations in life."

"You say that in jest?"

"Not at all. The market gardener, with whom I live, feeds me. He has no money, nor have I."

Raisky shrugged his shoulders, felt in his pockets, produced his pocket book and laid some notes on the table.

"You have counted wrong," said Mark. "There are only eighty here."

"I have no more money on me. My aunt keeps my money, and I will send you the balance to-morrow."

"Don't forget. This is enough for the moment and now I want to sleep."

"My bed is at your disposal, and I will sleep on the divan. You are my guest."

"I should be worse than a Tatar if I did that," murmured Mark, already half asleep. "Lie down on your bed. Anything will do for me."

In a few minutes he was sleeping the sleep of a tired, satisfied and drunken man worn out with cold and weariness. Raisky went to the window, raised the curtain, and looked out into the dark, starlit night. Now and then a flame hovered over the unemptied bowl, flared up and lighted up the room for a moment. There was a gentle tap on the door.

"Who is there?" he asked.

"I, Borushka. Open quickly. What are you doing there," said the anxious voice of Tatiana Markovna.

Raisky opened the door, and saw his aunt before him, like a white-clad ghost.

"What is going on here. I saw a light through the window, and thought you were asleep. What is burning in the bowl."

"Rum."

"Do you drink punch at night?" she whispered, looking first at him, then at the bowl in amazement.

"I am a sinner, Grandmother. Sometimes I drink."

"And who is lying there asleep?" she asked in new terror as she gazed on the sleeping Mark.

"Gently, Grandmother, don't wake him. It is Mark."

"Mark! Shall I send for the police! What have you to do with him? You have been drinking punch at night with Mark? What has come over you, Boris Pavlovich?"

"I found him at Leonti's, we were both hungry. So I brought him here and we had supper."

"Why didn't you call me. Who served you, and what did they bring you?"

"Marina did everything."

"A cold meal. Ah, Borushka, you shame me."

"We had plenty to eat."

"Plenty, without a single hot dish, without dessert. I will send up some preserves."

"No, no ... if you want anything, I can wake Mark and ask him."

"Good heavens! I am in my night-jacket," she whispered, and drew back to the door. "How he sleeps, all rolled up like a little dog. I am ashamed, Boris Pavlovich, as if we had no beds in the house. But put out the flames. No dessert!"

Raisky extinguished the blue flame and embraced the old lady. She made the sign of the Cross over him, looked round the room once more, and went out on tiptoe. Just as he was going to lie down again there was another tap on the door, he opened it immediately.

Marina entered, bearing a jar of preserves; then she brought a bed and two pillows. "The mistress sent them," she said.

Raisky laughed heartily, and was almost moved to tears.

CHAPTER X

Early in the morning a slight noise wakened Raisky, and he sat up to see Mark disappear through the window. He does not like the straight way, he thought, and stepped to the window. Mark was going through the park, and vanished under the thick trees on the top of the precipice. As he had no inclination to go to bed again, he put on a light overcoat and went down into the park too, thinking to bring Mark back, but he was already far below on the bank of the Volga. Raisky remained standing at the top of the precipice. The sun had not yet risen, but his rays were already gilding the hill tops, the dew covered fields were glistening in the distance, and the cool morning wind breathed freshness. The air grew rapidly warmer, giving promise of a hot day. Raisky walked on in the park, and the rain began to fall. The birds sang, as they darted in all directions seeking their morning meal, and the bees and the humble-bees hummed over the flowers. A feeling of discomfort came over Raisky. He had a long day before him, with the impressions of yesterday and the day before still strong upon him. He looked down on the unchanging prospect of smiling nature, the woods and the melancholy Volga, and felt the caress of the same cooling breeze. He went forward over the courtyard, taking no notice of the greetings of the servants or the friendly advances of the dogs.

He intended to go back to his room to turn the tenseness of his mood to account as an artistic motive in his novel; but as he hurried past the old house, he noticed that the door was half open, and went in. Since his arrival he had only been here for a moment with Marfinka, and had glanced into Vera's room. Now it occurred to him to make a closer inspection. Passing through his old bedroom and two or three other rooms, he came into the corner room, then with an expression of extreme astonishment in his face he stood still.

Leaning on the window-sill, so that her profile was turned towards him, stood a girl of two or three and twenty, looking with strained curiosity, as if she were following some one with her eyes, down to the bank of the Volga. He was startled by the white, almost pallid face under the dark hair, the velvet-black eyes with their long lashes. Her face, still looking anxiously into the distance, gradually assumed an indifferent expression. The girl glanced hastily over park and courtyard, then as she turned and caught sight of him, shrank back.

"Sister Vera!" he cried.

Her face cleared, and her eyes remained fixed on him with an expression of modest curiosity, as he approached to kiss her.

She drew back almost imperceptibly, turning her head a little so that his lips touched her cheek, not her mouth, and they sat down opposite the window.

Impatient to hear her voice he began: "How eagerly I have expected you, and you have stayed away so long."

"Marina told me yesterday that you were here."

Her voice, though not so clear as Marfinka's, was still fresh and youthful.

"Grandmother wanted to send you word of my arrival, but I begged her not to tell you. When did you return? No one told me you were here."

"Yesterday, after supper. Grandmother and my sister don't know I am here yet. No one saw me but Marina."

She threw some white garments that lay beside her into the next room, pushed aside a bundle and brought a table to the window. Then she sat down again, with a manner quite unconstrained, as if she were alone.

"I have prepared coffee," she said. "Will you drink it with me. It will be a long time before it is ready at the other house. Marfinka gets up late."

"I should like it very much," he replied, following her with his eyes. Like a true artist he abandoned himself to the new and unexpected impression.

"You must have forgotten me, Vera," he remarked after a pause, with an affectionate note in his voice.

"No," she said, as he poured out the coffee, "I remember everything. How was it possible to forget you when Grandmother was for ever talking about you?"

He would have liked to ask her question after question, but they crowded into his brain in so disconnected a fashion that he did not know where to begin.

"I have already been in your room. Forgive the intrusion," he said.

"There is nothing remarkable here," she said hastily, looking around as if something not intended for strange eyes might be lying about.

"Nothing remarkable, quite right. What book is that?"

He put out his hand for the book under her hand; she rapidly drew it away and put it behind her on the shelf.

"You hide it as you used to hide the currants in your mouth. But show it me."

"Do you read books that may not be seen?" he said, laughingly as she shook her head.

"Heavens! how lovely she is!" he thought. And he wondered how such beauty could have lost its way in such an outlandish place. He wanted to touch some answering chord in her heart, wanted her to reveal something of her feelings, but his efforts only produced a greater coldness.

"My library was in your hands?"

"Yes, but later Leonid Ivanovich took it over, and I was glad to be relieved of the charge."

"But he must have left you a few books?"

"Oh no! I read what I liked, and then surrendered the books."

"What did you like?"

She looked out of the window as she answered: "A great many. I have really forgotten."

"Do you care for music?"

She looked at him inquiringly before she said, "Does that mean that I play myself, or like to hear music?"

"Both."

"I don't play, but I like to hear music, but what music is there here?"

"But what are your particular tastes?" Again she looked at him inquiringly. "Do you like housekeeping, or needlework. Do you do embroidery?"

"No, Marfinka likes and understands all those things."

"But what do you like? A book only occupies you for a short time. You say that you don't do any needlework, but you must like something, flowers perhaps."

"Flowers, yes, in the garden, but not in the house where they have to be tended. I love this corner of God's earth, the Volga, the precipice, the forest and the garden—these are the things I love," she said, looking contentedly at the prospect from the window.

"What ties bind you to this little place?"

She gave no answer, but her eyes wandered lovingly over the trees and the rising ground, and finally rested on the dazzling mirror of water.

"It is a beautiful place," admitted Raisky, "but the view, the river bank, the hills, the forest—all these things would became tedious if they were not inhabited by living creatures which share our feelings and exchange ideas with us."

She was silent.

"Vera!" said Raisky after a pause.

"Ah!" she said, as if she had only just heard his remarks, "I don't live alone; Grandmother, Marfinka...."

"As if you shared your sympathies and thoughts with them. But perhaps you have a congenial spirit here?"

Vera nodded her head.

"Who is that happy individual?" he stammered, urged on by envy, terror and jealousy.

"The pope's wife with whom I have been stopping," said Vera as she rose and shook the crumbs from her apron. "You must have heard of her."

"The pope's wife!" he repeated.

"When she is here with me we both admire the Volga, we are never tired of talking about it. Will you have some more coffee? May I have it cleared away?"

"The pope's wife," he repeated thoughtfully, without hearing her question, and the smile on her lips passed unobserved.

"Will you have some more coffee?"

"No. Do you care for Grandmother and Marfinka?"

"Whom else should I hold dear?"

"Well—me," he retorted, jesting.

"You too," she said, looking gaily at him, "if you deserve it."

"How does one earn this good fortune?" he asked ironically.

"Love, they say, is blind, gives herself without any merit, is indeed blind," she rejoined.

"Yet sometimes love comes consciously, by way of confidence, esteem and friendship. I should like to begin with the last, and end with the first. So what must one do, dear sister, to attract your attention."

- 73 -

"Not to make such round eyes as you are doing now for instance, not to go into my room—without me, not to try to find out what my likes and dislikes are...."

"What pride! Tell me, Sister, forgive my bluntness: Do you pride yourself on this? I ask because Grandmother told me you were proud."

"Grandmother must have her finger in everything. I am not proud. In what connection did she say I was?"

"Because I have made a gift of these houses and gardens to you and Marfinka. She said that you would not accept the gift. Is that true? Marfinka has accepted on the condition that you do not refuse. Grandmother hesitated, and has not come to a final decision, but waits, it seems, to see what you will say. And how shall you decide. Will a sister take a gift from a brother?"

"Yes, I accept ... but no, I can buy the estate. Sell it to me.... I have money, and will pay you 50,000 roubles for it."

"I will not do it that way."

She looked thoughtfully out on the Volga, the precipice, and the park.

"Very well. I agree to anything you please, so long as we remain here."

"I will have the deed drawn up."

"Yes, thank you!" she said, stretching out both hands to him.

He pressed her hands, and kissed Vera on the cheek. She returned the pressure of his hands and kissed the air.

"You seem really to love the place and this old house."

"And you, do you mean to stay here long?"

"I don't know. It depends on circumstances—on you."

"On me?"

"Come over to the other house."

"I will follow you. I must first put things straight here. I have not yet unpacked."

The less Raisky appeared to notice Vera, the more friendly Vera was to him, although, in spite of her aunt's wishes she neither kissed him nor addressed him as "thou." But as soon as he looked at her overmuch or seemed to hang on her words, she became suspicious, careful and reserved. Her coming made a change in the quiet circle, putting everything in a different light. It might happen that she said nothing, and was hardly seen for a couple of days, yet Raisky was conscious every moment of her whereabouts and her doings. It was as if her voice penetrated to him through any wall, and as if her doings were reflected in any place where he was. In a few days he knew her habits, her tastes, her likings, all that love on her outer life. But the indwelling spirit, Vera herself, remained concealed in the shadows. In her conversation she betrayed no sign of her active imagination and she answered a jest with a gay smile, but Raisky rarely made her laugh outright. If he did her laughter broke off abruptly to give place to an indifferent silence. She had no regular employment. She read, but was never heard to speak of what she read; she did not play the piano, though she sometimes struck discords and listened to their effects.

Raisky noticed that their aunt was liberal with observation and warnings for Marfinka; but she said nothing to Vera, no doubt in the hope that the good seed sown would bear fruit.

Vera had moments when she was seized with a feverish desire for activity; and then she would help in the house, and in the most varying tasks with surprising skill. This thirst for occupation came on her especially when she read reproach in her aunt's eyes. If she complained that her guests were too much for her, Vera would not bring herself to assist immediately, but presently she would appear in the company with a bright face, her eyes gleaming with gaiety, and astonished her aunt by the grace and wit with which she entertained the visitors. This mood would last a whole evening, sometimes a whole day, before she again relapsed into shyness and reserve, so that no one could read her mind and heart.

That was all that Raisky could observe for the time, and it was all the others saw either. The less ground he had to go on however, the more active his imagination was in seeking to divine her secret.

She came over every day for a short time, exchanged greetings with her aunt and her sister, and returned to the other house, and no one knew how she passed her time there. Tatiana Markovna grumbled a little to herself, complained that her niece was moody, and shy, but did not insist.

For Raisky the whole place, the park, the estate with the two houses, the huts, the peasants, the whole life of the place had lost its gay colours. But for Vera he would long since have left it. It was in this melancholy mood that he lay smoking a cigar on the sofa in Tatiana Markovna's room. His aunt who was never happy unless she was doing something, was looking through some accounts brought her by Savili; before her lay on pieces of paper samples of hay and rye. Marfinka was working at a piece of lace. Vera, as usual, was not there.

Vassilissa announced visitors; the young master; from Kolchino.

"Nikolai Andreevich Vikentev, please enter."

Marfinka coloured, smoothed her hair, gave a tug to her fichu, and cast a glance in the mirror. Raisky shook his finger at her, making her colour more deeply.

"The person who stayed one night here," said Vassilissa to Raisky, "is also asking for you."

"Markushka?" asked Tatiana Markovna in a horrified tone.

"Yes," said Vassilissa.

Raisky hurried out.

"How glad he is, how he rushes to meet him. Don't forget to ask him for the money. Is he hungry? I will send food directly," cried his aunt after him.

There stepped, or rather sprang into the room a fresh-looking, well-built young man of middle height of about twenty-three years of age. He had chestnut hair, a rosy face, grey-blue keen eyes, and a smile which displayed a row of strong teeth. He laid on a chair with his hat a bunch of cornflowers and a packet carefully done up in a handkerchief.

"Good-day, Tatiana Markovna; Good-day, Marfa Vassilievna," he cried. He kissed the old lady's hand, and would have raised Marfinka's to his lips, but she pulled it away, though he found time to snatch a hasty kiss from it.

"You haven't been to see us for three weeks," said Tatiana Markovna, reproachfully.

"I could not come. The Governor would not let me off. Orders were given to settle up all the business in the office," said Vikentev, so hurriedly that he nearly swallowed some of the words.

"That is absurd; don't listen to him, Granny," interrupted Marfinka. "He hasn't any business, as he himself said."

"I swear I am up to my neck in work. We are now expecting a new chief clerk, and I swear by God we have to sit up into the night."

"It is not the custom to appeal to God over such trifles. It is a sin," said Tatiana Markovna severely.

"What do you mean? Is it a trifle when Marfa Vassilievna will not believe me, and I, by God—"

"Again?"

"Is it true, Tatiana Markovna, that you have a visitor? Has Boris Pavlovich arrived? Was it he I met in the corridor? I have come on purpose—"

"You see, Granny, he has come to see my cousin. Otherwise he would have stayed away longer, wouldn't he?"

"As soon as I could tear myself away, I came here. Yesterday I was at Kolchino for a minute, with Mama—"

"Is she well?"

"Thanks for the kind thought. She sends her kind regards and begs you not to forget her nameday."

"Many thanks. I only don't know whether I can come myself. I am old, and fear the crossing of the Volga."

"Without you, Granny, Vera and I will not go. We, too, are afraid of crossing the Volga."

"Be ashamed of yourself, Marfa Vassilievna. What are you afraid of? I will fetch you myself with our boat. Our rowers are singers."

"Under no circumstances will I cross with you. You never sit quiet in the boat for a minute. What have you got alive in that handkerchief? See, Granny, I am sure it's a snake."

"I have brought you a carp, Tatiana Markovna, which I have caught myself. And these are for you, Marfa Vassilievna. I picked the cornflowers here in the rye."

"You promised not to pick any without me. Now you have not put in an appearance for more than two weeks. The cornflowers are all withered, and what can I do with them?"

"Come with me, and we'll pick some fresh ones."

"Wait," called Tatiana Markovna. "You can never sit quiet, you have hardly had time to show your nose, the perspiration still stands on your forehead, and you are aching to be off. First you must have breakfast. And you, Marfinka, find out if that person, Markushka, will have anything. But don't go yourself, send Egorka."

Marfinka seized the carp's head with two fingers, but when he began to wave his tail hither and thither, she uttered a loud cry, hastily dropped him on the floor, and fled down the corridor.

Vikentev hurried after, and a few moments later Tatiana Markovna heard a gay waltz in progress and a vigorous stampede, as if someone were rolling down the steps. Soon the two of them tore across the courtyard to the garden, Marfinka leading, and from the garden came the sound of chattering, singing and laughter. Tatiana Markovna shook her head as she looked through the window. Cocks, hens and ducks fled in panic, the dogs dashed barking at Marfinka's heels, the servants put their heads out of the windows of their quarters, in the garden the tall plants swayed hither and hither, the flower beds were broken by the print of flying feet, two or three vases were overturned, and every bird sought refuge in the depths of the trees.

A quarter of an hour later, the two culprits sat with Tatiana Markovna as politely as if nothing had happened. They looked gaily about the room and at one another, as Vikentev wiped the perspiration from his face and Marfinka fanned her burning face with her handkerchief.

"You are a nice pair," remarked Tatiana Markovna.

"He is always like that," complained Marfinka, "he chased me. Tell him to sit quiet."

"It wasn't my fault, Tatiana Markovna. Marfa Vassilievna told me to go into the garden, and she herself ran on in front."

"He is a man. But it does not become you, who are a girl, to do these things."

"You see what I have to endure through you," said Marfinka.

"Never mind, Marfa Vassilievna. Granny is only scolding a little, as she is privileged to do."

"What do you say, Sir?" said Tatiana Markovna, catching his words. "Come here, and since your Mama is not here, I will box your ears for you."

"But, Tatiana Markovna, you threaten these things and never do them," he said, springing up to the old lady and bowing his head submissively.

"Do box his ears well, Granny, so that his ears will be red for a month."

"How did you come to be made of quicksilver?" said Tatiana Markovna, affectionately. "Your late father was serious, never talked at random, and even disaccustomed your mother from laughter!"

"Ah, Marfa Vassilievna," broke in Vikentev. "I have brought you some music and a new novel."

"Where are they?"

"I left them in the boat. That's the fault of the carp. I will go and fetch them now."

In a moment he was out of the door, and Marfinka would have followed if her aunt had not detained her.

"What I wanted to say to you is——" she began.

She hesitated a little, as if she could not make up her mind to speak. Marfinka came up to her, and the old lady smoothed her disordered hair.

"What then, Granny?"

"You are a good child, and obey every word of your grandmother's. You are not like Veroshka...."

"Don't find fault with Veroshka, Granny!"

"No, you always defend her. She does indeed respect me, but she retains her own opinion and does not believe me. Her view is that I am old, while you two girls are young, know everything, and read everything. If only she were right. But everything is not written in books," she added with a sigh.

"What do you want to say to me?" asked Marfinka curiously.

"That a grown girl must be a little more cautious. You are so wild, and run about like a child."

"I am not always running about. I work, sew embroider, pour out tea, attend to the household. Why do you scold me, Grandmother," she asked with tears in her eyes. "If you tell me I must not sing, I won't do it."

"God grant that you may always be as happy as a bird. Sing, play——"

"Then, why scold me?"

"I don't scold you; I only ask you to keep within bounds. You used to run about with Nikolai Andreevich——"

Marfinka reddened and retired to her corner.

"That is no harm," continued Tatiana Markovna. "There is nothing against Nikolai Andreevich, but he is just as wild as you are. You are my dearest child, and you will remember what is due to your dignity."

Marfinka blushed crimson.

"Don't blush, darling. I know that you will do nothing wrong, but for other people's sake you must be careful. Why do you look so angry. Come and let me kiss you."

"Nikolai Andreevich will be here in a moment, and I don't know how to face him."

Before Tatiana Markovna could answer Vikentev burst in, covered with dust and perspiration, carrying music and a book which he laid on the table by Marfinka.

"Give me your hand, Marfa Vassilievna," he cried, wiping his forehead. "How I did run, with the dogs after me!"

Marfinka hid her hand, bowed, and returned with dignity:

"Je vous remercie, monsieur Vikentev, vous êtes bien amiable."

He stared first at Marfinka, then at her aunt, and asked whether she would try over a song with him.

"I will try it by myself, or in company with Grandmother."

"Let us go into the park, and I will read you the new novel," he then said, picking up the book.

"How could I do such a thing?" asked Marfinka, looking demurely at her aunt. "Do you think I am a child?"

"What is the meaning of this, Tatiana Markovna," stammered Vikentev in amazement. "Marfa Vassilievna is unendurable." He looked at both of them, walked into the middle of the room, assumed a sugary smile, bowed slightly, put his hat under his arm, and struggling in vain to drag his gloves on his moist hands began: "*Mille pardons, mademoiselle, de vous avoir dérangée. Sacrebleu, ca n'entre pas. Oh mille pardons, mademoiselle.*"

"Do stop, you foolish boy!"

Marfinka bit her lips, but could not help laughing.

"Just look at him, Granny! How can anybody keep serious when he mimics Monsieur Charles so nicely?"

"Stop, children," cried Tatiana Markovna, her frown relaxing into smiles. "Go, and God be with you. Do whatever you like."

CHAPTER XI

Raisky's patience had to suffer a hard trial in Vera's indifference. His courage failed him, and he fell into a dull, fruitless boredom. In this idle mood he drew village scenes in his sketch album—he had already sketched nearly every aspect of the Volga to be seen from the house or the cliff—and he made notes in his note books. He hoped by these occupations to free himself from his obsessing thoughts of Vera. He knew he would do better to begin a big piece of work, instead of these trifles. But he told himself that Russians did not understand hard work, or that real work demanded rude strength, the use of the hands, the shoulders and the back. He thought that in work of this kind a man lost consciousness of his humanity, and experienced no pleasures in his exertions; he shouldered his burden like a horse that seeks to ward off the whip with his tail. Rough manual labour left no place for boredom. Yet no one seeks distractions in work, but in pleasure. Work, not appearances, he repeated, oppressed by the overpowering dulness which drove him nearly mad, and created a frame of mind quite contrary to his gentle temperament. I have no work, I cannot create as do artists who are absorbed in their work, and are ready to die for it.

He took his cap and strolled into the outlying parts of the town, then into the town, where he observed every passer-by, stared into the houses, down the streets, and at last found himself standing before the Koslov's house. Being told that Koslov was at the school, he inquired for Juliana Andreevna. The woman who had opened the door to him, looked at him askance, blew her nose with her apron, wiped it with her finger, and vanished into the house for good. He knocked again, the dogs barked, and then appeared a little girl, holding her finger to her mouth, who stared at him and departed. He was about to knock again, but, instead, turned to go. As he passed through the little garden he heard voices, Parisian French, and a woman's voice; he heard laughter and even a kiss.

"Poor Leonti!" he whispered. "Or rather, blind Leonti!"

He stood uncertain whether to go or stay, then hastened his steps, and determined to have speech with Mark. He sought distraction of some kind to rid himself of his mood of depression, and to drive away the insistent thoughts of Vera. Passing the warped houses, he left the town and passed between two thick hedges beyond which stretched on both sides vegetable gardens.

"Where does the market gardener, Ephraim, live?" he asked, addressing a woman over the hedge who was working in the beds.

Silently, without pausing in her work, she motioned with her elbow to a hut standing isolated in the field. As he climbed over the fence, two dogs barked furiously at him. From the door of the hut came a healthy young woman with sunburnt face and bare arms, holding a baby.

She called off the dogs with curses, and asked Raisky whom he wished to see. He was looking curiously round, since he did not understand how anyone except the peasant and his wife could be living there. The hut, against which were propped spades, rakes and other tools, planks and pails, had neither yard nor fence; two windows looked out on the vegetable garden, two others on the field. In the shed were two horses, here was a pig surrounded by a litter of young, and a hen wandered around with her chickens. A little further off stood some cars and a big telega.

"Does Mark Volokov live here?" asked Raisky.

The woman pointed to the telega in silence.

"That's his room," she said, pointing to one of the windows. "He sleeps in the telega."

"At this time of day?"

"He only came home this morning, probably rather drunk."

Raisky approached the telega.

"What do you want of him?" asked the woman.

"To visit him."

"Let him sleep."

"Why?"

"I am frightened here alone with him, and my husband won't be here yet. I hope he'll sleep."

"Does he insult you?"

"No, it would be wicked to say such a thing. But he is so restless and peculiar that I am afraid of him."

She rocked the child in her arms, and Raisky looked curiously under the straw covering. Suddenly Mark's tangled hair and beard emerged and the woman vanished into the hut as he cried, "Fool, you don't know how to receive visitors."

"Good-day! What has brought you here?" cried Mark as he crawled out of the telega and stretched himself. "A visit, perhaps."

"I was taking a walk out of sheer boredom."

"Bored! with two beautiful girls at home. You, an artist, and you are taking a walk out of sheer boredom. Don't your affections prosper?" he winked. "They are lovely children, especially Vera?"

"How do you know my cousins, and in what way do they concern you?" asked Raisky drily.

"Don't be vexed. Come into my drawing-room."

"Tell me rather why you sleep in the telega. Are you playing at Diogenes?"

"Yes, because I must."

They entered the hut and went into a boarded compartment, where stood Mark's bed with a thin old mattress, a thin wadded bed-cover and a tiny pillow. Scattered on a shelf on the wall, and on the table lay books, two guns hung on the wall, linen and clothes were tumbled untidily on the only chair.

"This is my salon, sit down on the bed, and I will sit on the chair. Let us take off our coats, for it is infernally hot. No ceremony, as there are no ladies. That's right. Do you want anything? There is nothing but milk and eggs. If you don't want any, give me a cigar."

"Many thanks. I have already breakfasted, and it will presently be dinner time."

"Yes! You live with your Aunt. Weren't you expelled after having harboured me in the night?"

"On the contrary, she reproached me with having allowed you to go to bed without any dessert, and for not having demanded pillows."

"And didn't she rail against me?"

"As usual, but...."

"I know it is habit and does not come from her heart. She has the best heart one can wish for, better than any here. She is bold, full of character, and with a solid understanding; now indeed her brain is weakening...."

"That is your opinion? You have found someone for whom you have sympathy?"

"Yes, especially in one respect. She cannot endure the Governor any more than I can. I don't know what her reasons are; his position is enough for me. We neither of us like the police; we are oppressed by them. The old lady is compelled by them to carry out all sorts of repairs; to me they pay far too much attention, find out where I live, whether I go far from the town, and whom I visit."

Both fell silent.

"Now we have nothing more to talk about. Why did you come here?" asked Mark.

"Because I was bored."

"Fall in love."

Raisky was silent.

"With Vera," continued Mark. "Splendid girl, and she is related to you. It must be easy for you to begin a romance with her."

Raisky made an angry gesture, to which Mark replied by a burst of laughter.

"Call the ancient wisdom to your help," he said. "Show outward coldness when you are inwardly consumed, indifference of manner, pride, contempt—every little helps. Parade yourself before her as suits your calling."

"My calling?"

"Isn't it your calling to be eccentric?"

"Perhaps," remarked Raisky indifferently.

"I, for instance," said Mark, "should make direct for my goal, and should be sure of victory. You may do the same, but you would do so penetrated by the conviction that you stood on the heights and had drawn her up to you, you idealist. Show that you understand your calling, and you may succeed. It's no use to wear yourself out with sighs, to be sleepless, to watch for the raising of the lilac curtain by a white hand, to wait a week for a kindly glance."

Raisky rose, furious.

"Ah, I have hit the bull's eye."

Raisky put compulsion on himself to restrain his rage, for every involuntary expression or gesture of anger would have meant nothing less than acquiescence.

"I should very well like to fall in love, but I cannot," he yawned, counterfeiting indifference. "It is unsuited to my years and doesn't cure my boredom."

"Try it," teased Mark. "Let us have a wager that in a week you will be as enamoured as a young cat. And within two months, or perhaps one, you will have perpetrated so many follies that you will not know how to get away from here."

"If I am, with what will you pay?" asked Raisky in a tone bordering on contempt.

"I will give you my trousers or my gun. I possess only two pairs of trousers. The tailor has recovered a third pair for debt. Wait, I will try on your coat. Why, it fits as if I were poured into a mould. Try mine."

"Why?"

"I should like to see whether it suits you. Please try it on, do."

Raisky was indulgent enough to allow himself to be persuaded, and put on Mark's worn, dirty coat.

"Well, does it suit?"

"It fits!"

"Wear it then. You don't wear a coat long, while for me it lasts for two years. Besides, whether you are contented or not I shan't take yours off my shoulders. You would have to steal it from me."

Raisky shrugged his shoulders.

"Does the wager hold!" asked Mark.

"What put you on to that—you will excuse me—ridiculous idea?"

"Don't excuse yourself. Does it hold?"

"The wager is not equal. You have no possessions."

"Don't be disturbed on that account. I shall not have to pay. If my prophecy comes true, then you will pay me three hundred roubles, which would come in very conveniently."

"What nonsense," said Raisky, as he stood up and reached for his cap and stick.

"At the latest you will be in love in a fortnight. In a month you will be groaning, wandering about like a ghost, playing your part in a drama, or possibly in a tragedy, and ending, as all your like do, with some piece of folly. I know you, I can see through you."

"But if, instead my falling in love with her, she were to fall in love with me...."

"Vera! with you!"

"Yes, Vera, with me."

"Then I will find a double pledge, and bring it to you."

"You are a madman!" said Raisky, and went without bestowing a further glance on Mark.

"In one month's time I shall have won three hundred roubles," Mark cried after him.

Raisky walked angrily home. "I wonder where our charmer is now," he wondered gloomily. "Probably sitting on her favourite bench, admiring the view. I will see." As he knew Vera's habits, he could say with nearly complete certainty where she would be at any hour of the day. He went over to the precipice, and saw her, as he had thought, sitting on the bench with a book in her hand. Instead of reading she looked out, now over the Volga, now into the bushes. When she saw Raisky, she rose slowly and walked over to the old house. He signed to her to wait for him, but she either did not perceive the sign, or did not wish to do so. When she reached the courtyard she quickened her steps, and disappeared within the door of the old house.

Raisky could hardly control his rage. "And a stupid girl like that thinks that I am in love with her," he thought. "She has not the remotest conception of manners." In offering the wager, Mark had stirred up all the bitterness latent in him. He hardly looked at Vera when he sat opposite her at dinner. If he happened to raise his eyes, it was as if he were dazed by a flash of lightning. Once or twice she had looked at him in a kind, almost affectionate way, but his wild glance betrayed to her the agitation, of which she deemed herself to be the cause, and to avoid meeting his eyes she bent her head over her empty plate.

"After dinner, I shall drive with Marfinka to the hay harvest," said Tatiana Markovna to Raisky. "Will you bestow on your meadows the honour of your presence, Sir?"

"I have no inclination to go," he murmured.

"Does the world go so hard with you?" asked Tatiana Markovna. "You are indeed weighed down with work."

He looked at Vera, who was mixing red wine with water. She emptied her glass, rose, kissed her aunt's hand, and went out.

Raisky too rose, and went to his room. His aunt, Marfinka, and Vikentev, who had just happened to turn up, drove to the hay harvest, and the afternoon peace soon reigned over the house. One man crawled into the hayrick, another in the outhouse, another slept in the family carriage itself, while others took advantage of the mistress's absence to go into the outskirts of the town.

Raisky's thoughts were filled with Vera. Although he had sworn to himself to think of her no more, he could not conquer his thoughts. Where was she? He would go to her and talk it all over. He was inspired only with curiosity, he assured himself. He took his cap and hurried out. Vera was neither in the room nor in the old house; he searched for her in vain on the field, in the vegetable garden, in the thicket on the cliff, and went to look for her down along the bank of the Volga. When he found no one he turned homewards, and suddenly came across her a few steps from him, not far from the house.

"Ah!" he cried, "there you are. I have been hunting for you everywhere."

"And I have been waiting for you here," she returned.

He felt as if he were suddenly enveloped in winter in the soft airs of the South.

"You—waiting for me," he said in a strange voice, and looked at her in astonishment.

"I wanted to ask you why you pursue me?"

Raisky looked at her fixedly.

"I hardly ever speak to you."

"It is true that you rarely talk to me, but you look at me in such a wild and extraordinary fashion that it constitutes a kind of pursuit. And that is not all; you quietly follow my steps. You get up earlier than I do, and wait for me to wake, draw my curtains back, and open the window; whatever way I take in the park, and wherever I sit down, I must meet you."

"Very rarely."

"Three or four times a week. It would not be often and would not annoy me, quite the reverse, if it occurred without intention. But in your eyes and steps I see only one thing, the continual effort to give me no peace, to master my every glance, word and thought."

He was amazed at her boldness and independence, at the freedom of her speech. He saw before him, as he imagined, the little girl who had nervously concealed herself from him for fear that her egoism might suffer through the inequality of her brains, her ideas and her education. This was a new figure, a new Vera.

"What if all this exists only in your imagination?" he said undecidedly.

"Don't lie to me," she interrupted. "If you are successful in observing my every footstep, my every moment, at least permit me to be conscious of the discomfort of such observation. I tell you plainly that it oppresses me; it is slavery; I feel like a prisoner."

"What do you ask of me?"

"My freedom."

"Freedom—I am your chevalier—therefore...."

"Therefore you will not leave a poor girl room to breathe. Tell me, what reason have I given you to regard me differently from any other girl?"

"Beauty adores admiration; it is her right."

"Beauty has also a right to esteem and freedom. Is it an apple hanging on the other side of the hedge, that every passer-by can snatch at?"

"Don't agitate yourself, Vera!" he begged, taking her hands. "I confess my guilt. I am an artist, have a susceptible temperament, and perhaps abandoned myself too much to my impressions. Then I am no stranger. Let us be reconciled, Vera. Tell me your wishes, and they shall be sacredly fulfilled. I will do what pleases you, will avoid what offends you, in order to deserve your friendship."

"I told you from the beginning, you remember, how you could show me your sympathy, by not observing me, by letting me go my way and taking no notice of me. Then I will come of myself, and we will fix the hours that we will spend together, reading or walking."

"You ask me, Vera, to be utterly indifferent to you?"

"Yes."

"Not to notice how lovely you are? To look at you as if you were Grandmother. But even if I adore your beauty in silence from a distance, you would know it, and can you forbid me that? Passion may melt the surface and there may steal into your heart an affection for me. Don't let me leave you without any hope. Can you not give me any?"

"I cannot!"

"How can you tell? There may come a time."

"No, Cousin, never."

Unmanned by terror, he collected his strength to say breathlessly:

"You are no longer free? You love?"

She knit her brow and looked down on the Volga.

"And is there any sin if I do? Will you not permit it, Cousin?" she asked ironically.

"I! I, who bring you the lofty philosophy of freedom, how should I not permit you to love. Love independently of everybody, conceal nothing, fear neither Granny nor anyone else. The dawn of freedom is red in the sky, and shall woman alone be enslaved? You love. Say so boldly, for passion is happiness, and allow others at least to envy you."

"I concede no one the right to call me to account; I am free."

"But you are afraid of Grandmother."

"I am afraid of no one. Grandmother knows it, and respects my freedom. And my wish is that you should follow her example. That is all I wanted to say," she concluded as she rose from the bench.

"Yes, Vera, now I understand, and am in accord with you," he replied, rising also. "Here is my hand on it, that from to-day you will neither hear nor notice my presence."

She gave her hand, but drew it rapidly back as he pressed it to his lips.

"We will see," she said. "But if you don't keep your word, we will see—"

"Say all you have to say, Vera, or my head will go to pieces."

Vera looked long at the prospect before her before she ended with decision:

"Then however dearly I love this place, I will leave it."

"To go where?"

"God's world is wide. Au revoir, Cousin!"

A few days later Raisky got up about five o'clock. The sun was already full on the horizon, a wholesome freshness rose from garden and park, flowers breathed a deeper perfume, and the dew glittered on the grass. He dressed quickly and went out into the garden, when he suddenly met Vera.

"It is not intentional, not intentional, I swear," he stammered in his first surprise.

They both laughed. She picked a flower, threw it to him, and gave him her hand; and in reply to the kiss he gave she kissed him on the forehead.

"It was not intentional, Vera," he repeated. "You see yourself."

"I see you are good and kind."

"Generous," he added.

"We have not got to generosity yet," she said laughing, and took his arm. "Let us go for a walk; it's a lovely morning."

He felt unspeakably happy.

"What coat are you wearing?" she asked in surprise as they walked. "It is not yours."

"Ah, it is Mark's."

"Is he here? How did you come by his coat?"

"Are you frightened? The whole house fears him like fire?" And he explained how he got the coat. She listened absently as they went silently down the main path of the garden, Vera with her eyes on the ground.

Against his will he felt impelled to seek another argument with her.

"You seem to have something on your mind," she began, "which you do not wish to tell."

"I did wish to, but I feared the storm I might draw upon myself."

"You did not wish to discuss beauty once more?"

"No, no, I want to explain what my feeling for you is. I am convinced that this time I am not in error. You have opened to me a special door of your heart, and I recognise that your friendship would bring great happiness, and that its soft tones would bring colour into my dull life. Do you think, Vera, that friendship is possible between a man and a woman?"

"Why not? If two such friends can make up their minds to respect one another's freedom, if one does not oppress the other, does not seek to discover the secret of the other's heart, if they are in constant, natural intercourse, and know how to respect secrets...."

His eyes blazed. "Pitiless woman," he broke in.

She had seen the glance, and lowered her eyes.

"We will go in to Grandmother. She has just opened the window, and will call us to tea?"

"One word more, Vera. You have wisdom, lucidity, decision...."

"What is wisdom?" she asked mischievously.

"Observation and experience, harmoniously applied to life."

"I have hardly any experience."

"Nature has bestowed on you a sharp eye and a clear brain."

"Is not such a possession disgraceful for a girl?"

"Your wholesome ideas, your cultivated speech...."

"You are surprised that a drop of village wisdom should have descended on your poor sister. You would have preferred to find a fool in my place, wouldn't you, and now you are annoyed?"

"No, Vera, you intoxicate me. You do indeed forbid me to mention your beauty by so much as a syllable, and will not hear why I place it so high. Beauty is the aim and at the same time the driving power of art, and I am an artist. The beauty of which I speak is no material thing, she does not kindle her fires with the glow of passionate desire alone; more especially she awakens the man in man, arouses thought, inspires courage, fertilises the creative power of genius, even when that genius stands at the culmination of its dignity and power; she does not scatter her beams for trifles, does not besmirch purity—she is womanly wisdom. You are a woman, Vera, and understand what I mean. Your hand will not be raised to punish the man, the artist, for this worship of beauty."

"According to you wisdom lies in keeping these rules before one's eyes as the guiding thread of life, in which case I am not wise, I have not 'received this baptism.'"

An emotion closely related to sadness shone in her eyes, as she gazed upwards for a moment before she entered the house. Raisky anxiously told himself that she was as enigmatic as night itself, and he wondered what was the origin of these foreign ideas and whether her young life was already darkened.

CHAPTER XII

On Sunday Tatiana Markovna had guests for the second breakfast. The covers had been removed from the purple damask-covered chairs in the reception room. Yakob had rubbed the eyes of the family portraits with a damp rag, and they appeared to look forth more sharply than on ordinary days. The freshly waxed floors shone. Yakob himself paraded in a dress coat and a white necktie, while Egorka, Petrushka and Stepka, the latter of whom had been fetched from the village and had not yet found his legs, had been put into old liveries which did not fit them and smelt of moth. The dining-room and the reception room had been fumigated just before the meal.

Tatiana Markovna herself, in a silk dress and shawl, with her cap on the back of her head, sat on the divan. Near her the guests had taken their places in accordance with their rank and dignity. The place of honour was occupied by Niel Andreevich Tychkov, in a dress coat with an order, an important old gentleman whose eyebrows met in his great fat face, while his chin was lost in his cravat. The consciousness of his dignity appeared in every gesture and in his condescending speech. Next him sat the invariably modest Tiet Nikonich, also in a dress coat, with a glance of devotion for Tatiana Markovna, and a smile for all. Then followed the priest in a silk gown with a broad embroidered girdle, the councillors of the local court, the colonel of the garrison, ladies from the town; young officials who stood talking in undertones in a corner; young girls, friends of Marfinka, who timidly clasped their damp hands and continually changed colour; finally a proprietor from the neighbourhood with three half-grown sons.

When the company had already been assembled for some little time at the breakfast-table, Raisky entered. He felt that he was playing the rôle of an actor, fresh to the place, making his first appearance on the provincial stage after the most varying reports had been spread about him.

Tatiana Markovna introduced him as "My nephew, the son of my late niece Sfonichka," though everybody knew who he was. Several people stood up to greet him. Niel Andreevich, who expected that he would come and speak to him, gave him a friendly smile; the ladies pulled their dresses straight and glanced at the mirror; the young officials who were standing eating off their plates in the corner shifted from one foot to the other; and the young girls blushed still more and pressed their hands as if danger threatened.

Raisky bowed to the assembled guests, and sat down beside his aunt on the divan.

"Look how he throws himself down," whispered a young official to his neighbour. "His Excellency is looking at him."

"Niel Andreevich has been wanting to see you for a long time," said Tatiana Markovna aloud, adding under her breath, "His Excellency, don't forget." In the same low tone Raisky asked who the little lady was with the fine teeth and the well-developed figure.

"Shame, Boris Pavlovich," and aloud, "Niel Andreevich, Borushka has been desiring to present himself to you for a long time."

Raisky was about to reply when Tatiana Markovna pressed his hand, enjoining silence.

"Why have you not given me the pleasure of a visit from you before," said Niel Andreevich with a kindly air. "Good men are always welcome. But it is not amusing to visit us old people, and the new generation do not care for us, do they? And you hold with the young people. Answer frankly."

"I do not divide mankind into the old and the new generation," said Raisky, helping himself to a slice of cake.

"Don't hurry about eating; talk to him," whispered Tatiana Markovna.

"I will eat and talk at the same time," he returned aloud.

Tatiana Markovna looked confused, and turned her back on him.

"Don't disturb him," continued Niel Andreevich. "Young people are like that. I am curious to know how you judge men, Boris Pavlovich."

"By the impression they produce on me."

"Admirable. I like you for your candour. Let us take an example. What is your opinion of me?"

"I am afraid of you."

Niel Andreevich laughed complacently.

"Tell me why. You may speak quite plainly."

"Why I am afraid of you? They say you find fault with everybody," he went on, heedless of Tatiana Markovna's efforts to interrupt. "My Grandmother tells me that you lectured one man for not having attended Mass."

Tatiana Markovna went hot all over, and taking off her cap, put it down behind her.

"I am glad she told you that. I like to have my doings correctly reported. Yes, I do lecture people sometimes. Do you remember?" he appealed to the young men at the door.

"At your service, your Excellency," answered one of them quickly, putting one foot forward and his hands behind his back. "I once received one."

"And why?"

"I was unsuitably dressed."

"You came to me one Sunday after Mass. I was glad to see you, but instead of appearing in a dress coat, you came in a short jacket."

At this point Paulina Karpovna rustled in, wearing a muslin dress with wide sleeves so that her white arms were visible almost to the shoulder. She was followed by a cadet.

"What heat! *Bonjour, Bonjour*," she cried, nodding in all directions, and then sat down on the divan beside Raisky.

"There is not room here," he said, and sat down on a chair beside her.

"Ah, Dalila Karpovna," remarked Niel Andreevich. "Good-day. How are you?"

"Good-day," she answered drily, turning away.

"Why don't you bestow a kind glance on me, and let me admire your swanlike neck!"

The young officials in the corner giggled, the ladies smiled, and Paulina Karpovna whispered to Raisky: "The rude creature. The first word he speaks is folly."

"Ah, you despise an old man. But if I were to seek for your hand? Do I look like a bridegroom, or am I too old for you?"

"I decline the honour. *Bonjour*, Natalie Ivanovna, where did you buy that pretty hat, at Madame Pichet's?"

"My husband ordered it from Moscow, as a surprise for me."

"Very pretty."

"But listen seriously," cried Niel Andreevich insistently. "I am going to woo you in earnest. I need a housekeeper, a modest woman, who is no coquette, and has no taste for finery, who never glances at another man, and you are an example."

Paulina Karpovna pretended not to hear, but fanned herself and attempted to draw Raisky into a conversation.

"In our esteem," went on Niel Andreevich, pitilessly, "you are a model for our mothers and daughters. At church your eyes remain fixed on the sacred picture without a moment's diversion, and never even perceive the presence of young men...."

The giggling in the corner increased, the ladies made faces in their efforts to restrain their laughter, and Tatiana Markovna tried to divert Niel Andreevich's attention from her guest, by herself addressing her, but he returned to the attack.

"You are as retiring as a nun," he went on, "never display your arms and shoulders, but bear yourself in accordance with your years."

"Why don't you leave me alone?" returned Paulina Karpovna, and turning to Raisky she added: *"Est-il bête, grossier."*

"Because I wish to marry you, we are a suitable pair."

"It will be difficult to find a wife for you."

"We are well matched. I was still an assessor when you married the late Ivan Egorovich. And that must be—"

"How hot it is! Stifling! Let us go into the garden. Please give me my mantilla, Michel," she said turning to the cadet who had come with her.

At this moment Vera appeared, and the company rose and crowded round her, so that the conversation took another turn. Raisky was bored by the guests, and by the exhibition he had just witnessed. He would have left the room, but that Vera's presence provided a strong incentive to remain. Vera looked quickly round at the guests, said a few words here and there, shook hands with the young girls, smiled at the ladies, and sat down on a chair by the stove. The young officials smoothed their coats, Niel Andreevich kissed her hand with evident pleasure, and the girls fixed their eyes on her. Meanwhile Marfinka was busily employed in pouring out time, handing dishes and particularly in entertaining her friends.

"Vera Vassilievna, my dear, do take my part," cried Niel Andreevich.

"Is any one offending you?"

"Indeed there is. There is Dalila, no, Pelageia Karpovna—"

"Impertinent creature," said that lady aloud, as she rose and went quickly towards the door.

Tatiana Markovna also rose. "Where are you going, Paulina Karpovna?" she cried. "Marfinka, do not let her go."

"No, no, Tatiana Markovna," came Paulina Karpovna's voice from the hall, "I am always grateful to you, but I do not wish to meet such a loon. If my husband were alive, no man would dare...."

"Do not be vexed; he means nothing by it, but is in reality a decent old gentleman."

"Please let me go. I will come again and see you when he is not here," she said as she left the house in tears.

In the room she had left everyone was in gay humour, and Niel Andreevich condescended to share the general laughter, in which however, neither Raisky nor Vera joined. Paulina Karpovna might be eccentric, but that did not excuse either the loonish amusement of the people assembled or the old man's attacks. Raisky remained gloomily silent, and shifted his feet ominously.

"She is offended and has departed," remarked Niel Andreevich, as Tatiana Markovna, visibly agitated returned, and resumed her seat in silence. "It won't do her any harm, but will be good for her health. She shouldn't appear naked in society. This is not a bathing establishment."

At this point the ladies lowered their eyes, and the young girls grew crimson, and pressed their hands nervously together.

"Neither should she stare about her in church and have young men following her footsteps. Come, Ivan Ivanovich, you were once her indefatigable cavalier. Do you still visit her?" he asked a young man severely.

"Not for a long time, your Excellency. I got tired of forever exchanging compliments."

"It's a good thing you have given it up. What an example she sets to women and young girls, going about dressed in pink with ribbons and frills, when she is over forty. How can anybody help reading her a lecture? You see," he added turning to Raisky, "that I am only a terror to evildoers. Who has made you fear me?"

"Mark," answered Raisky, to the excitement of all present.

"What Mark?" asked Niel Andreevich, frowning.

"Mark Volokov, who is in exile here."

"Ah! that thief. Do you know him?"

"We are friends."

"Friends!" hissed the old man. "Tatiana Markovna, what do I hear?"

"Don't believe him, Niel Andreevich. He does not know what he is talking about. What sort of a friend of yours is he?"

"Why, Grandmother, did he not sup here with me and spend the night? Didn't you yourself give orders to have a soft bed made up for him?"

"Boris Pavlovich, for pity's sake, be silent," whispered his aunt angrily.

But Tychkov was already looking at her with amazement, the ladies with sympathy, while the men stared and the young girls drew closer to one another. Vera looked round the company, thanking Raisky by a friendly glance, and Marfinka hid behind her aunt.

"What a confession! You admitted this Barabbas under your roof," said Niel Andreevich.

"Not I, Niel Andreevich. Borushka brought him in at night, and I did not even know who was sleeping in his room."

"You go round with him at night? Don't you know that he is a suspicious character, an enemy of the administration, a renegade from Church and Society. So he has been telling you about me?"

"Yes," Raisky said.

"By his description I am a wild beast, a devourer of men."

"No, you do not devour them, but you allow yourself, by what right God only knows, to insult them."

"And did you believe that?"

"Until to-day, no."

"And to-day?"

"To-day, I believe it," agreed Raisky to the terror and agitation of the company. Most of the officials present escaped to the hall, and stood near the door listening.

"How so," asked Niel Andreevich haughtily.

"Because you have just insulted a lady."

"You hear, Tatiana Markovna."

"Boris Pavlovich, Borushka," she said, seeking to restrain him.

"That old fashion-plate, that frivolous, dangerous woman!"

"What do her faults matter to you. Who gave you the right to judge other people?"

"Who gave you the right, young man, to reproach me? Do you know that I have been in the service for forty years, and that no minister has ever made the slightest criticism to me."

"My right is that you have insulted a lady in my house. I should be a miserable creature to permit that. If you don't understand that, the worse for you."

"If you receive a person who is, to the knowledge of the whole town, a frivolous butterfly, dressing in a way unsuited to her age, and leaving unfulfilled her duties to her family...."

"Well, what then?"

"Then both you and Tatiana Markovna deserve to hear the truth. Yes, I have been meaning to tell you for a long time, Matushka."

"Frivolity, flightiness and the desire to please are not such terrible crimes. But the whole town knows that you have accumulated money through bribery that you robbed your own nieces and had them locked up in an asylum. Yet my Grandmother and I have received you in our house, and you take it upon yourself to lecture us."

The guests who heard this indictment were horror-stricken. The ladies hurried out into the hall without taking leave of their hostess, the rest followed them like sheep, and soon all were gone. Tatiana Markovna motioned Marfinka and Vera to the door, but Marfinka alone obeyed the indication. As for Niel Andreevich he had become deadly pale.

"Who," he cried, "who has brought you these tales? Speak! That brigand Mark? I am going straight to the Governor. Tatiana Markovna, if this young man again sets foot in your house, you and I are strangers. Otherwise within twenty four hours, both he and you and your whole household shall be transferred to a place where not even a raven can penetrate with food. Who? Who told him? I will know. Who? Speak," he hissed, gasping for breath, and hardly knowing what he said.

"Stop talking rubbish, Niel Andreevich," commanded Tatiana Markovna, rising suddenly from her place. "You will explode with fury. Better drink some water. You ask who has said it. There is no secret about it, for I have said it, and it is common knowledge in the town."

"Tatiana Markovna!" shrieked Niel Andreevich. "You have your deserts. Why make so much noise about it? In another person's house you attack a woman, and that is not the action of a gentleman."

"How dare you speak like that to me?"

Raisky would have thrown himself on him if his aunt had not waved him aside. Then with the commanding dignity she knew how to assume, she put on her cap, wrapt herself in her shawl, and went right up to Niel Andreevich, while Raisky looked on in amazement, with a sense of his own smallness in her majestic presence.

"Who are you?" she began. "A clerk in the chancellery, an upstart. And yet you dare to address a noblewoman with violence. You have too good an opinion of yourself, and have asked for your lesson, which you shall have from me once and for all. Have you forgotten the days when you used to bring documents from the office to my father, and did not dare to sit down in my presence, when you used to receive gifts from my hand on feast-days? If you were an honest man no one would reproach you. But you have, as my nephew says, accumulated stolen wealth, and it has been endured out of weakness. You should hold your tongue, and repent in your old age of your evil life. But you are bursting, intoxicated with pride. Sober yourself and bow your head. Before you stands Tatiana Markovna Berezhkov, and also my nephew Boris Pavlovich Raisky. If I had not restrained him he would have thrown you out of the house, but I prefer that he should not soil his hands with you; the lackeys are good enough."

As she stood there with blazing eyes, she bore a close resemblance to a portrait of one of her ancestors that hung on the wall. Tychkov turned his eyes this way and that seemingly beside himself with rage.

"I shall write to St. Petersburg," he gasped, "the town is in danger." Then he slunk out, so agitated by her furious aspect that he dared not raise his eyes to her face.

Tatiana Markovna maintained her proud bearing, though her fingers grasped nervously at her shawl. Raisky approached her hesitatingly, seeing in her, not his aunt, but another, and to him an almost unknown woman.

"I did not understand the majesty of your temperament. But I make my bow, not as a grandson before to an honoured grandmother, but as man to woman. I offer you my admiration and respect, Tatiana Markovna, best of women," he said, kissing her hand.

"I accept your courtesy, Boris Pavlovich, as an honour which I have deserved. Do you accept for your honourable championship the kiss, not of a grandmother, but of a woman."

As she kissed him on the cheek, he received another kiss from the other side.

"This kiss is from another woman," said Vera in a low voice as she left the room, before Raisky's outstretched arms could reach her.

"Vera and I have not spoken to one another, but we have both understood you. We do, in fact, talk very little, but we resemble one another," said Tatiana Markovna.

"Granny, you are an extraordinary woman!" cried Raisky, looking at her with as much enthusiasm as if he saw her for the first time.

"Drive to the Governor's, Borushka, and tell him exactly what has happened so that the other party may not be first with his lying nonsense. I am going to beg Paulina Karpovna's pardon."

CHAPTER XIII

For three days the impression of this Sunday morning breakfast remained with Raisky. He had been surprised by this sudden transformation of Tatiana Markovna from grandmother and kindly hostess into a lioness, but he had been still more agitated by Vera's kiss. He could have wept for emotion, and would like to have built new hopes on it, but it was a kiss that led no further, a flash of lightning immediately extinguished.

Raisky kept his promise, and neither went to Vera's room, nor followed her; he saw her only at meals and then rarely talked to her. He succeeded in hiding from her the fact that she still occupied his thoughts; he would like to have wiped out of her recollection his hasty revelation of himself to her.

Then he began a portrait of Tatiana Markovna, and occupied himself seriously with the plan of his novel. With Vera as the central figure, and the scene his own estate and the bank of the Volga his fancy took shape and the secret of artistic creation became clear to him.

It chanced once or twice that he found himself walking with Vera. Gaily and almost indifferently he poured out for her his store of thought and knowledge, even of anecdote, as he might do to any amiable, clever stranger, without second thoughts or any wish to reap an advantage. He led in fact a peaceful, pleasant life, demanding nothing and regretting nothing. He perceived with satisfaction that Vera no longer avoided him, that she confided in him and drew closer to him; she would herself come to his room to fetch books, and he made no effort to retain her.

They often spent the afternoon with Tatiana Markovna. Vera apparently liked to hear him talk, and smiled at his jokes, though from time to time she would get up suddenly in the middle of a sentence when he was reading aloud or talking, and with some slight excuse, go out and not appear again for hours. He made no effort to follow her.

He found recreation with friends in the town, driving occasionally with the Governor or taking part with Marfinka and Vera in some rural entertainment.

The month which Mark had set as a limit for their wager, was nearly over, and Raisky felt himself free from passion. At least he thought so, and put down all his symptoms to the working of his imagination and to curiosity. On some days even Vera appeared to him in the same light as Marfinka. He saw in them two charming young girls, only late left school with all the ideas and adorations of the schoolgirl, with the schoolgirl's dream-theory of life, which is only shattered by experience. He told himself that he was absolutely cold and indifferent, and in a position truthfully to call himself her friend. He would shortly leave the place, but before that he must visit "Barabbas," take his last pair of trousers, and warn him against making a wager.

He went to Leonti to ask where Mark was to be found and discovered them both at breakfast.

"You might develop into a decent individual," cried Mark to him, "if you were a little bolder."

"You mean if I had the boldness to shoot my neighbour or to storm an inn by night."

"How will you take an inn by storm? Besides, there is no need, since your aunt has her own guesthouse. Many thanks for having chased that old swine from your house, I am told in conjunction with Tatiana Markovna. Splendid!"

"Where did you hear that?"

"The whole town is talking of it. I wanted to come and show my respect to you, when I suddenly heard that you were on friendly terms with the Governor, had invited him to your house, and that you and your aunt had stood on your hind paws before him. That is abominable, when I thought you had only invited him to show him the door."

"That is what is called bourgeois courage, I believe."

"I don't know what it is called, but I can best give you an example of the kind of courage. For some time the police inspector has been sniffing round our vegetable garden, so probably his Excellency has been kind enough to show an interest in me, and to enquire after my health and amusements. Well, I am training a couple of bull-dogs, and I hadn't had them a week before the garden was clear of cats. I have them ready at dark, and if the Colonel or his suite arrive, I shall let my beasts loose. Of course it will happen by accident."

"I have come to say goodbye, for I am leaving here shortly."

"You are going away?" asked Mark in astonishment, then added in a low, serious voice, "I should like to have a word with you."

"Speak, by all means. Is it a question of money again?"

"Money as far as I am concerned, but it is not of that I wish to speak to you. I will come to you later. I cannot speak of that now," he said looking significantly at Koslov's wife to indicate that he could not explain himself in her presence.

"No one will let you go?" whispered Juliana Andreevna. "I have not once spoken to you out of hearing of my husband."

"Have you brought the money with you," asked Mark suddenly, "the three hundred roubles for the wager?"

"Where is the pair of trousers?" asked Raisky ironically.

"I am not joking; you must pay me my three hundred roubles."

"Why? I am not in love as you see."

"I see that you are head over ears in love."

"How do you see that."

"In your face."

"The month is past, and with it the wager at an end. As I don't need the trousers I will make you a present of them to go with the coat."

"How can you go away?" complained Leonti. "And the books—"

"What books?"

"Your books. See for yourself by the catalogue that they are all right."

"I have made you a present of them."

"Be serious for a moment. Where shall I send them?"

"Goodbye. I have no time to spare. Don't come to me with the books, or I will burn them. And you, wise man, who can tell a lover by his face, farewell. I don't know whether we shall meet again."

"Where is the money? It isn't honest not to surrender it. I see the presence of love, which like measles has not yet come out, but soon will. Your face is already red. How tiresome that I fixed a limit, and so lose three hundred roubles by my own stupidity."

"Goodbye."

"You will not go," said Mark with decision.

"I shall have another opportunity of seeing you, Koslov. I am not starting until next week."

"You will not go," repeated Mark.

"What about your novel?" asked Leonti. "You intended to finish it here."

"I am already near the end of it, though there is still some arranging to be done, which I can do in St. Petersburg."

"You will not end your romance either, neither the paper one nor the real one." said Mark.

Raisky was about to answer, but thought better of it, and was quickly gone.

"Why do you think he won't finish the novel?" asked Leonti.

"He is only half a man," replied Mark with a scornful, bitter laugh.

Raisky walked in the direction of home. His victory over himself seemed so assured that he was ashamed of his earlier weakness. He pictured to himself how he would now appear to her in a new and surprising guise, bold, deliberately scornful, with neither eyes nor desire for her beauty; and he pictured her astonishment and sorrow.

In his impatience to see the effect of this new development in himself he stole into her room and crossed the carpet without betraying his presence. She sat with her elbows on the table, reading a letter, written as he noticed on blue paper in irregular lines and sealed with common blackish-brown sealing wax.

"Vera!" he said in a low voice. She shrank back with such obvious terror that he too trembled, then quickly put the letter in her pocket.

They looked at one another without stirring.

"You are busy. Excuse my coming," he said, and took a step backward, as if to leave her.

She made no answer, but, gradually recovering her self-possession, and without removing her eyes from his face she advanced towards him with her hand still in her pocket.

"It must be a very interesting letter and a great secret," he said with a forced laugh, "since you conceal it so quickly."

With her eyes still upon him she sat down on the divan.

"Show me the letter," he laughed, betraying his agitation by a tremor of the voice. "You will not show it?" he went on as she looked at him in amazement and pressed her hand tighter in her pocket.

She shook her head.

"I don't need to read it. What possible interest could I have in another person's letter? I only wanted a proof of your confidence, of your friendly disposition towards me. You see my indifference. See, I am not as I was," he said, telling himself at the same time that the letter obsessed him.

She tried, to read in his face the indifference in which he was insisting. His face indeed wore an aspect of indifference, but his voice sounded as if he were pleading for alms.

"You will not show it," he said. "Then God be with you," and he turned to the door.

"Wait," she said, putting her hand in her pocket and drawing out a letter which she showed him.

He looked at both sides, and glanced at the signature, Pauline Kritzki.

"That is not the letter," he said, returning it.

"Do you see another?" she asked drily.

He replied that he had not, fearing that she might accuse him of spying, and at her request began to read:

"Ma belle chamante divine Vera Vassilievna! I am enraptured and fall on my knees before your dear, noble, handsome cousin; he has avenged me, and I am triumphant and weep for joy. He was great. Tell him that he is ever my knight, that I am his devoted slave. Ah, how I admire him, I would say—the word is on the tip of my tongue—but I dare not. Yet why should I not? Yes, I love him, I adore him. Everyone must adore him...."

Here Raisky attempted to return the letter, but Vera bade him continue, as there was a request for him. He skipped a few lines and proceeded:—

"Implore your cousin (he adores you. Do not deny it, for I have seen his passionate glances. What would I not give to be in your place).

"Implore your cousin, darling Vera Vassilievna, to paint my portrait. I don't really care about the portrait, but to be with an artist to admire him, to speak to him, to breathe the same air with him! *Ma pauvre tête, je deviens folle. Je compte sur vous, ma belle et bonne amie, et j'attends la réponse.*"

"What answer shall I give her?" asked Vera, as Raisky laid the letter on the table.

He was thinking of the other letter, wondering why she had hidden it, and did not hear her question.

"May I write that you agree?"

"God forbid! on no account."

"How is it to be done then? She wants to breathe the same air as you."

"I should stifle in that atmosphere."

"But if I ask you to do it?" whispered Vera.

"You, what difference can it make to you?" he asked trembling.

"I should like to say something pleasant to her," she returned, but did not add that she seized this means of detaching him from herself. Paulina Karpovna would not lightly let him out of her hands.

"Should you accept it as a sign of friendship if I fulfilled your wish? Well, then," as she nodded, "I make two conditions, one that you should be present at the sittings. Otherwise I should be clearing out at the first sitting. Do you agree?" Then, as she nodded unwillingly, "the second is that you show me the other letter."

"Which letter?"

"The one you hid so quickly in your pocket."

"There isn't another."

"You would not have hidden this letter in terror; will you show the other?"

"You are beginning again," she said reproachfully.

"You need not trouble. I was only jesting. But for God's sake do not look on me as a despôt or a spy; it was mere curiosity. God be with you and your secrets."

"I have no secrets," she returned drily as he rose to go.

"Do you know that I am soon leaving?" he asked suddenly.

"I heard so; is it true?"

"Why do you doubt?"

She dropped her eyes and said nothing.

"You will be glad for me to go?"

"Yes," she answered in a whisper.

"Why," he said sadly, and came nearer.

She thought for a moment, drew out another letter, glanced through it, carefully scratching out a word or a line here and there, and handed it to him.

"Read that letter," she said, again slipping her hand into her pocket.

He began to read the delicate handwriting: "I am sorry, dear Natasha," and then asked, "Who is Natasha?"

"The priest's wife, my school friend."

"Ah! the pope's wife. It is your own letter. That is interesting," and he became absorbed in the reading.

"I am sorry, dear Natasha," the letter ran, "that I have not written to you since my return. As usual I have been idle, but I had other reasons, which you shall learn. The chief reason you already know (here some words were scratched out), which agitates me very much. But of that we will speak when we meet.

"The other reason is the arrival of our relative, Boris Pavlovich Raisky. For my misfortune he scarcely ever leaves the house, so that for a fortnight I did hardly anything except hide from him. What an abundance of reason, of different kinds of knowledge, of brilliance, of talent he brought with him, and with it all what unrest. He upsets the whole household. He had hardly arrived before he was seized with the firm conviction that not only the estate, but all that lived on it, were his property. Taking his stand on a relationship, which hardly deserves the name, and on the fact that he knew us when we were little, he treated us as if we were children or schoolgirls. Although I have hidden myself from him, I have only just succeeded in preventing him from seeing how I sleep and dream, and what I hope and wait for.

"This pursuit has almost made me ill, and I have seen no one, written to no one. I feel like a prisoner. It is as if he were playing with me, perhaps quite against his own will. One day he is cold and indifferent, the next his eyes are ablaze, and I fear him as I would a madman. The worst of all seems to me to be that he does not know himself, so that no reliance can be placed on his plans and promises; he decides on one course, and the next day takes another. He himself says he is nervous, susceptible and passionate, and he may be right. He is no play actor, and does not disguise himself; he is, I think, too sensible and well-bred, indeed, too honest, for that.

"He is by way of being an artist, draws, writes, improvises very nicely on the piano, and dreams of art. Yet it seems to me that he does substantially nothing, but is spending his life, as he says, in the adoration of beauty; he is a lover by temperament, like (do you remember?) Dashenka Sfemechkin, who fell in love with a Spanish prince, whose portrait she had seen in a German calendar, and would admit no one, not even the piano-tuner, Kish. But Boris Pavlovich is full of kindness and honour, is upright, gay, original, but all these qualities are so disconnected and uncertain in their expression that we don't know what to make of them. Now he seeks my friendship, but I am afraid of him, am afraid he may do anything, am afraid (here some lines were crossed out). Ah, if only he would go away. It is terrible to think he may one day (here again words were crossed out).

"And I need one thing—rest. The doctor says I am nervous, must spare myself, and avoid all agitation. Thank God, he is also attached to Grandmother, and I am left in peace. I do not want to step out of the circle I have drawn for myself; and nobody else should cross the line. In its sanctity lies my peace and my whole happiness.

"If Raisky oversteps this line, the only course that remains to me is to fly from here. That is easy to say, but where? And then I have some conscience about it, because he is so good, so kind to me and my sister, and means to make a gift to us of this place, this Paradise, where I have learned to live and not to vegetate. It lies on my conscience that he should squander these undeserved tokens of affection, that he tries to be brilliant for my sake, and to awaken in me some affection, although I have denied him every hope. Ah, if he only knew how vain his efforts are.

"Now I will tell you about *him*...."

The letter went no further, and Raisky looked at the lines as if he were trying to read behind them. Vera had said practically nothing about herself; she remained in the shadow, while the whole garish light fell on him.

"There was another letter," he said sharply, "written on blue paper."

Vera had not left the room, but someone's hand was on the lock.

"Who is there?" asked Raisky with a start.

In the doorway appeared Vassilissa's anxious face.

"It's I," she said in a low voice. "It's a good thing you are here, Boris Pavlovich; they are asking for you. Please make haste. There is nobody in the hall. Yakob is at church. Egorka has been sent to the Volga for some fish, and I am alone with Pashutka."

"Who is asking for me?"

"A gendarme from the Governor. The Governor asks you to go to see him, at once, if possible, if not to-morrow morning. The business is pressing."

"Very well. I will go."

"Please, as quickly as possible. Then *he* has also come."

"Who?"

"The man they would like to horsewhip. He has made himself at home in the hall, and is waiting for you. The Mistress and Marfa Vassilievna have not yet returned from the town."

"Didn't you ask his name?"

"He gave his name, but I have forgotten. He is the man who stayed the night with you when you were drinking. Please, Boris Pavlovich, be quick. Pashutka and I have locked ourselves in."

"Why?"

"Because we were afraid. I climbed out of the window into the yard to come and tell you. If only he does not nose anything out."

Raisky went with her, laughing. He sent a message by the gendarme that he would be with the Governor in an hour. Then he sought out Mark and led him into his room.

"Do you wish to spend the night with me?" he asked ironically.

"I am indeed a nightbird," answered Mark, who looked anxious. "I receive too much attention in the daytime, and it puts less shame on your Aunt's house. The magnificent old lady, to show Tychkov the door. But I have come to you on important business," he said, looking serious.

"You have business! That is interesting."

"Yes, more serious than yours. To-day I was at the police-station, not exactly paying a call. The police inspector had invited me, and I was politely fetched with a pair of grey horses."

"What has happened?" "A trifling thing. I had lent books to one or two people...."

"Perhaps mine, that you had taken from Leonti?"

"Those and others—here is the list," he said, handing him a slip of paper.

"To whom did you give the books?"

"To many people, mostly young people. One fool, the son of an advocate, did not understand some French phrases, and showed the book to his mother, who handed it on to the father, and he in his turn to the magistrate. The magistrate, having heard of the name of the author, made a great commotion and informed the Governor. At first the lad would not give me away, but when they applied the rod to him he gave my name, and to-day they summoned me to court."

"And what line did you adopt?"

"What line?" said Mark laughing, as he looked at Raisky. "They asked me whose books they were, and where I had got them, and I said from you; some you had brought with you; others, Voltaire, for instance, I had found in your library."

"I'm much obliged. Why did you put this honour on me?"

"Nobody will meddle with you, since you are in his Excellency's favour. Then you are not living here under official compulsion. But I shall be sent off to a third place of exile; this is already the second. At any other time this would be a matter of indifference to me, but just now, for the time being, at least, I should like to stay here."

"And what else?"

"Nothing. I only wanted to tell you what I have done, and to ask whether you will take it on yourself or not."

"But what if I won't, and I don't intend to."

"Then instead of your name I will give Koslov's. He is growing mouldy here. Let him go to prison. He can take up his Greeks again later."

"No, he will never take them up again if he is robbed of his position, and of his bread and butter."

"There you are right, my conclusions were illogical. It would be better for you to take it on yourself."

"What are you to me that I should do so?"

"On the former occasion I needed money, and you had what I lacked. This is the same case. No one will touch you, while I should be sent off. I am now logical enough."

"You ask a remarkable service. I am just going to the Governor, who has sent for me. Good-bye."

"He has sent for you, then?"

"What am I to do? What should I say?"

"Say that you are the hero of the piece, and the Governor will quash the whole matter, for he does not like sending special reports to St. Petersburg. With me it is quite different. I am under police supervision, and it is his duty to return a report every month as to my circumstances and my mode of life. However," he added with apparent indifference, "do as you like. And now come, for I have no more time either. Let us go as far as the wood together, and I will climb down the precipice. I will wait at the fisherman's on the island to see how the matter ends."

At the edge of the precipice Mark vanished into the bushes. Raisky drove to the Governor's, and returned home about two o'clock in the morning.

Although he had gone so late to bed, he rose early. The windows of Vera's room were still darkened. She is still sleeping, he thought, and he went into the garden, where he walked up and down for an hour, waiting for the drawing back of the lilac curtain. He hoped Marina would cross the yard, but she did not come. Then Tatiana Markovna's window was opened, the pigeons and the sparrows began to gather on the spot were they were wont to receive crumbs from Marfinka, doors opened and shut, the grooms and the servants crossed the yard, but the lilac curtain remained untouched. The gloomy Savili came out of his room and looked silently round the yard. When Raisky called him he came towards him with slow steps.

"Tell Marina to let me know when Vera Vassilievna is dressed."

"Marina is not here."

"Where is she?"

"She started at dawn to accompany the young lady over the Volga."

"What young lady, Vera Vassilievna?"

"Yes."

"How did they go, and with whom?"

"In the *brichka*, with the dun horse. They will return in the evening," he added.

"Do you think they will return to-day?" asked Raisky with interest.

"Assuredly. Prokor with the horse, and Marina too. They will see the young lady safely there, and return immediately."

Raisky looked at Savili without seeing him, and they stood opposite one another for some time speechless.

"Have you any further orders?" Savili asked at length.

Raisky recovered himself, and inquired whether Savili was awaiting Marina. Savili replied by a curse on his wife.

"Why do you beat her?" asked Raisky. "I have been intending for a long time to advise you to leave her alone."

"I don't beat her any more."

"Since when?"

"For the last week, since she has stayed quietly at home."

"Go, I have no orders. But do not beat Marina. It will be better both for you and her if you give her complete liberty."

Raisky passed on his way with bent head, glancing sadly at Vera's window. Savili's eyes too were on the ground, and he had forgotten to put his cap on again in his amazement at Raisky's last words.

"Passion once more!" thought Raisky. "Alas, for Savili, and for me!"

CHAPTER XIV

Since Vera's departure Raisky had experienced the meaning of unmitigated solitude. He felt as if he were surrounded by a desert, now that he was deprived of the sight of her, although nature around him was radiant and smiling. Tatiana Markovna's anxious solicitude, Marfinka's charming rule, her songs, her lively chatter with the gay and youthful Vikentev, the arrival and departure of guests, the eccentricities of the freakish Paulina Karpovna—none of these things existed for him. He only saw that the lilac curtain was motionless, the blinds had been drawn down, and that Vera's favourite bench remained empty.

He did not want to love Vera, and if he had wished it he ought still to resist, for Vera had denied him every hope; indeed her beauty seemed to have lost its power over him, and he was now drawn to her by a different attraction.

"What is Vera's real nature?" he asked his aunt one day.

"You see for yourself. She recognises only her own understanding and her own will. She was born in my arms, and has spent her whole life with me, yet I do not know what is in her mind, what are her likes and dislikes. I do not force her, or worry her, so that she can hardly think herself unfortunate. You see for yourself that my girls live with me as free as the birds of the air."

"You are right, Grandmother. It is not fear, or anxiety, or the power of authority that binds you to them, but the tenderest of home ties. They adore you, and so they ought to do, but it is the fruit of their upbringing. Why should worn-out conceptions of duty be pressed upon them, and why should they live like caged birds? Let them dip into the reservoir of life itself. A bird imprisoned in a cage loses the capacity for freedom, and, even if the door of his cage is opened, he will not take flight."

"I have never tried to exercise restraint on Marfinka or Vera. Supposing a respectable, rich man of old and blameless family were to ask for Marfinka's hand, and she refused it, do you think I should persuade her?"

"Well, Granny, I leave Marfinka to you, but do not attempt to do anything with Vera. You must not restrain her in any way, must leave her her freedom. One bird is born for the cage, another for freedom. Vera will be able to direct her own life."

"Do I restrain or repress her? I am like the police inspector who only sees that there is an outward semblance of order; I do not penetrate below the surface unless my assistance is invited."

"Tell me, Grandmother, what sort of a woman is this priest's wife, and what are the links that bind her to Vera?"

"Natalie Ivanovna and Vera made friends at a boarding school. She is a good, modest woman."

"Is she sensible? Possibly a woman of weight and character?"

"Oh no! She is not stupid, is fairly educated, a great reader, and fond of dress. The pope, who is much liked by the local landowner, is not poor, and lives in comfort on his own land. He is a sensible man, belongs to the younger generation, but he leads too worldly a life for the priesthood, as is the custom in landed society. He reads French books, and smokes, for instance; things that are unsuited to the priestly garb. Every glance of Veroshka's, every mood of hers is sacred to Natalie Ivanovna; whatever she may say is wise and good. This suits Vera, who does not want a friend, but an obedient servant; that is why she loves the pope's wife."

"And Vera loves you too?" asked Raisky, who wanted to know if Vera loved anybody else except the pope's wife.

"Yes, she loves me," answered Tatiana Markovna with conviction, "but in her own fashion. She never shows it, and never will, though she loves me and would be ready to die for me."

"And you love Vera?"

"Ah, how I love her!" she sighed, and tears stood in her eyes. "She does not know, but perhaps one day she may learn."

"Have you noticed how thoughtful she has been for some time. Is she not in love?" he added in a half-whisper, but immediately regretted the question, which it was too late to withdraw. His aunt started back as if a stone had hit her.

"God forbid!" she cried, making the sign of the Cross. "This sorrow has been spared us. Do not disturb my peace, but confess, as you would to the priest, if you know anything."

Raisky was annoyed with himself, and made an effort, partially successful, to pacify his aunt.

"I have not noticed anything more than you have. She would hardly be likely to say anything to me that she kept secret from you."

"Yes, yes, it is true she will say nothing. The pope's wife knows everything, but she would rather die than betray Vera's secrets. Her own secrets she scatters for anyone to pick up, but not Vera's."

"With whom could she fall in love?" remarked Tatiana Markovna after a silence. "There is no one here."

"No one?" interrupted Raisky quickly.

Tatiana Markovna shook her head, then went on after a while:—

"There might be the Forester. He is an excellent individual, and has shown an inclination, I notice. He would be certainly an admirable match for Vera, but...."

"Well?"

"She is so strange. Heaven knows how any one would dare, how any man would woo her. He is splendid—well-established and rich. The wood alone yields thousands."

"Is the Forester young, educated, a man that counts?"

Vassilissa entered and announced Paulina Karpovna.

"The evil one himself has brought her," grumbled Tatiana Markovna. "Show her in, and be quick with breakfast."

CHAPTER XV

One evening a thunderstorm was brewing. The black clouds lay entrenched beyond the Volga, and the air was as hot and moist as in a bathhouse. Here and there over the fields and roads rose pillars of dust.

In the house Tatiana Markovna sent her household hurrying to close the stove pipes, the doors and the windows. She was not only afraid of a thunderstorm herself, but she was not pleased if her fear was not shared by everybody else—that would be freethinking. So at each flash of lightning everyone must make the sign of the Cross, on pain of being thought a blockhead. She chased Egorka from the ante-room into the servants' room, because during the approach of the storm he would not stop giggling with the maids.

The storm approached majestically, with the dull distant noise of the thunder, with a storm of sand, when suddenly there was a flash of lightning over the village and a sharp clap of thunder.

Disregarding the passionate warnings of his aunt, Raisky took his cap and umbrella and hurried into the park, anxious to see the landscape under the shadow of the storm, to find new ideas for his drawings, and to observe his own emotions. He descended the cliff, and passed through the undergrowth by a winding, hardly perceptible path. The rain fell by bucketfuls, one flash of lightning followed another, the thunder rolled, and the whole prospect was veiled in mist and cloud. He soon regretted his intention. His soaked umbrella did not protect him from the rain, which whipped his face and poured down on his clothes, and his feet sank ankle-deep in the muddy ground. He was continually knocking against and stumbling over unevennesses in the ground or tree stumps, treading in holes and pools. He was obliged to stand still until a flash of lightning lighted up a few yards of the path. He knew that not far away lay a ruined arbour, dating from the time when the precipice formed part of the garden. Not long before he had seen it in the thicket, but now it was indiscoverable, however much he would have preferred to observe the storm from its shelter. And since he did not wish to retrace the horrible path by which he had come, he resolved to make his way to the nearest carriage road, to climb over the twisted hedge and to reach the village.

He could hardly drag his soaked boots free of the mud and weeds, and he was dazzled by the lightning and nearly deafened by the noise. He confessed that he might as well have admired the storm from the shelter of the house. In the end he struck the fence, but when he tried to leap over it he slipped and fell in the ditch. With difficulty he dragged himself out and clambered over. There was little traffic on the steep and dangerous ridge, used for the most part as a short cut by empty one-horse carriages with their quiet beasts.

He closed his dripping umbrella, and put it under his arm. Dazzled by the lightning, slipping every minute, he toiled painfully up the slope, and when he reached the summit he heard close by the noise of wheels, the neighing of horses and the cry of the coachman. He stood on one side and pressed himself against the fence to allow the passage of the carriage, since the road was very narrow. In a flash of lightning Raisky saw before him a char-à-banc with several persons in it, drawn by two well-kept, apparently magnificent horses. In the light of another flash he was amazed to recognise Vera.

"Vera," he cried loudly.

The carriage stood still.

"Who is there? Is it you, cousin, in this weather?"

"And you?"

"I am hurrying home."

"So do I want to. I came down the precipice, and lost my way in the bushes.

"Who is driving you? Is there room for me."

"Plenty of room," said a masculine voice. "Give me your hand to get up." Raisky gave his hand, and was hauled up by a strong arm. Next to Vera sat Marina, and the two, huddled together like wet chickens, were trying to protect themselves from the drenching rain by the leather covering.

"Who is with you?" asked Raisky in a low voice. "Whose horses are these, and who is driving?"

"Ivan Ivanovich."

"I don't know him."

"The Forester," whispered Vera, and he would have repeated her words if she had not nudged him to keep silence. "Later," she said.

He remembered the talk with his aunt, her praises of the Forester, her hints of his being a good match. This then was the hero of the romance, the Forester. He tried to get a look at him, but only saw an ordinary hat with a wide brim, and a tall, broad-shouldered figure wrapped in a rain coat.

The Forester handled the reins skilfully as he drove up the steep hill, cracked his whip, whistled, held the horses' heads with a firm hand when they threatened to shy at a flash of lightning, and turned round to those sheltered in the body of the vehicle.

"How do you feel, Vera Vassilievna," he inquired anxiously. "Are you very cold and wet?"

"I am quite comfortable, Ivan Ivanovich; the rain does not catch me."

"You must take my raincoat. God forbid that you should take cold. I should never forgive myself all my life for having driven you."

"You weary me with your friendly anxiety. Don't bother about anything but your horses."

"As you please," replied Ivan Ivanovich with hasty obedience, turning to his horses, and he cast only an occasional anxious glance towards Vera.

They drove past the village to the door of the new house. Ivan Ivanovich jumped down and hammered on the door with his riding whip. Handing over the care of his horses to Prokor, Tarasska and Egorka, who hurried up for the purpose, he stood by the steps, took Vera in his arms, and carried her carefully and respectfully, like a precious burden, through the ranks of wide-eyed lackeys and maid-servants bearing lights, to the divan in the hall.

Raisky followed, wet and dirty, without once removing his eyes from them.

The Forester went back into the ante-room, made himself as respectable as he could, shook himself, pushed his fingers through his hair, and demanded a brush.

Meanwhile Tatiana Markovna bade Vera welcome and reproached her for venturing on such a journey; she must change her clothes throughout and in a few moments the samovar would be brought in, and supper served.

"Quick, quick, Grandmother!" said Vera, rubbing herself affectionately against her. "Let us have tea, soup, roast and wine. Ivan Ivanovich is hungry." She knew how to quiet her aunt's anxiety.

"That's splendid. It shall be served in a minute. Where is Ivan Ivanovich?"

"I am making myself a bit decent," cried a voice from the ante-room.

Egor, Yakob and Stepan hummed round the Forester as if he had been a good horse. Then he entered the hall and respectfully kissed the hands of

Tatiana Markovna, and of Marfinka, who had only just decided to get out of bed, where she had hidden herself for fear of the storm.

"It is not necessary, Marfinka," said her aunt, "to hide from the storm. You should pray to God, and will not then be struck."

"I am not afraid of thunder and lightning, of which the peasants are usually the victims, but it makes me nervous," replied Marfinka.

Raisky, with the water still dripping off him, stood in the window watching the guest. Ivan Ivanovich Tushin was a tall, broad-shouldered man of thirty-eight, with strongly-marked features, a dark, thick beard, and large grey rather timid eyes, and hands disproportionately large, with broad nails. He wore a grey coat and a high-buttoned vest, with a broad turned-down home-spun collar. He was a fine man, but with marked simplicity, not to put a fine point on it in his glance and his manners. Raisky wondered jealously whether he was Vera's hero. Why not? Women like these tall men with open faces and highly developed muscular strength. But Vera—

"And you, Borushka," cried Tatiana Markovna suddenly, clapping her hands. "Look at your clothes. Egorka and the rest of you! Where are you? There is a pool on the floor round you, Borushka. You will be ill. Vera was driving home, but there was no reason for you to go out into the storm. Go and change your clothes, Borushka, and have some rum in your tea. Ivan Ivanovich, you ought to go with him. Are you acquainted? My nephew Boris Raisky—Ivan Ivanovich Tushin."

"We have already made acquaintance," said Tushin, with a bow. "We picked up your nephew on the way. Many thanks, I need nothing, but you, Boris Pavlovich, ought to change."

"You must forgive an old woman for telling you you are all half mad. No animal leaves his hole in weather like this. Yakob, shut the shutters closer. Fancy crossing the Volga in weather like this."

"My carriage is solid, and has a cover. Vera Vassilievna sat as dry as if she were in a room."

"But in this terrible storm."

"Only old women are afraid of a storm."

"I'm much obliged."

"I beg your pardon," said Tushin in embarrassment. "It slipped from my tongue. I meant ordinary women."

"God will forgive you," laughed Tatiana Markovna. "It won't indeed hurt you, but Vera! Were you not afraid?"

"One does not think of fear with Ivan Ivanovich."

"If Ivan Ivanovich went bear-hunting, would you go with him?"

"Yes, Grandmother. Take me with you sometimes, Ivan Ivanovich."

"With pleasure, Vera Vassilievna, in winter. You have only to command."

"That is just like her, not to mind what her Grandmother thinks."

"I was joking, Grandmother."

"I know you would be equal to it. Had you no scruples about hindering Ivan Ivanovich; this distance...."

"It is my fault. As soon as I heard from Natalie Ivanovna that Vera Vassilievna wanted to come home, I asked for the pleasure," he said looking at Vera with a mixed air of modesty and respect.

"A nice pleasure in this weather."

"It was lighter while we were driving, and Vera Vassilievna was not afraid."

"Is Anna Ivanovna well?"

"Thank you. She sends her kindest regards, and has sent you some preserves, also some peaches out of the orangery, and mushrooms. They are in the char-à-banc."

"It is very good of her. We have no peaches. I have put aside for her some of the tea that Borushka brought with him."

"Many thanks."

"How could you let your horses climb the hill in such weather? Were they terrified by the storm?"

"My horses obey me like dogs. Should I have driven Vera Vassilievna if there were any danger?"

"You are a good friend," interrupted Vera. "I have absolute trust both in you, and in your horses."

At this moment Raisky returned, having changed his clothes. He had noticed the glance which Vera gave Tushin, and had heard her last remark.

"Thank you, Vera Vassilievna," answered Tushin. "Don't forget what you have just said. If you ever need anything, if...."

"If there is another such raging storm," said Tatiana Markovna.

"Any storm," added Tushin firmly.

"There are other storms in life," said Tatiana Markovna with a sigh.

"Whatever they are, if they break on you, Vera Vassilievna, seek refuge in the forest over the Volga, where lives a bear who will serve you, as the fairytale tells."

"I will remember," returned Vera laughing. "If a sorcerer wants to carry me off, as in the fairy-tale, I will take refuge in the wood."

Raisky saw Tushin's glance of devotion and modest reserve, he heard his words, so quietly and modestly spoken, and thought the letter written on the blue paper could be from no one else. He looked at Vera to see if she were moved or would relapse into a stony silence, but she showed no sign. Vera appeared to him in a new light. In her manner and her words to Tushin he saw simplicity, trust, gentleness and affection such as she showed to no one else, not even to her aunt or to Marfinka.

"She is on her guard with her Grandmother," he thought, "and takes no heed of Marfinka. But when she looks at Tushin, speaks to him, or gives her hand it is plain to see that they are friends."

The Forester, who had business to do in the town, stayed for three days with Tatiana Markovna, and for three days Raisky sought for the key to this new character and to his place in Vera's heart.

They called Ivan Ivanovich the "Forester," because he lived on his estate in the midst of the forest. He loved the forest, growing new timber on the one hand and on the other allowing it to be cut down and loaded up on the Volga for sale. The several thousand *dessiatins* of surrounding forest were exceedingly well managed, and nothing was lacking; there was even a steam saw. He attended to everything himself, and in his spare time hunted and fished and amused himself with his bachelor neighbours. From time to time he sought a change of scene, and then arranged with his friends to drive in a three-horse carriage, drawn by fresh horses, forty versts away to the seat of a landed proprietor, where for three days the fun was fast enough. Then they returned, put up with Tushin, or waked the sleepy town. In these festivals all class distinctions were lost.

After this dissipation he would again remain lost to the world for three months in his forest home, see after the wood cutting, and go hunting with two servants, and occasionally have to lie up with a wounded arm. The life suited him. He read works on agriculture and forestry, took counsel with his German assistant, an experienced forester, who was nevertheless not allowed to be the master. All orders must come from Tushin himself, and were carried out by the help of two foremen and a gang of hired labourers.

In his spare time he liked to read French novels, the only distraction that he permitted himself. There was nothing extraordinary in a retired life like this in the wide district in which he lived.

Raisky learnt that Tushin saw Vera at the pope's house, that he went there expressly when he heard that Vera was a visitor. Vera herself told him so. She and Natalie Ivanovna, too, visited Tushin's property, known as "Smoke," because far away from the hills could be seen the smoke rising from the chimneys of the house in the depth of the forest.

Tushin lived with his spinster sister, Anna Ivanovna, to whom Tatiana Markovna was much attached. Tatiana Markovna was delighted when she came to town. There was no one with whom she liked more to drink coffee, no one to whom she gave her confidence in the same degree; they shared the same liking for household management, the same deep-rooted self-esteem and the same respect for family tradition.

Of Tushin himself there was little more to say than was revealed on a first occasion; his character lay bare to the daylight, with no secret, no romantic side. He possessed more than plain good sense, for his understanding did not derive from the brain alone, but from the heart and will. Men of his type, especially when they care nothing for the superfluous things of life, but keep their eyes fixed undeviatingly on the necessary, do not make themselves noticed in the crowd and rarely reach the front of the world's stage.

Raisky noticed in the Forester's behaviour towards Vera a constant adoration expressed by his glance and his voice, and sometimes by his timidity; on her side an equally constant confidence, frankness and affection, nothing more. He did not surprise in her a single sign or gesture, a single word or glance that might have betrayed her. Tushin showed pure esteem and a consistent readiness to serve her as her bear, and no more. Surely he was not the man who wrote the letter on the blue paper.

After the Forester had taken his leave, the household fell back into its regular routine. Vera seemed untroubled and in possession of a quiet happiness, and showed herself kind and affectionate to her aunt and Marfinka. Yet there were days when unrest suddenly came upon her, when she went hastily to her room in the old house, or descended the precipice into the park, and displayed a gloomy resentment if Raisky or Marfinka ventured to disturb her solitude. After a short interval she resumed an even, sympathetic temper, helped in the household, looked over her aunt's accounts, and even paid visits to the ladies in the town. She discussed literary questions with Raisky, who realised from the opinions she expressed that her reading was wide and enticed her into thorough-going discussions. They read together, though not regularly. Sometimes a wild intoxication flared up in her, but it was a disconcerting merriment. One evening, when she suddenly left the room, Tatiana Markovna and Raisky exchanged a long questioning glance.

"What do you think of Vera?" she began. "She seems to have recovered from her malady of the soul."

"I think it is more serious than before."

"What is the matter with you, Borushka? You can see how gay and friendly she has become."

"Is she like the Vera you have known. I fear that this is not gladness, but rather agitation, even intoxication."

"You are right. She is changed."

"Don't you notice that she is ecstatic?"

"Ecstatic?" repeated Tatiana Markovna anxiously. "Why do you say that, especially just at night? I shan't sleep. The ecstasy of a young girl spells disaster."

CHAPTER XVI

Not only Raisky, but Tatiana Markovna gave up her attitude of acquiescence, and secretly began to watch Vera narrowly. Tatiana Markovna became thoughtful, she even neglected the affairs of the house and farm, left the keys lying on the table, did not speak to Savili, kept no accounts, and did not drive out into the fields. She grew melancholy as she sought in vain how she might seek from Vera a frank avowal, or find means to avert misfortune.

Vera in love, in an ecstasy! It seemed to her more than small-pox or measles, worse even than brain fever. And with whom was she in love? God grant that it were Ivan Ivanovich. If Vera were married to him, she herself would die in peace. But her feminine instinct told her that whatever deep affection the Forester cherished for Vera, it was reciprocated by nothing more than friendship.

Who then was the man? Of the neighbouring landowners there was only Tushin whom she saw and knew anything of. The young men in the town, the officers and councillors, had long since given up any hope of being received into her favour.

She looked keenly and suspiciously at Vera when she came to dinner or tea, and tried to follow her into the garden, but as soon as Vera was aware of her aunt's presence she quickened her steps and vanished into the distance.

"Spirited away like a ghost!" said Tatiana Markovna to Raisky. "I wanted to follow her, but where, with my old limbs? She flits like a bird into the woods, into the bushes, over the precipice."

Raisky went immediately into the park, where he met Yakob, and asked him if he had seen the young lady.

"I saw Vera Vassilievna just now by the chapel."

"What was she doing there?"

"Praying."

Raisky went to the chapel, wondering to himself how she had come to take refuge in prayer. On the left there lay in the meadow between the park and the road, a lonely, weather-beaten, half-ruined wooden chapel, adorned with a picture of the Christ, a Byzantine painting in a bronze frame. The ikon had grown dark with age, the paint had been cracked in many places, so that the Christ face was hardly recognisable, but the eyelids were still plainly discernible, and the eyes looked out dreamily on the worshippers; the folded hands were also preserved.

Raisky advanced noiselessly over the grass. Vera was standing with her back to him, her face turned towards the ikon, unconscious of his approach. On the grass by the chapel lay her straw hat and sunshade. Her hands did not make the sign of the Cross, her lips uttered no prayers, her whole body appeared motionless, as if she hardly breathed; her whole being was at prayer.

Involuntarily Raisky too held his breath. Is she begging for happiness, or is she confiding her sorrow to the Crucified?

Suddenly she awoke from her prayer, turned and started when she caught sight of Raisky.

"What are you doing here?" she said severely.

"Yakob met me and said you were here; so I came. Grandmother...."

"Since you mention Grandmother, I will point out that she has been watching me for some time. Do you know the reason?" she asked, looking straight into his eyes.

"I think she always does."

"No, it was not her idea to watch me. Tell me without concealing anything, have you communicated to her your suppositions about love and a letter written on blue paper?"

"I think not of the letter."

"Then of love. I must know what you said?"

"We were speaking of you. Grandmother has her own questionings as to why you are so serious one moment and so gay the next. I said (it is a long time ago) that perhaps you were in love."

"And Grandmother?"

"She was terrified."

"Why?"

"Chiefly because of your evident excitement."

"Grandmother's peace of mind is dear to me; dearer, perhaps, than you think."

"She told me herself that she believed in your boundless love for her."

"Thank God! I am grateful to you for repeating this to me. Go to Grandmother and destroy this curiosity of hers about my being in love, in ecstasy. It cannot be difficult for you, and you will fulfil my wishes if you love me."

"What would I not do to prove it to you. Later in the evening...."

"No, this minute. When I come to dinner her eyes are to look on me as before, do you understand?"

"Well, I will go!" promised Raisky, but did not stir.

"Make haste!"

"And you?"

For answer she pointed in the direction of the house.

"One word more," she said, detaining him. "You must never, never talk about me to Grandmother, do you understand?"

"Agreed, sister."

She motioned him to be gone, and when turning into an avenue he looked round for a moment, she had vanished. She had, as Grandmother said, disappeared like a ghost. A moment later there was the report of a gun from the precipice. Raisky wondered who was playing tricks there, and went towards the house.

Vera appeared punctually at the midday meal. Keenly as he looked at her, Raisky could observe no change in her. Tatiana Markovna glanced at him once or twice in inquiry, but was visibly reassured when she saw no signs of anything unusual. Raisky had executed Vera's commission, and had alleviated her acutest anxiety, but it was impossible to reassure her completely.

Tatiana Markovna was saddened and wounded by the lack of confidence shown her by Vera, her niece, her daughter, her dearest child, entrusted to her care by her mother. Terror overcame her. She lay awake anxiously through the night, she questioned Marina, sent Marfinka to find out what Vera was doing, but without result. Suddenly there occurred to her what seemed to her a good plan; as she put it to Raisky, she would make use of allegory. She remembered that she possessed a moral tale which she had read and wept over in her own youth. Its theme was the disastrous consequences which followed on passion and disobedience to parents. A young man and a girl loved one another, and met against the will of their parents. She stood on the balcony beckoning and talking to him, and they wrote one another long epistles. Others intervened, the young girl lost her reputation, and the young man was sent to some vague place in America by his father.

Like many others Tatiana Markovna pinned her faith to the printed word, especially when the reading was of an edifying character. So she took her talisman from the shelf, where it lay hidden under a pile of rubbish, and laid it on the table near her work basket. At dinner she declared to the two sisters her desire that they should read aloud to her on alternate evenings, especially in bad weather, since she could not read very much on account of her eyes. Generally speaking, she was not an enthusiastic reader, and only liked to listen when Tiet Nikonich read aloud to her on agricultural matters or hygiene, or about distressing occurrences of murder or arson.

Vera said nothing, but Marfinka asked immediately whether the book had a happy ending.

"What sort of book is it?" inquired Raisky, picking up the book and glancing at a page here and there. "What old rubbish have you discovered, Grandmother. I expect you read it when you were in love with Tiet Nikonich."

"Don't be foolish, Boris Pavlovich. You are not asked to read."

Raisky took his departure, and the room was left to the reading party.

Vera was unendurably bored, but she never refused assent to any definitely expressed wish of her aunt's. At last, after three or four evenings, the point was reached where the lovers exchanged their vows. The tale was faultlessly moral and horribly dull. Vera hardly listened. At each word of love her aunt looked at her to see whether she was touched, whether she blushed or turned pale, but Vera merely yawned.

On the last evening when only a few chapters were left, Raisky stayed in the room when the table was cleared and the reading began. Vikentev, too, was present. He could not sit quiet, but jumped up from time to time, ran to Marfinka, and begged to be allowed to take his share in the reading. When they gave him the book he inserted long tirades of his own in the novel, or read with a different voice suited to each character. He made the heroine lisp in a mournful whisper, the hero speak with his own natural voice, so that Marfinka blushed and looked angrily at him, and the stern father spoke with the voice of Niel Andreevich. At last Tatiana Markovna took the book from him with an intimation to him to behave reasonably, whereupon he continued his studies in character-mimicry for Marfinka's benefit behind her back. When Marfinka betrayed him he was requested to go into the garden until supper time and the reading went on without him. The catastrophe of the tale approached at last, and when the last word was read and the book shut there was silence.

"What stupid nonsense," said Raisky at length, and Marfinka wiped away a tear.

"What do you think, Veroshka?" asked Tatiana Markovna.

Vera made no reply, but Marfinka decided it was a horrid book because the lovers had suffered so cruelly.

"If they had followed the advice of their parents, things would not have come to such a pass. What do you think, Veroshka?"

Vera got up to go, but on the threshold she stopped.

"Grandmother," she said, "why have you bothered me for a whole week with this stupid book?" And without waiting for an answer she glided away, but Tatiana Markovna called her back.

"Why, Vera, I meant to give you pleasure."

"No, you wanted to punish me for something. In future I would rather be put for a week on bread and water," and kneeling on the footstool at her aunt's feet she added, "Good-night, Grandmother."

Tatiana Markovna stooped to kiss her and whispered. "I did not want to punish you, but to guard you against getting into trouble yourself."

"And if I do," whispered Vera in reply, "will you have me put in a convent like Cunigunde?"

"Do you think I am a monster like those bad parents? It's wicked, Vera, to think such things of me."

"I know it would be wicked, Grandmother, and I don't think any such thing. But why warn me with such a silly book?"

"How should I warn you and guard you, my dear. Tell me and set my mind at rest."

"Make the sign of the Cross over me," she said after a moment's hesitation, and when her aunt had made the holy sign, Vera kissed her hand and left the room.

"A wise book," laughed Raisky. "Well, has the beautiful Cunigunde's example done any good?"

Tatiana Markovna was grieved and in no mood for joking, and sent for Pashutka to take the book to the servants' room.

"You have brought Vera up in the right way," said Raisky. "Let Egorka and Marina read your allegory together, and the household will be impeccable."

Vikentev called Marfinka into the garden, Raisky went to his room, and Tatiana Markovna sat for a long time on the divan, absorbed in thought. She had lost all interest in the book, was herself sickened by its pious tone, and was really ashamed of having had recourse to so gross a method. Marina, Yakob and Vassilissa came one after another to say that supper was ready, but Tatiana Markovna wanted none, Vera declined, and to Marina's astonishment even Marfinka, who never went supperless to bed, was not hungry.

Meanwhile Egorka had got wind of the universal loss of appetite. He helped himself to a considerable slice from the dish with his fingers to taste, as he told Yakob, whom he invited to share the feast. Yakob shook his head and crossed himself, but nevertheless did his share, so that when Marina came to clear the table the fish and the sweets were gone.

The mistress's preparations for rest were made, and quiet reigned in the house. Tatiana Markovna rose from the divan and looked at the ikon. She crossed herself, but she was too restless for prayer, and did not kneel down as usual. Instead she sat down on the bed and began to go over her passage of arms with Vera. How could she learn what lay on the girl's heart. She remembered the proverb that wisdom comes with the morning, and lay down, but not that night to sleep, for there was a light tap on the door, and she heard Marfinka's voice, "Open the door. Grandmother. It's me."

"What's the matter, my dear?" she said, as she opened the door. "Have you come to say good-night. God bless you! Where is Nikolai Andreevich?"

But she was terrified when she saw Marfinka's face.

"Sit down in the armchair," she said, but Marfinka clung to her.

"Lie down, Grandmother, and I will sit on the bed beside you. I will tell you everything, but please put out the light."

Then Marfinka began to relate how she had gone with Vikentev into the park to hear the nightingales sing, how she had first objected because it was so dark.

"Are you afraid?" Vikentev had asked.

"Not with you," and they had gone on hand in hand.

"How dark it is! I won't go any farther. Don't take hold of my hand!" She went on involuntarily, although Vikentev had loosed her hand, her heart beating faster and faster. "I am afraid, I won't go a step farther." She drew closer to him all the same, terrified by the crackling of the twigs under her feet.

"Here we will wait. Listen!" he whispered.

The nightingale sang, and Marfinka felt herself enveloped in the warm breath of night. At intervals her hand sought Vikentev's, but when he touched hers she drew it back.

"How lovely, Marfa Vassilievna! What an enchanted night!"

She nudged him not to disturb the song.

"Marfa Vassilievna," he whispered, "something so good, so wonderful is happening to me, something I have never felt before. It is as if everything in me was astir. At this moment," he went on as she remained silent, "I should like to fling myself on horseback, and ride, ride, till I had no breathe left, or fling myself into the Volga and swim to the opposite bank. Do you feel anything like that?"

"Let us go away from here. Grandmother will be angry."

"Just a minute more. How the nightingale does sing! What does he sing?"

"I don't know."

"Just what I should like to say to you, but don't know how to say."

"How do you know what he sings? Can you speak nightingale language?"

"He is singing of love, of my love for you," and startled by his own words he drew her hand to his lips and covered it with kisses.

She drew it back, and ran at full speed down the avenue towards the house; on the steps she waited a moment to take breath.

"Not a step farther," she cried breathlessly, clinging to the doorpost as he overtook her. "Go home."

"Listen, Marfa Vassilievna, my angel," he cried, falling on his knees. "On my knees I swear...."

"If you speak another word, I go straight to Grandmother."

He rose, and led her by force into the avenue.

"What are you doing? I will call, I won't listen to your nightingale."

"You won't listen to it, but you will to me."

"Let me go. I will tell Grandmother everything."

"You must tell her to-night, Marfa Vassilievna. We have come too near to one another that if we were suddenly separated.... Should you like that, Marfa Vassilievna? If you like I will go away for good."

She wept and seized his hand in panic, when he drew back a step.

"You love me, you love me," he cried.

"Does your mother know what you are saying to me?"

"Not yet."

"Ought you to say it then? Is it honourable?"

"I shall tell her to-morrow."

"What if she will not give her blessing?"

"I won't obey."

"But I will. I will take no step without your Mother's and Grandmother's consent," she said, turning to go.

"As far as I am concerned, I am sure of my Mother's consent. I will hurry now to Kolchino, and my Mother will send you her consent to-morrow. Marfa Vassilievna, give me your hand."

"What will Grandmother say? If she does not forgive me I shall die of shame," she said, and she hurried into the house.

"Heavens, what will Grandmother say?" she wondered, shutting herself up in her room, and shaking with fever. How should she tell her grandmother, and should she tell Veroshka first. She decided in favour of her grandmother, and when the house was quiet slipped to her room like a mouse.

The two talked low to one another for a long time. Tatiana Markovna made the sign of the cross over her darling many times, until she fell asleep on her shoulder. Then she carefully laid the girl's head on the pillow, rose, and prayed with many tears. But more heartily than for Marfinka's happiness she prayed for Vera, with her grey head bowed before the cross.

CHAPTER XVII

Vikentev kept his word, and on the very next day brought his mother to Tatiana Markovna, he himself taking refuge in his office, where he sat on pins and needles.

His mother, still a young woman, not much over forty, as gay and full of life as he himself was, had plenty of practical sense. They kept up between themselves a constant comic war of words; they were for ever disputing about trifles, but when it came to serious matters, she proclaimed her authority to him with quite another voice and another manner. And though he indeed usually began by protesting, he submitted to her will, if her request was reasonable. An unseen harmony underlay their visible strife.

That night, after Marfinka had left him, Vikentev had hurried to Kolchino. He rushed to his mother, threw his arms round her and kissed her. When, nearly smothered by his embrace, she thrust him from her, he fell on his knees and said solemnly: "Mother, strike me if you will, but listen. The supreme moment of my life has arrived. I have...."

"Gone mad," she supplied, looking him up and down.

"I am going to be married," he said, almost inaudibly.

"What? Mavra, Anton, Ivan, Kusma! Come here, quick!"

Mavra alone responded to the call.

"Call everybody. Nikolai Andreevich has gone mad."

"I am not joking, and I must have an answer tomorrow."

"I will have you locked up," she said, seriously disturbed at last.

Far into the night the servants heard heated arguments, the voices of the disputants now rising almost to a shout, then laughter, then outbursts of anger from the mistress, a gay retort from him, then dead silence, the sign of restored tranquillity. Vikentev had won the victory, which was indeed a foregone conclusion, for while Vikentev and Marfinka were still uncertain of their feelings, Tatiana Markovna and Marfa Egorovna had long before realised what was coming, and both, although they kept their own counsel, had weighed and considered the matter, and had concluded that the marriage was a suitable one.

"What will Tatiana Markovna say?" cried Marfa Egorovna to her son the next morning as the horses were being put in. "If she does not agree, I will never forgive you for the disgrace it will bring on us, do you hear?"

She herself, in a silk dress and a lace mantle, with yellow gloves and a coquettish fan, might have been a fiancée. When Tatiana Markovna was informed of the arrival of Madame Vikentev, she had her shown into the reception room. Before she herself changed her dress to receive her, Vassilissa had to peer through the doorway to see what kind of toilette the guest had made. Then Tatiana Markovna donned a rustling silk dress with a silver sheen, over which she wore her Turkish shawl; she even tried to put on a pair of diamond earrings, but gave up the attempt impatiently, telling herself that the holes in her ears had grown together. Then she sent word to Vera and Marfinka to change their dresses. In passing she told Vassilissa to set out the best table linen, and the old silver and glass for the breakfast and the dinner table. The cook was ordered to serve chocolate in addition to the usual dishes, and sweets and champagne were ordered. With folded hands, adorned for the occasion with old and costly rings, she stepped solemnly into the reception room. But when she caught sight of her guest's pleasant face she all but forget the importance of the moment, but pulled herself together in time, and resumed her serious aspect.

Marfa Egorovna rose in friendly haste to meet her hostess, and began: "What ideas my mad boy has!" but restrained herself when she saw Madame Berezhkov's attitude. They exchanged ceremonious greetings. Tatiana Markovna asked the visitor to sit on the divan, and seated herself stiffly beside her.

"What is the weather like?" she asked. "Had you a windy crossing over the Volga?"

"There was no wind."

"Did you come by the ferry?"

"In the boat. The calèche was brought over on the ferry."

"Yakob, Egorovna, Petrushka? Where are you? Why don't you come when you are called? Take out the horses, give them fodder, and see that the coachman is well looked after."

The servants, who had rushed in to answer the summons, hurried out. Of course the horses had been taken out while Tatiana Markovna was dressing, and the coachman was already sitting in the servants' room, doing full justice to the beer set before him.

"No, no, Tatiana Markovna," protested the visitor, "I have come for half an hour on business."

"Do you think you will be allowed to go?" asked Tatiana Markovna in a voice that permitted no reply. "You have come a long way from over the

Volga. Is this the first year of our acquaintance? Do you want to insult me?"

"Ah, Tatiana Markovna, I am so grateful to you, so grateful! You are just like a relative, and how you have spoilt my Nikolai!"

"I feel sometimes as if he were my own son," burst from Tatiana Markovna, whose dignity could hold out no longer against these friendly advances.

"Yes, you are so kind to him, Tatiana Markovna, that, presuming on your kindness, he has taken it into his head...."

"Well?"

"He begged me to come over to see you, and he asks for the hand of Marfa Vassilievna. Marfa Vassilievna agrees; she loves Nikolai."

"Because Marfinka took upon herself to answer his declaration she is now shut up in her room, in her petticoat, without shoes," lied her aunt. Then in order to lay full stress on the importance of the moment, she added: "I have given orders not to admit your son, so that he may not play with a poor girl's affections."

It was impossible for Marfa Egorovna not to recognise the provocation of these remarks.

"If I had foreseen this," she said angrily, "I would have given him a different answer. He assured me—and I was so willing to believe him—of your affection for him, and for me. Pardon my mission, Tatiana Markovna, and pray let that poor child out of her room. The blame rests with my boy only, and he shall be punished. Have the kindness to order my carriage."

She placed her hand on the bell, but Tatiana Markovna detained her.

"Your horses are taken out. You will stay with me, Marfa Egorovna, to-day, to-morrow, all the week."

"But since you are so angry with Marfa Vassilievna and my son, who does indeed deserve to be punished?"

The wrinkles in Tatiana Markovna's face faded, and her eyes gleamed with joy. She threw her shawl and cap on the divan.

"I can't keep it up any longer!" she exclaimed. "Take off your hat and mantilla. We are only teasing one another, Marfa Egorovna. I shall have a grandson, you a daughter. Kiss me, dear! I wanted to keep up the old customs, but there are cases which they don't fit. We knew what must be the upshot of this. If we hadn't wished it we should not have allowed them to go and listen to the nightingales."

"How you frightened me!" cried Marfa Egorovna.

"He had to be frightened. I will read him a lesson."

Mother and aunt had gone a long way into the future, and when they were about as far as the christening of the third child, Marfa Egorovna noticed in the garden among the bushes a head which was now hidden, then again cautiously raised to reconnoitre. She recognised her son, and pointed him out to Tatiana Markovna. They called him, but when he at last decided to enter, he hung about in the ante-room, as if he were making himself presentable.

"You are welcome, Nikolai Andreevich," said Tatiana Markovna pointedly, while his mother looked at him ironically.

"Good morning, Tatiana Markovna," he stammered at last, and kissed the old lady's hand. "I have bought tickets for the charity concert, for you and Mama, for Vera Vassilievna and Marfa Vassilievna and for Boris Pavlovich. It's a splendid concert ... the first singer in Moscow...."

"Why do we need to go to concerts?" interrupted Tatiana Markovna, looking at him sideways. "The nightingales sing so finely here. In the evening we go into the garden, and can hear them for nothing."

Marfa Egorovna bit her lip, but Vikentev stood transfixed.

"Sit down, Nikolai Andreevich," continued the old lady seriously and reproachfully, "and listen to what I have to say. What does your conscience tell you? How have you rewarded my confidence?"

"Don't make fun of me ... it's unkind."

"I am not joking. It wasn't right of you, my friend, to speak to Marfinka, and not to me. Supposing I had not consented?"

"If you had not consented I would have...."

"What?"

"Oh, I would have gone away from here, joined the Hussars, have contracted debts, and gone to wrack and ruin."

"Now he threatens! You should not be so bent on your own way, young man."

"Give me Marfa Vassilievna, and I will be more tranquil than water, humbler than the grass."

"Shall we give him Marfinka, Marfa Egorovna?"

"He hasn't deserved it, Tatiana Markovna. And it is really too early. Perhaps in two years' time...."

He flew to his mother and shut her mouth with a kiss. Then he received from Tatiana Markovna the sign of the cross, and a kiss on the forehead.

"Where is Marfa Vassilievna?" he shouted joyfully.

"You must have patience," admonished his grandmother, "we will fetch her."

Tatiana Markovna and Marfa Egorovna found Marfinka hidden in the corner behind the curtains of her bed, close by the ikons. She covered her blushing face in her hands.

Vera received the news from her aunt with quiet pleasure, saying that she had expected it for a long time.

"God grant that you may follow her example," said Tatiana Markovna.

"If you love me as I love you, Grandmother, you will bestow all your care and thought on Marfinka. Take no thought for me."

"My heart aches for you, Veroshka."

"I know, and that grieves me. Grandmother," she said with a despairing note, "it is killing me to think that your heart aches on my account."

"What do you say, Veroshka? open your heart to me. Perhaps I can comprehend, and if you have grief, help to assuage it."

"If trouble overtakes me, Grandmother, and I cannot conquer it myself, I will come to you and to none other, God only excepted. But do not make me suffer any more, or allow yourself to suffer."

"Will it not be too late when trouble has once overtaken you?" whispered her aunt. Then she added aloud, "I know that you are not like Marfinka, and I will not disturb you."

A long sigh escaped her as she left the room with quick steps and bent head. Vera's distress was the only cloud on her horizon, and she prayed earnestly that it might pass and not gather into a black storm cloud. Vera sought to calm her own agitation by walking up and down the garden, but only succeeded gradually. As soon as she caught sight of Marfinka and Vikentev in the arbour, she hurried to them, looked affectionately into her sister's face, kissed her eyes, her lips, her cheeks, and embraced her warmly.

"You must be happy," she said with tears in her eyes.

"How lovely you are Veroshka, and how good! We are not a bit like sisters. There is nobody in the neighbourhood fit to marry you, is there, Nikolai Andreevich?"

Vera pressed her hand in silence.

"Nikolai Andreevich, do you know what she is?"

"An angel," answered Vikentev as promptly as a soldier answers his officer.

"An angel," mimicked Vera laughing, and pointing to a butterfly hovering over a flower. "There is an angel. But if you even touch him the colour of his wings will be spoiled, and he will perhaps even lose a wing. You must spoil her, love and caress her, and God forbid that you ever wound her. If you ever do," she threatened, smiling, "you will have to reckon with me."

Within a week of this happy occasion the house was restored to its ordinary routine. Marfa Egorovna drove back to Kolchino, but Vikentev became a daily visitor, and almost a member of the family. He and Marfinka no longer jumped and ran like children, though they occasionally had a lively dispute, half in jest, half in earnest. They sang and read together, and the pure, fresh poetry of youth, plain for all to read, welled up in their frank, unspoiled hearts.

The wedding being fixed for the autumn, preparations for Marfinka's house-furnishing and trousseau were being gradually pushed forward. From the cupboards of the house were brought old lace, silver and gold plate, glass, linen, furs, pearls, diamonds and all sorts of treasures, to be divided by Tatiana Markovna with Jew-like exactness into two equal shares, with the aid of jewellers, workers in gold, and others.

"That is yours, Vera, and there is Marfinka's share. You are not to receive a pearl or on ounce more than the other. See for yourselves."

Vera pushed pearls and diamonds into a heap with a declaration that she needed very little. This only angered Tatiana Markovna, who began the work of division all over again. Raisky sent to his former guardian for the diamonds and silver that had been his mother's portion, and bestowed these also on the sisters, but his aunt hid the treasure in the depths of her coffers.

"You will want them yourself." she said, "on the day when you take it into your head to marry."

The estate with all that belonged to it he had made over in the names of the sisters, a gift for which each of them thanked him after her fashion.

Tatiana Markovna wrinkled her forehead, and looked askance at him, but she could not long maintain this attitude, and ended by embracing him.

In various rooms, in Tatiana Markovna's sitting room, in the servants' room, and even in the reception room, tables were covered with linen. The marriage bed, with its lace pillow-cases and cover was being prepared, and every morning there came dressmakers and seamstresses. Only Raisky and Vera remained untouched by the universal gay activity. Even when Raisky sought distraction in riding or visiting, there was in fact no one else in the world for him but Vera. He avoided too frequent visits to Koslov on account of Juliana Andreevna.

He did not visit Paulina Karpovna, but she came the oftener, and bored him and Tatiana Markovna by her pose, retiring or audacious, as the case might be. Tatiana Markovna especially was annoyed by her unasked for criticisms of the wedding preparations, and by her views on marriage generally. Marriage, she declared, was the grave of love, elect souls were bound to meet in spite of all obstacles, even outside the marriage bond, and so forth. While she expounded these doctrines she cast languishing eyes on Raisky.

Neither did the young people who now often came to the house to dance, awaken any interest in Raisky or Vera. These two were only happy under given circumstances; he—with her, she—when unseen by anyone she could flit like a ghost to the precipice to lose herself in the undergrowth, or when she drove over the Volga to see the pope's wife.

CHAPTER XVIII

The weather was gloomy. Rain fell unintermittently, the sky was enshrouded in a thick cloud of fog, and on the ground lay banks of mist. No one had ventured out all day, and the family had already gone early to bed, when about ten o'clock the rain ceased, Raisky put on his overcoat to get a breath of air in the garden. The rustle of the bushes and the plants from which the rain was still dripping, alone broke the stillness of the night. After a few turns up and down he turned his steps to the vegetable garden, through which his way to the fields lay. Here and there a glimmering star hung above in the dense darkness, and before him the village lay like a dark spot on the dark background of the indistinguishable fields beyond. Suddenly he heard a slight noise from the old house, and saw that a window on the ground floor had been opened. Since the window looked out not into the garden, but on to the field, he hastened to reach the grove of acacias, leapt the fence and landed in a puddle of water, where he stood motionless.

"Is it you?" said a low voice from the window. It was Vera's voice.

Though his knees trembled under him, he was just able to answer in the same low tone, "Yes."

"The rain has kept me in all day, but to-morrow morning at ten. Go quickly; some one is coming."

The window was closed quietly, and Raisky cursed the approaching footsteps that had interrupted the conversation. It was then true, and the letter written on blue paper not a dream. Was there a rendezvous? He went in the direction of the steps.

"Who is there?" cried a voice, and Raisky was seized from behind.

"The devil," cried Raisky, pushing Savili away, "since when have you taken upon yourself to guard the house?"

"I have the Mistress's orders. There are so many thieves and vagabonds in the neighbourhood, and the sailors from the Volga do a lot of mischief."

"That is a lie. You are out after Marina, and you ought to be ashamed of yourself."

He would have gone, but Savili detained him.

"Allow me, Sir, to say a word or two about Marina. Exercise your merciful powers, and send the woman to Siberia."

"Are you out of your senses?"

"Or into a house of detention for the rest of her life."

"I'm much more likely to send you, so that you cease to beat her. What are you doing, spying here in this abominable way?" said Raisky between his teeth, as he cast a glance at Vera's window. In another moment he was gone.

Raisky hardly slept at all that night, and he appeared next morning in his aunt's sitting-room with dry, weary eyes. The whole family had assembled for tea on this particular bright morning. Vera greeted him gaily, as he pressed her hand feverishly and looked straight into her eyes. She returned his gaze calmly and quietly.

"How elegant you are this morning," he said.

"Do you call a simple straw-coloured blouse elegant?" she asked.

"But the scarlet band on your hair, with the coils of hair drawn across it, the belt with the beautiful clasp, and the scarlet-embroidered shoes.... You have excellent taste, and I congratulate you."

"I am glad that I meet with your approval, but your enthusiasm is rather strange. Tell me the reason of this extraordinary tone."

"Good, I will tell you. Let us go for a stroll."

He saw that she gave him a quick glance of suspicion as he proposed an appointment with her for ten o'clock. After a moment's thought she agreed, sat down in a corner, and was silent. About ten o'clock she picked up her work and her parasol, and signed to him to follow her as she left the house. She walked in silence through the garden, and they sat down on a bench at the top of the cliff.

"It was by chance," said Raisky, who was hardly able to restrain his emotion, "that I have learnt a part of your secret."

"So it seems," she answered coldly. "You were listening yesterday."

"Accidentally, I swear."

"I believe you."

"Vera, there is no longer any doubt that you have a lover. Who is he?"

"Don't ask."

"Who is there in the world who could desire your happiness more ardently than I do? Why have you confidence in him and not in me?"

"Because I love him."

"The man you love is to be envied, but how is he going to repay you for the supreme happiness that you bring him? Be careful, my friend. To whom do you give your confidence?"

"To myself."

"Who is the man?"

Instead of answering him she looked full in his face, and he thought that her eyes were as colourless as those of a watersprite, and there lay hidden in them a maddening riddle. From below in the bushes there came the sound of a shot. Vera rose immediately from the bench, and Raisky also rose.

"HE?" he asked in a dull voice. "It is ten o'clock."

She approached the precipice, Raisky following close at her heels. She motioned him to come no farther.

"What is the meaning of the shot?"

"He calls."

"Who?"

"The writer of the blue letter. Not a step further unless you wish that I leave here for ever."

She rapidly descended the precipice, and in a few moments had vanished behind the brushwood and the trees. He called after her to take care, but in reply heard only the crackling of the dry twigs beneath her feet. Then all was still. He was left to torment himself with wondering who the object of her passion could be.

It was none other than Mark Volokov, pariah, cynic, gipsy, who would ask the first likely man he met for money, who levelled his gun on his fellow-men, and, like Karl Moor, had declared war on mankind—Mark Volokov, the man under police supervision.

It was to meet this dangerous and suspicious character that Vera stole to the rendezvous—Vera, the pearl of beauty in the whole neighbourhood, whose beauty made strong men weak; Vera, who had mastered even the tyrannical Tatiana Markovna; Vera, the pure maiden sheltered from all the winds of heaven. It would have seemed impossible for her to meet a man against whom all houses were barred. It had happened so simply, so easily, towards the end of the last summer, at the time that the apples were ripe. She was sitting one evening in the little acacia arbour by the fence near the old house, looking absently out into the field, and away to the Volga and the hills beyond, when she became aware that a few paces away the branches of the apple tree were swaying unnaturally over the fence. When she looked more closely she saw that a man was sitting comfortably on the top rail. He appeared by his face and dress to belong to the lower class; he was not a schoolboy, but he held in his hands several apples.

"What are you doing here?" she asked, just as he was about to spring down from the fence.

"I am eating," he said, after taking a look at her. "Will you try one?" he added, hitching himself along the fence towards her.

She looked at him curiously, but without fear, as she drew back a little.

"Who are you?" she said severely. "And why do you climb on to other people's fences."

"What can it matter to you who I am. I can easily tell you why I climb on other people's fences. It is to eat apples."

"Aren't you ashamed to take other people's apples?" she asked.

"They are my apples, not theirs; they have been stolen from me. You certainly have not read Proudhon. But how beautiful you are!" he added in amazement. "Do you know what Proudhon says?" he concluded.

"*La propriété c'est le vol.*"

"Ah, you have read Proudhon." He stared at her, and as she shook her head, he continued, "Anyway, you have heard it. Indeed, this divine truth has gone all round the world nowadays. I have a copy of Proudhon, and will bring it to you."

"You are not a boy, and yet you steal apples. You think it is not theft to do so because of that saying of Proudhon's."

"You believe, then, everything that was told you at school? But please tell me who you are. This is the Berezhkovs' garden. They tell me the old lady has two beautiful nieces."

"I too say what can it matter to you who I am?"

"Then you believe what your Grandmother tells you?"

"I believe in what convinces me."

"Exactly like me," he said, taking off his cap. "Is it criminal in your eyes to take apples?"

"Not criminal, perhaps, but not good manners."

"I make you a present of them," he said, handing her the remaining four apples and taking another bite out of his own.

He raised his cap once more and bid her an ironic good-day.

"You have a double beauty, you are beautiful to look at and sensible into the bargain. It is a pity that you are destined to adorn the life of an idiot. You will be given away, poor girl."

"No pity, if you please. I shall not be given away like an apple."

"You remember the apples; many thanks for the gift. I will bring you books in exchange, as you like books."

"Proudhon?"

"Yes, Proudhon and others. I have all the new ones. Only you must not tell your Grandmother and her stupid visitors, for although I do not know who they are, I don't think they would have anything to do with me."

"How do you know? You have only seen me for five minutes."

"The stag's breed is never hidden, one sees at once that you belong to the living, not to the dead-alive, and that is the main point. The rest comes with opportunity...."

"I have a free mind, as you yourself say, and you immediately want to overpower it. Who are you that you should take upon yourself to instruct me?"

He looked at her in amazement.

"You are neither to bring me books, nor to come here again yourself," she said, rising to go. "There is a watchman here, and he will seize you."

"That is like the Grandmother again. It smells of the town and the Lenten oil, and I thought that you loved the wide world and freedom. Are you afraid of me, and who do you think I am?"

"A seminarist, perhaps," she said laconically.

"What makes you think that?"

"Well, seminarists are unconventional, badly dressed, and always hungry. Go into the kitchen, and I will tell them to give you something to eat."

"That's very kind. Did anything else about the seminarists strike you?"

"I am not acquainted with any of them, and have seen very little of them at all; they are so unpolished, and talk so queerly...."

"They are our real missionaries, and what does it matter if they talk queerly? While we laugh at them they attack the enemy, blindly perhaps, but at any rate with enthusiasm."

"What enemy?"

"The world; they fight for the new knowledge, the new life. Healthy, virile youth needs air and food, and we need such men."

"We? Who?"

"The new-born strength of the world."

"Do you then represent the 'new-born strength of the world,'" she said, looking at him with observant, curious eyes, but without irony, "or is your name a secret?"

"Would it frighten you if I named it?"

"What could it mean to me if you did disclose it? What is it?"

"Mark Volokov. In this silly place my name is heard with nearly as much terror as if it were Pugachev or Stenka Razin."

"You are that man?" she said, looking at him with rising curiosity. "You boast of your name, which I have heard before. You shot at Niel Andreevich, and let a couple of dogs loose on an old lady. There are the manifestations of your 'new strength.' Go, and don't be seen here again."

"Otherwise you will complain to Grandmama?"

"I certainly shall. Good-bye."

She left the arbour and walked away without listening to his rejoinder. He followed her covetously with his eyes, murmuring as he sprang to the ground a wish that those apples also could be stolen. Vera, for her part, said not a word to her aunt of this meeting, but she confided nevertheless in her friend Natalie Ivanovna after exacting a promise of secrecy.

CHAPTER XIX

After leaving Raisky, Vera listened for a while to make sure he was not following her, and then, pushing the branches of the undergrowth aside with her parasol, made her way by the familiar path to the ruined arbour, whose battered doorway was almost barricaded by the fallen timbers. The steps of the arbour and the planks of the floor had sunk, and rotten planks cracked under her feet. Of its original furniture there was nothing left but two moss-grown benches and a crooked table.

Mark was already in the arbour, and his rifle and huntsman's bag lay on the table. He held out his hand to Vera, and almost lifted her in over the shattered steps. By way of welcome he merely commented on her lateness.

"The weather detained me," she said. "Have you any news?"

"Did you expect any?"

"I expect every day that you will be sent for by the military or the police."

"I have been more careful since Raisky played at magnanimity and took upon himself the fuss about the books."

"I don't like that about you, Mark, your callousness and malice towards everyone except yourself. My cousin made no parade of what he had done; he did not even mention it to me. You are incapable of appreciating a kindness."

"I do appreciate it in my own way."

"Just as the wolf in the fable appreciated the kindness of the crane. Why not thank him with the same simplicity with which he served you. You are a real wolf; you are for ever disparaging, detracting, or blaming someone, either from pride or...."

"Or what?"

"Or by way of cultivating the 'new strength.'"

"Scoffer!" he laughed, as he sat down beside her. "You are young, and still too inexperienced to be disillusioned of all the charm of the good old times. How can I instruct you in the rights of mankind?"

"And how am I to cure you of the slandering of mankind?"

"You have always a retort handy, and nobody could complain of dullness with you, but," he said, clutching meditatively at his head, "if I...."

"Am locked up by the police," she finished. "That seems to be all that your fate still lacks."

"But for you, I should long ago have been sent off somewhere. You are a disturbing element."

"Are you tired of living peaceably, and already craving for a storm? You promised me to lead a different life. What have you not promised me? And I was so happy that they even noticed my delight at home. And now you have relapsed into your old mood," she protested, as he seized her hand.

"Pretty hand!" he said, kissing it again and again without any objection from her, but when he sought to kiss her cheek she drew back.

"You refuse again. Is your reserve never to end? Perhaps you keep your caresses for...."

She drew her hand away hastily.

"You know I do not like jests of that kind. You must break yourself of this tone, and of wolfish manners generally; that would be the first step towards unaffected manhood."

"Tone and manners! You are a child still occupied with your ABC. Before you lie freedom, life, love, happiness, and you talk of tone and manners. Where is the human soul, the woman in you? What is natural and genuine in you?"

"Now you are talking like Raisky."

"Ah, Raisky! Is he still so desperate?"

"More than ever, so that I really don't know how to treat him."

"Lead him by the nose."

"How hideous! It would be best to tell him the truth about myself. If he knew all he would be reconciled and would go away, as he said he intended to do long ago."

"He will hate you, read you a lecture, and perhaps tell your Aunt."

"God forbid that she should hear the truth except from ourselves. Should I go away for a time?"

"Why? It could not be arranged for you to be away long, and if your absence was short he would be only the more agitated. When you were away what good did it do. There is only one way and that is to conceal the truth from him, to put him on a wrong track. Let him cherish his passion, read verses, and gape at the moon, since he is an incurable Romanticist. Later on he will sober down and travel once more."

"He is not a Romanticist in the sense you mean," sighed Vera. "You may fairly call him poet, artist. I at least begin to believe in him, in his delicacy and his truthfulness. I would hide nothing from him if he did not betray his passion for me. If he subdues that, I will be the first to tell him the whole truth."

"We did not meet," interrupted Mark, "to talk so much about him."

"Well, what have you done since we last met?" she asked gaily. "Whom have you met? Have you been discoursing on the 'new strength' or the 'dawn of the future,' or 'young hopes?' Every day I live in anxious expectation."

"No, no," laughed Mark. "I have ceased to bother about the people here; it is not worth while to tackle them."

"God grant it were so. You would have done well if you had acted up to what you say. But I cannot be happy about you. At the Sfogins, the youngest son, Volodya, who is fourteen, declared to his mother that he was not going any more to Mass. When he was whipped, and questioned, he pointed to his eldest brother, who had sneaked into the servants' room and there preached to the maids the whole evening that it was stupid to observe the fasts of the Church, to go through the ceremony of marriage, that there was no God...."

Mark looked at her in horror.

"In the servants' room! And yet I talked to him for a whole evening as if he were a man capable of reason, and gave him books...."

"Which he took straight to the bookseller. 'These are the books you ought to put on sale,' he said. Did you not give me your promise," she said reproachfully, "when we parted and you begged to see me again?"

"All that is long past. I have had nothing more to do with those people since I gave you that promise. Don't be angry, Vera. But for you I would escape from this neighbourhood to-morrow."

"Escape—where? Everywhere there are the same opportunities; boys who would like to see their moustaches grow quicker, servants' rooms, if independent men and women will not listen to your talk. Are you not ashamed of the part you play?" she asked after a brief pause. "Do you look on it as your mission?"

She stroked his bent head affectionately as she spoke. At her last words he raised his head quickly.

"What part do I play? I give a baptism of pure water."

"Are you convinced of the pureness of the water?"

"Listen, Vera. I am not Raisky," said Mark, rising. "You are a woman, or rather one should say a bud which has yet to unfold into womanhood. When that unfolding comes many secrets will be clear to you that have no part in a girl's dreams and that cannot be explained; experience is the sole key to these secrets. I call you to your initiation, Vera; I show you the path of life. But you stand hesitating on the threshold, and your advance is slow. The serious thing is that you don't even believe me."

"Do not be vexed," begged Vera affectionately. "I agree with you in everything that I recognise as right and honourable. If I cannot always follow you in life and in experience it is because I desire to know and see for myself the goal for which I am making."

"That is to say, that you wish to judge for yourself."

"And do you desire that I should not judge for myself?"

"I love you, Vera. Put your trust in me, and obey. Does the flame of passion burn in me less strongly than in your Raisky, for all his poetry. Passion is chary of words. But you will neither trust nor obey me."

"Would you have me not stand at the level of my personality? You yourself preached freedom to me, and now the tyrant in you appears because I do not show a slavish submission."

"Let us part, Vera, if doubt is uppermost with you and you have no confidence in me, for in that fashion we cannot continue our meetings."

"Yes, let us part rather than that you should exact a blind trust in you. In my waking hours and in my dreams I imagine that there lies between us no disturbance, no doubt. But I don't understand you, and therefore cannot trust you."

"You hide under your Aunt's skirts like a chicken under a hen, and you have absorbed her ideas and her system of morals. You, like Raisky, inshroud passion in fantastic draperies. Let us put aside all the other questions untouched. The one that lies before us is simple and straightforward. We love one another. Is that so or not?"

"What does that lead to, Mark!"

"If you don't believe me, look around you. You have spent your whole life in the woods and fields, and do you learn nothing from what you see in all directions?" he asked, pointing to a swarm of flying pigeons, and to the nesting swallows. "Learn from them; they deal in no subtleties!"

"Yes, they circle round their nests. One has flown away, probably in search of food."

"When winter comes they will all separate."

"And return in spring to the same nest."

"I believe you when you talk reasonably, Vera. You felt injured by my rough manners, and I am making every effort. I have transformed myself to the old-fashioned pattern, and shall soon shift my feet and smile when I make my bow like Tiet Nikonich. I don't give way to the desire to abuse or to quarrel with anybody, and draw no attention to my doings. I shall next be making up my mind to attend Mass, what else should I do?"

"You are in the mood for joking, but joking is not what I wanted," sighed Vera.

"What do you want me to do?"

"So far I have not even been able to persuade you to spare yourself for my sake, to cease your baptisms, to live like other people."

"But if I act in accordance with my convictions?"

"What is your aim? What do you hope to do?"

"I teach fools."

"Do you even know yourself what you teach, for what you have been struggling for a whole year? To live the life that you prescribe is not within the bounds of possibility. It is all very new and bold, but...."

"There we are again at the same old point. I can hear the old lady piping," he laughed scornfully, pointing in the direction of the house. "You speak with her voice."

"Is that your whole answer, Mark? Everything is a lie; therefore, away with it! But the absence of any notion of what truth is to supersede the lies makes me distrustful."

"You set reflexion above nature and passion. You are noble, and you naturally desire marriage. But that has nothing to do with love, and it is love and happiness that I seek."

Vera rose and looked at him with blazing eyes.

"If I wished only for marriage, Mark, I should naturally make another choice."

"Pardon me, I was rude," he said in real embarrassment, and kissed her hand. "But, Vera, you repress your love, you are afraid, and instead of giving yourself up to the pleasure of it you are for ever analysing."

"I try to find out who and what you are, because love is not a passing pleasure to me, but you look on it as a distraction."

"No, as a daily need of life, which is no matter for jesting. Like Raisky, I cannot sleep through the long nights, and I suffer nervous torture that I could not have believed possible. You say you love me; that I love you is plain? But I call you to happiness and you are afraid...."

"I do not want happiness for a month, for six months—"

"For your life long, and even after death?" asked Mark, scornfully.

"For life! I do not want to foresee an ultimate limit. I do not and will not believe in happiness with a term. But I do believe in another kind of intimate happiness, and I want...."

"To make me embrace the same belief."

"Yes, I know no other happiness, and I would scorn it if I knew it."

"Good-bye, Vera. You do not love me, but are for ever disputing, analysing either my character or the nature of happiness. We always get back to the point from which we started. I think it is your destiny to love Raisky. You can make what you will of him, can deck him out with all your Aunt's tags, and evolve a new hero of romance every day, for ever and ever. I haven't the time for that kind of thing. I have work to do."

"Ah work, and love, with happiness as an afterthought, a trifle...."

"Do you wish to build a life out of love after the old fashion, a life such as that lived by the swallows who leave their nest only to seek food."

"You would fly for a moment into a strange nest, and then forget."

"Yes, if forgetting is so easy; but if one cannot forget, one returns. But must I return if I don't want to? Is that compatible with freedom? Would you ask that?"

"I cannot understand a bird's life of that kind."

"Farewell, Vera. We were mistaken. I want a comrade, not a school girl."

"Yes, Mark, a comrade, strong like yourself, I agree. A comrade for the whole of life, is that not so?"

"I thought," said Mark as if he had not heard her last question, "that we should soon be united, and that whether we separated again must depend on temperament and circumstances. You make your analysis in advance, so that your judgment is as crooked and twisted as an old maid's could be. You don't look to the quarter whence truth and light must come. Sleep, my child. I was mistaken. Farewell once more. We will try to avoid one another in the future."

"We will try. But can we really not find happiness together? What is the hindrance?" she asked, in a low, agitated tone, touching his hand.

Mark shouldered his gun in silence, and walked out of the arbour into the brushwood. Vera stood motionless as if she were in a deep sleep. Overcome by grief and amazement, she could not believe he was really leaving her. Where there is no trust there is no love, she thought. She did not trust him, and yet, if she did not love him, why was her grief and pain at his going so great. Why did she feel that death itself would be welcome?

"Mark!" she cried in a low voice. He did not look round, and although she repeated the cry he strode forward. "Mark!" she cried breathlessly a third time, but he still pursued his path. Her face faded, but mechanically she picked up her handkerchief and her parasol and mounted the cliff. Were truth and love to be found there where her heart called her? Or did truth lie in the little chapel that she was now approaching?

For four days Vera wandered in the park, and waited in the arbour, but Mark did not come. There was no reply to the call of her heart. She no longer hid her movements from Raisky, who came upon her from time to time in the chapel. She allowed him to accompany her to the little village church on the hill where she usually went alone. She remained on her knees with bowed head for a long time, while he stood motionless behind her. Then without a word or a glance, she took his arm, to return wearily to the old house, where they parted. Vera knew nothing of his secret suffering, of the passionate love which attracted him to her, the double love of a man for a woman, and of an artist for his ideal.

Raisky wondered what the shots meant. It need not necessarily be love that drove her to the rendezvous. There might be a secret of another kind, but the key to the mystery lay in her heart. There was no salvation for her except in love, and he longed to give her protection and freedom.

Again he found her at twilight praying in the chapel, but this time she was calm and her eyes clear. She gave him her hand, and was plainly pleased to see him.

"You cannot imagine, Vera," he said, "how happy it makes me to see you calmer. What has given you peace?"

She glanced towards the chapel.

"You don't go down there any more?" he said, pointing to the precipice.

She shook her head.

"Thank God!" he cried. "If you are going home now, take my arm," he said, and they walked together along the path leading across the meadow. "You have been fighting a hard and despairing battle, Vera. So much you do not conceal. Are you going to conquer this agonising and dangerous passion?"

"And if I do, Cousin?" she asked despondently.

"The richer for a great experience, strengthened against future storms, your portion will be a great happiness, sufficient to fill your whole life."

"I cannot comprehend any other happiness," she said, thoughtfully. She stood still, leaning her head on his shoulder, and her eyes filled with tears. He did not know that he had probed her wound by touching on the very point that had caused her separation from Mark.

At that moment there was the report of a shot in the depths below the precipice, and the sound was re-echoed from the hills. Raisky and Vera both started. She stood listening for a moment. Her eyes, still wet with tears, were wide and staring now. Then she loosed her hold of his arm, and hurried in the direction of the precipice, with Raisky hurrying at her heels. When she had gone half way, she stopped, laid her hand on her heart, and listened once more.

"A few minutes ago your mind was made up, Vera!"

Raisky's face was pale, and his agitation nearly as great as hers. She did not hear his words, and she looked at him without seeing him. Then she took a few steps in the direction of the precipice, but suddenly turned to go slowly towards the chapel.

"I am not going," she whispered. "Why does he call me? It cannot be that he has changed his attitude in the last few days."

She sank down on her knees before the sacred picture, and covered her face with her hands. Raisky came up to her, and implored her not to go. She herself gazed at the picture with expressionless, hopeless eyes. When she rose she shuddered, and seemed unaware of Raisky's presence.

A shot sounded once more. With a cry Vera ran over the meadow towards the cliff. Perhaps my conviction has conquered, she thought. Why else should he call her? Her feet hardly seemed to touch the grass as she ran into the avenue that led to the precipice.

CHAPTER XX

Vera came that night to supper with a gloomy face. She eagerly drank a glass of milk, but offered no remark to anyone.

"Why are you so unhappy, Veroshka?" asked her aunt. "Don't you feel well."

"I was afraid to ask," interposed Tiet Nikonich politely. "I could not help noticing, Vera Vassilievna, that you have been altered for some time; you seem to have grown thinner and paler. The change becomes your looks, but the symptoms ought not to be overlooked, as they might indicate the approach of illness."

"I have a little tooth-ache, but it will soon pass," answered Vera unwillingly.

Tatiana Markovna looked away sadly enough, but said nothing, while Raisky tapped his plate absently with a fork, but ate nothing, and maintained a gloomy silence. Only Marfinka and Vikentev took every dish that was offered them, and chattered without intermission.

Vera soon took her leave, followed by Raisky. She went into the park, and stood at the top of the cliff looking down into the dark wood below her; then she wrapped herself in her mantilla, and sat down on the bench. Silently she acceded to Raisky's request to be allowed to sit down beside her.

"You are in trouble, and are suffering, Vera."

"I have tooth-ache."

"It is your heart that aches, Vera. Share your trouble with me."

"I make no complaint."

"You have an unhappy love affair, with whom?"

She did not answer. She knew that her hopes were still not dead, mad though they might be. What if she went away for a week or two to breathe, to conjure up her strength.

"Cousin," she said at last, "to-morrow at daybreak I am going across the Volga, and may stay away longer than usual. I have not said good-bye to Grandmother. Please say it for me."

"I will go away too."

"Wait, Cousin, until I am a little calmer. Perhaps then I can confide in you, and we can part like brother and sister, but now it is impossible. Still, in case you do go away, let us say good-bye now. Forgive me my strange ways, and let me give you a sister's kiss."

She kissed him on the forehead and walked quickly away, but she had only taken a few steps before she paused to say: "Thank you for all you have done for me. I have not the strength to tell you how grateful I am for your friendship, and above all for this place. Farewell, and forgive me."

"Vera," he cried in painful haste. "Let me stay as long as you are here or are in the neighbourhood. Even if we don't see one another, I yet know where you are. I will wait till you are calmer, till you fulfil your promise, and confide in me, as you have said you would. You won't be far away, and we can at least write to one another. Give me at least this consolation, for God's sake," he murmured passionately. "Leave me at least that Paradise which is next door to Hell."

She looked at him with a distraught air, and bent her head in assent. But she saw the glow of delight which swept over his agitated face, and wondered sorrowfully why *he* did not speak like that.

"I will put off my journey till the day after tomorrow. Good-night!" she said, and gave him her hand to kiss before they separated.

Early next day Vera gave Marina a note with instructions to deliver it and to wait for the answer. After the receipt of the answer she grew more cheerful and went out for a walk along the riverside. That evening she told her aunt that she was going on a visit to Natalie Ivanovna, and took leave of them all, promising Raisky not to forget him.

The next day a fisherman from the Volga brought him a letter from Vera, in which she called him "dear cousin," and seemed to look forward to a happier future. Into the friendly tone of the letter he contrived to read tender feeling, and he forgot, in his delight, his doubts, his anxiety, the blue letters, and the precipice. He wrote and dispatched immediately a brief, affectionate reply.

Vera's letter aroused in him the artist sense, and drove him to set out his chaotic emotions in defined form. He sought to crystallise his thoughts and affections; his very passion took artistic shape, and assumed in the clear light Vera's charming features.

"What are you scribbling day and night?" inquired Tatiana Markovna. "Is it a play or another novel?"

"I write and write, Granny, and don't know myself how it will end."

"It doesn't matter what the child does so long as he is amused," she remarked, not altogether missing the character of Raisky's occupation. "But why do you write at night, when I am so afraid of fire, and you might fall asleep over your drama. You will make yourself ill, and you often look as yellow as an over-ripe gherkin as it is."

He looked in the glass, and was struck with his own appearance. Yellow patches were visible on the nose and temples, and there were grey threads in his thick, black hair.

"If I were fair," he grumbled, "I should not age so quickly. Don't bother about me, Granny, but leave me my freedom. I can't sleep."

"You too ask me for freedom, like Vera. It is as if I held you both in chains," she added with an anxious sigh. "Go on writing, Borushka, but not at night. I cannot sleep in peace, for when I look at your window the light is always burning."

"I will answer for it, Grandmother, that there shall be no fire, and if I myself were to be burnt...."

"Touch wood! Do not tempt fate. Remember the saying that 'my tongue is my enemy.'"

Suddenly Raisky sprang from the divan and ran to the window.

"There is a peasant bringing a letter from Vera," he cried, as he hurried out of the room.

"One might think it was his father in person," said Tatiana Markovna to herself. "How many candles he burns with his novels and plays, as many as four in a night!"

Again Raisky received a few lines from Vera. She wrote that she was longing to see him again, and that she wanted to ask for his services. She added the following postscript:—

"Dear Friend and Cousin, you taught me to love and to suffer, and poured the strength of your love into my soul. This it is that gives me courage to ask you to do a good deed. There is here an unhappy man who has been driven from his home and lies under the suspicion of the Government. He has no place to lay his head, and everyone, either from indifference or fear, avoids him. But you are kind and generous, and cannot be indifferent; still less will you hesitate to do a deed of pure charity. The wretched man has not a kopek, has no clothes, and autumn is coming on.

"If your heart tells you, as I don't doubt it will, what to do, address the wife of the acolyte, Sekleteia Burdalakov, but arrange it so that neither Grandmother, nor anyone at home, knows anything of it. A sum of three hundred roubles will be sufficient, I think, to provide for him for a whole year, perhaps two hundred and fifty would suffice. Will you put in a cloak and a warm vest (in my firm belief in your kind heart and your love to me, I enclose the measures taken by the village tailor) to protect him from the cold.

"I don't like to ask you for a rug for him; that would be to make an unfair use of kindness. In the winter the poor exile will probably leave the place, and will bless you, and to some degree me as well. I would not have troubled you, but you know that my Grandmother has all my money, which is therefore inaccessible."

"What on earth is the meaning of this postscript?" cried Raisky. "The whole note is certainly not from her hand; she could not have written like this."

He threw himself on the divan in a fit of nervous laughter. He was in Tatiana Markovna's sitting-room, with Vikentev and Marfinka. At first the lovers laughed, but stopped when they saw the violent character of his mirth. Tatiana Markovna, who came in at this moment, offered him some drops of cordial in a teaspoon.

"No, Grandmother," he cried, still laughing violently. "Don't give me drops, but three hundred roubles."

"What do you want the money for?" said Tatiana Markovna hesitating. "Is it for Markushka again. You had much better ask him to return the eighty roubles he has had."

He entered into the spirit of the bargain, and eventually had to content himself with two hundred and fifty roubles, which he dispatched next day to the address given. He also ordered the cloak and vest, and bought a warm rug, to be sent in a few days.

"I thank you heartily, and with tears, dear Cousin," ran the letter he received in return for his gifts. "I cannot express in writing the gratitude I feel. Heaven, not I, will reward you. How delighted the poor exile was with your gift. He laughed for joy, and is wearing the new things. He immediately paid his landlord his three months' arrears of rent, and a month in advance. He only allowed himself to spend three roubles in cigars, which he has not smoked for a long time, and smoking is his only passion."

Although the apocryphal nature of this remarkable missive was quite clear to Raisky, he did not hesitate to add a box of cigars to his gift for the "poor exile." It was enough for him that Vera's name was attached to this pressing request. He observed the course of his own passion as a physician does disease. As he watched the clouds driven before the wind, or looked at the green carpet of the earth, now taking on sad autumnal hues, he realised that Nature was marching on her way through never ending change, with not a moment's stagnation. He alone brooded idly with no prize in view. He asked himself anxiously what his duty was, and begged that Reason would shed some light on his way, give him boldness to leap over the funeral pyre of his hopes. Reason told him to seek safety in flight.

He drove into the town to buy some necessities for the journey, and there met the Governor who reproached him with having hidden himself for so long. Raisky excused himself on the ground of ill-health, and spoke of his approaching departure.

"Where are you going?"

"It is all one to me," returned Raisky gloomily. "Here I am so bored that I must seek some distraction. I intend going to St. Petersburg, then to my estate in the government of R—— and then perhaps abroad."

"I don't wonder that you are bored with staying in the same spot, since you avoid society, and must need distraction. Will you make an expedition with me? I am starting on a tour of the district to-morrow, why not come with me? You will see much that is beautiful, and, being a poet, you will collect new impressions. We will travel for a hundred versts by river. Don't forget your sketch-book."

Raisky shook the Governor's proffered hand, and accepted. The Governor showed him his well-equipped travelling carriage, declared that his kitchen would travel with him, and cards should not be forgotten, and promised himself a gayer journey than would have been possible in the sole society of a busy secretary.

Raisky felt a relief in the firm determination he now made to conquer his passion, and decided not to return from this journey, but to have his effects sent after him. While he was away he wrote in this sense to Vera, telling her that his life in Malinovka had been like an evil dream full of suffering, and that if he ever saw the place again it would be at some distant date.

A day or two later he received a short answer from Vera dated from Malinovka. Marfinka's birthday fell during the next week, and when the festival was over she was to go on a long visit to her future mother-in-law. If Raisky did not make some sacrifice and return, a sacrifice to her grandmother and herself, Tatiana Markovna would be terribly lonely.

Next evening he had a letter from Vera acquiescing in his intention of leaving Malinovka without seeing her again, and saying that immediately after the dispatch of this letter she would go over to her friend on the other side of the Volga, but she hoped that he would go to say good-bye to

Tatiana Markovna and the rest of the household, as his departure without any farewell must necessarily cause surprise in the town, and would hurt Tatiana Markovna's feelings.

This answer relieved him enormously. On the afternoon of the next day, when he alighted from the carriage in the outskirts of the town and bade his travelling host good-bye, he was in good enough spirits as he picked up his bag and made his way to the house.

Marfinka and Vikentev were the first to meet him, the dogs leaped to welcome him, the servants hurried up, and the whole household showed such genuine pleasure at his return that he was moved almost to tears. He looked anxiously round to see if Vera was there, but one and another hastened to tell him that Vera had gone away. He ought to have been glad to hear this news, but he heard it with a spasm of pain. When he entered his aunt's room she sent Pashutka out and locked the door.

"How anxiously I have been expecting you!" she said. "I wanted to send a messenger for you."

"What is the matter?" he exclaimed, pale with terror in fear of bad news of Vera.

"Your friend Leonti Ivanovich is ill."

"Poor fellow! What is wrong? Is it dangerous? I will go to him at once."

"I will have the horses put in. In the meantime I may as well tell you what is known all over the town. I have kept it secret from Marfinka only, and Vera already knows it. His wife has left him, and he has fallen ill. Yesterday and the day before the Koslovs' cook came to fetch you."

"Where has she gone?"

"Away with the Frenchman, Charles, who was suddenly called to St. Petersburg. She pretended she was going to stay with her relations in Moscow and said that Monsieur Charles would accompany her so far. She extracted from Koslov a pass giving her permission to live alone, and is now with Charles in St. Petersburg."

"Her relations with Charles," replied Raisky, "were no secret to anybody except her husband. Everyone will laugh at him, but he will understand nothing, and his wife will return."

"You have not heard the end. On her way she wrote to her husband telling him to forget her, not to expect her return, because she could no longer endure living with him."

"The fool! Just as if she had not made scandal enough. Poor Leonti! I will go to him, how sorry I am for him."

"Yes, Borushka, I am sorry for him too, and should like to have gone to see him. He has the simple honesty of a child. God has given him learning, but no common sense, and he is buried in his books. I wonder who is looking after him now. If you find he is not being properly cared for, bring him here. The old house is empty, and we can establish him there for the time being. I will have two rooms got ready for him."

"What a woman you are, Grandmother. While I am thinking, you have acted."

When he reached Koslov's house he found the shutters of the grey house were closed, and he had to knock repeatedly before he was admitted. He passed through the ante-room into the dining-room and stood uncertain before the study door, hesitating whether he should knock or go straight in. Suddenly the door opened, and there stood before him, dressed in a woman's dressing-gown and slippers, Mark Volokov, unbrushed, sleepy, pale, thin and sinister.

"The evil one has brought you at last," he grumbled half in surprise and half in vexation. "Where have you been all this time? I have hardly slept for two nights. His pupils are about in the day time, but at night he is alone."

"What is the matter with him?"

"Has no one told you. That she-goat has gone. I was pleased to hear it, and came at once to congratulate him, but I found him with not a drop of blood in his face, with dazed eyes, and unable to recognise anyone. He just escaped brain fever. Instead of weeping for joy, the man has nearly died of sorrow. I fetched the doctor, but Koslov sent him away, and walked up and down the room like one demented. Now he is sleeping, so we will not disturb him. I will go, and you must stay, and see that he does not do himself some injury in a fit of melancholy. He listens to no one, and I have been tempted to smack him." Mark spit with vexation. "You can't depend on his idiot of a cook. Yesterday the woman gave him some tooth powder instead of his proper powder. I am going to dismiss her to-morrow."

Raisky watched him in amazement, and offered his hand.

"What favour is this?" said Mark bitterly, and without taking the proffered hand.

"I thank you for having stood by my old friend."

Mark seized Raisky's hand and shook it.

"I have been looking for some means of serving you for a long time."

"Why, Volokov, are you for ever executing quick changes like a clown in a circus?"

"What the devil have I to do with your gratitude? I am not here for that, but on Koslov's account."

"God be with you and your manners, Mark Ivanovich!" replied Raisky. "In any case, you have done a good deed."

"More praise. You can be as sentimental as you like for all I care...."

"I will take Leonti home with me," resumed Raisky. "He will be absolutely at home there, and if his troubles do not blow over he will have his own quiet corner all his life."

"Bravo! that is deeds, not words. Koslov would wither without a home and without care. It is an excellent idea you have taken into your head."

"It comes not from me, but from a woman, and not from her head, but from her heart. My Aunt...."

"The old lady has a sound heart. I must go and breakfast with her one day. It is a pity she has amassed so many foolish ideas. Now I am going. Look after Koslov, if not personally, through some one else. The day before yesterday his head had to be cooled all day, and at night cabbage leaves should be laid on it. I was a little disturbed, because in his dazed state he got the cabbage and began to eat it. Good-bye! I have neither slept nor eaten, though Avdotya has treated me to a horrible brew of coffee...."

"Allow me to send the coachman home to fetch some supper," said Raisky.

"I would rather eat at home."

"Perhaps you have no money," said Raisky nervously drawing out his pocket book.

"I have money," said Mark enigmatically, hardly able to restrain a callous laugh, "I am going to the bath-house before I have my supper, as I haven't been able to undress here. I have changed my quarters, and now live with a clerical personage."

"You look ill, thin, and your eyes...."

Mark's face grew more evil and sinister than before.

"You too look worse," he said. "If you look in the glass you will see yellow patches and hollow eyes."

"I have many causes of anxiety."

"So have I. Good-bye," said Mark, and was gone.

Raisky went into the study and walked up to the bed on tiptoe.

"Who is there?" asked Leonti feebly.

When Leonti recognised Raisky he pushed his feet out of bed, and sat up.

"Is he gone?" he asked weakly. "I pretended to be asleep. You have not been for so long, and I have been expecting you all the time. The face of an old comrade is the only one that I can bear to see."

"I have been away, and heard when I returned of your illness."

"It is gossip. There is a conspiracy to say I am ill, which is all foolish talk. Mark, who even fetched a doctor, has been hanging about here as if he were afraid I should do myself an injury," said Leonti and paced up and down the room.

"You are weak, and walk with difficulty," said Raisky. "It would be better for you to lie down."

"I am weak, that is true," admitted Leonti.

He bent over the chair-back to Raisky, embraced him, and laid his face against his hair. Raisky felt hot tears on his forehead and cheeks.

"It is weakness," sobbed Leonti. "But I am not ill, and have not brain fever. They talk, but don't understand. And I understood nothing either, but now that I see you, I cannot keep back my tears. Don't abuse me like Mark, or laugh at me, as they all do, my colleagues and my sympathetic visitors. I can discern malicious laughter on all their faces."

"I respect and understand your tears and your sorrow," said Raisky, stifling his own tears.

"You are my kind old comrade. Even at school you never laughed at me, and do you know why I weep?"

Leonti took a letter from his desk and handed it to Raisky. It was the letter from Juliana Andreevna of which Tatiana Markovna had spoken. Raisky glanced through it.

"Destroy it," he said. "You will have no peace while it is in your possession."

"Destroy it!" said Leonti, seizing the letter, and replacing it in the desk. "How is it possible to think of such a thing, when these are the only lines she has written me, and these are all that I have as a souvenir?"

"Leonti! Think of all this as a malady, a terrible misfortune, and don't succumb to it. You are not an old man, and have a long life before you."

"My life is over, unless she returns to me," he whispered.

"What! You could, you would take her back!"

"You, too, Boris, fail to understand me!" cried Leonti in despair, as he thrust his hands into his hair and strode up and down. "People keep on saying I am ill, they offer sympathy, bring a doctor, sit all night by my bedside, and yet don't guess why I suffer so wildly, don't even guess at the only remedy there is for me. She is not here," he whispered wildly, seizing Raisky by the shoulders and shaking him violently. "She is not here, and that is what constitutes my illness. Besides, I am not ill, I am dead. Take me to her, and I shall rise again. And you ask whether I will take her back again! You, a novelist, don't understand simple things like that!"

"I did not know that you loved her like that," said Raisky tenderly. "You used to laugh and say that you had got so used to her that you were becoming faithless to your Greeks and Romans."

"I chattered, I boasted," laughed Leonti bitterly, "and was without understanding. But for this I never should have understood. I thought I loved the ancients, while my whole love was given to the living woman. Yes, Boris, I loved books and my gymnasium, the ancients and the moderns, my scholars, and you, Boris; I loved the street, this hedge, the service tree there, only through my love for her. Now, nothing of all this matters. I knew that as I lay on the floor reading her letter. And you ask whether I would receive her. God in Heaven! If she came, how she should be cherished!" he concluded, his tears flowing once more.

"Leonti, I come to you with a request from Tatiana Markovna, who asks you," he went on, though Leonti walked ceaselessly up and down, dragging his slippers and appeared not to listen, "to come over to us. Here you will die of misery."

"Thank you," said Leonti, shaking his head. "She is a saint. But how can a desolate man carry his sorrow into a strange house?"

"Not a strange house, Leonti, we are brothers, and our relation is closer than the ties of blood."

Leonti lay down on the bed, and took Raisky's hand.

"Pardon my egoism," he said. "Later, later, I will come of my own accord, will ask permission to look after your library, if no hope is left me."

"Have you any hope?"

"What! Do you think there is no hope?"

Raisky, who did not wish to deprive his friend of the last straw, nor to stir useless hope in him, hesitated, before he answered after a pause: "I don't know what to say to you exactly, Leonti. I know so little of your wife that I cannot judge her character."

"You know her," said Leonti in a dull voice. "It was you who directed my attention to the Frenchman, but then I did not understand you, because nothing of the kind had entered my head. But if he leaves her," he said, with a gleam of hope in his eyes, "she will perhaps remember me."

"Perhaps," said Raisky. "To-morrow I will come to fetch you. Good-bye for the present. To-night I will either come myself or send someone who will stay with you."

Leonti did not hear, and did not even see Raisky go.

When he reached home, Raisky gave his aunt an account of Leonti's condition, telling her that there was no danger, but that no sympathy would help matters. Yakob was sent to look after the sick man and Tatiana Markovna did not forget to send an abundant supper, with tea, rum, wine and all sorts of other things.

"What are these things for, Grandmother?" asked Raisky. "He doesn't eat anything."

"But the other one, if he returns?"

"What other one?"

"Who but Markushka? He will want something to eat. You found him with our invalid."

"I will go to Mark, Granny, and tell him what you say."

"For goodness' sake don't do that, Borushka. Mark will laugh at me."

"No, he will be grateful and respectful, for he understands you. He is not like Niel Andreevich."

"I don't want his gratitude and respect. Let him eat, and be satisfied, and God be with him. He is a ruined man. Has he remembered the eighty roubles?"

CHAPTER XXI

Raisky laughed as he went out into the garden. He looked sadly at the closed shutters of the old house, and stood for a long time on the edge of the precipice, looking down thoughtfully into the depths of the thicket and the trees rustling and cracking in the wind. Then he turned to look at the long avenues, here forming gloomy corridors, and then opening out into open stately spaces, at the flower gardens now fading under the approach of autumn, at the kitchen garden, and at the distant glimmer of the rising moon, and at the stars. He looked out over the Volga, gleaming like steel in the distance. The evening was fresh and cool, and the withered leaves were falling with a gentle rustle around him. He could not take his eyes from the river, now silvered by the moon, which separated him from Vera. She had gone without leaving a word for him. A word from her would have brought tenderness and would have drowned all bitterness, he thought. But she was gone without leaving a trace or any kind remembrance. With bent head and full of anxious thought he made his way along the dark avenues.

Suddenly delicate fingers seized his shoulders, and he heard a low laugh.

"Vera!" he cried, seizing her hand violently. "You here, and not away over the Volga!"

"Yes, here, not over there." She put her arm in his and asked him, laughing, whether he thought she would let him go without saying good-bye.

"Witch!" he said, not knowing whether fear or joy was uppermost. "I was this very moment complaining that you had not left a line for me, and now I can't understand, as everyone in the house told me you had gone away yesterday."

"And you believed it," she said laughing. "I told them to say so, to surprise you. They were humbugging.... To go away without two words," she asked triumphantly, "or to stay, which is better?"

Her gay talk, her quick gestures, the mockery in her voice, all these things seemed unnatural, and he recognised beneath it all weariness, strain, an effort to conceal the collapse of her strength. When they reached the end of the avenue he tried to lead her to an open spot, where he could see her face.

"Let me look at you! How gay and merry you are, Vera!" he said timidly.

"What is there to see?" she interrupted impatiently, and tried to draw him into the shadow again. He felt that her hands were trembling, and for the moment his own passion was stilled, and he shared her suffering.

"Why do you look at me like that? I am not crazy," she said, turning her face away.

He was stricken with horror. The insane are always assuring everyone of their sanity. What was wrong with Vera? She did not confide in him, she would not speak out, she was determined to fight her own battles. Who could support and shelter her? An inner voice told him that Tatiana Markovna alone could do it.

"Vera, you are ill," he said earnestly. "Give Grandmother your confidence."

"Silence! Not a word of Grandmother! Goodbye! To-morrow we will go for a stroll, do some shopping, go down by the river, anything you like."

"I will go away, Vera," he cried, filled with inexpressible fear. "I am worn out. Why do you deceive me? Why did you call me back to find you still here? Was it to mock my sufferings?"

"So that we could suffer together," she answered. "Passion is beautiful, as you yourself have said; it is life itself. You have taught me how to love, have educated passion in me, and now you may admire the result of your labour," she ended, drawing in a deep breath of the cool evening air.

"I warned you, Vera. I told you passion was a fierce wolf."

"No, worse, it is a tiger. I could not believe what you said, but I do now. Do you know the picture in the old house which represents a tiger showing his teeth at a seated Cupid? I never understood the picture, which seemed meaningless, but now I understand it. Passion is a tiger, lying there apparently so peaceful and inviting, until he begins to howl and to whet his teeth."

Raisky pursued the comparison in the hope that he might learn the name of Vera's lover.

"Your comparison is false, Vera. There are no tigers in our Northern climate. I am nearer the mark when I compare passion to a wolf."

"You are right," she said with a nervous laugh. "A real wolf. However carefully you feed him he looks always to the woods. You are all wolves, and *he*, too, is a wolf."

"Who?" he asked in an expressionless voice. "Tushin is a bear, a genuine Russian bear. You may lay your hand on his shaggy head, and sleep; your rest is sure, for he will serve you all his life."

"Which of the animals am I?" he asked gaily, noting that Tushin was not the man. "Don't beat about the bush, Vera, you may say I am an ass."

"No," she said scornfully. "You are a fox, a nice, cunning fox, with a gift for deception. That's what you are. Why don't you say something?" she went on, as he kept an embarrassed silence.

"Vera, there are weapons to be used against wolves, for me, to go away; for you, not to go down there," he said, pointing to the precipice.

"Tell me how to prevent myself from going there. Teach me, since you are my mentor, how not to go. You first set the house on fire, and then talk of leaving it. You sing in praise of passion, and then...."

"I meant another kind of passion. Where both parties to it are honourable, it means the supreme happiness in life, and its storms are full of the glow of life...."

"And where there is no dishonour, no precipice yawns? I love, and am loved, yet passion has me in its jaws. Tell me what I should do."

"Confess all to Grandmother," whispered Raisky, pale with terror, "or permit me to talk to her."

"To shame me and ruin me? Who told me I need not obey her?"

"At one moment you are on the point of telling your secret, at another you hide behind it. I am in the dark, and feel my way in uncertainty. How can I, when I do not know the whole truth, diagnose the case?"

"You know what is wrong with me? Why do you say you are in the dark. Come," she said, leading him into the moonlight. "See what is wrong with me."

He stood transfixed with terror and pity. Pale, haggard, with wild eyes and tightly pressed lips, this was quite another Vera. Strands of hair were loose from beneath her hood, and fell in gipsy-like confusion over her forehead and temples, and covered her eyes and mouth with every quick movement she made. Her shoulders were negligently clad in a satin wrap trimmed with swansdown, held in place by a loosely tied knot of silk.

"Well," she said, shaking her hair out of her eyes. "What has happened to the beauty whose praise you sang?"

"Vera," he said, "I would die for you. Tell me how I may serve you."

"Die!" she exclaimed. "Help me to live. Give me that beautiful passion which sheds its glorious light over the whole of life. I see no passion but this drowning tiger passion. Give me back at least my old strength, you, who talk of going to my Grandmother to place her and me on the same bier. It is too late to tell me to go no more to the precipice."

She sat down on the bench and looked moodily straight before her.

"You yourself, Vera, dreamed of freedom, and you prided yourself on your independence."

"My head burns. Have pity on your sister! I am ashamed to be so weak."

"What is it, dear Vera?"

"Nothing. Take me home, help me to mount the steps. I am afraid, and would like to lie down. Pardon me for having disturbed you for nothing, for having brought you here. You would have gone away and forgotten me. I am only feverish. Are you angry with me?"

Too dejected to reply, he gave her his arm, took her as far as her room, and struck a light.

"Send Marina or Masha to stay in my room, please. But say nothing to Grandmother, lest she should be alarmed and come herself. Why are you looking at me so strangely? God knows what I have been saying to you, to plague you and to avenge myself of all my humiliations. Tell Grandmother that I have gone to bed to be up early in the morning, and I pray you bless me in your thoughts, do you hear?"

"I hear," he said absently, as he pressed her hand and went out in search of Masha.

He looked forward with anxiety to Vera's awakening. He seemed to have forgotten his own passion since his imagination had become absorbed in the contemplation of her suffering.

"Something is wrong with Vera," said Tatiana Markovna, shaking her grey head as she saw how grimly he avoided her questioning glance.

"What can it be?" asked Raisky negligently, with an effort to assume indifference.

"Something is wrong, Borushka. She looks so melancholy and is so silent, and often seems to have tears in her eyes. I have spoken to the doctor, but he only talks the old nonsense about nerves," she said, relapsing into a gloomy silence.

Raisky looked anxiously for Vera's appearance next morning. She came at last, accompanied by the maid, who carried a warm coat and her hat and shoes. She said good morning to her aunt, asked for coffee, ate her roll with appetite, and reminded Raisky that he had promised to go shopping with her in the town and to take a walk in the park. It amazed him that she should be once more transformed, but there was a certain audacity in her gestures and a haste in her speech which seemed forced and alien from her usual manner and reminded him of her behaviour the day before.

She was plainly making a great effort to conceal her real mood. She chatted volubly with Paulina Karpovna, who had turned up unexpectedly and was displaying the pattern of a dress intended for Marfinka's trousseau. That lady's visit was really directed towards Raisky, of whose return she had heard. She sought in vain an occasion to speak with him alone, but seized a moment to sit down beside him, when she made eyes at him and said in a low voice: *"Je comprends; dites tout, du courage."*

Raisky wished her anywhere, and moved away. Vera meanwhile put on her coat and asked him to come with her. Paulina Karpovna wished to accompany them, but Vera declined on the ground that they were walking and had far to go, that the ground was damp, and that Paulina's elegant dress with a long train was unsuited for the expedition.

"I want to have you this whole day for myself," she said to Raisky as they went out together, "indeed every day until you go."

"But, Vera, how can I help you when I don't know what is making you suffer. I only see that you have your own drama, that the catastrophe is approaching, or is in process. What is it?" he asked anxiously, as she shivered.

"I don't feel well, and am far from gay. Autumn is beginning. Nature grows dark and sinister, the birds are already deserting us, and my mood, too, is autumnal. Do you see the black line high above the Volga? Those are the cranes in flight. My thoughts, too, fly away into the distance."

She realised halfway that this strange explanation was unconvincing, and only pursued it because she did not wish to tell the truth.

"I wanted to ask you, Vera, about the letters you wrote to me."

"I am ill and weak; you saw what an attack I had yesterday. I cannot remember just now all that I wrote."

"Another time then!" he sighed. "But tell me, Vera, how I can help you. Why do you keep me back, and why do you want to spend these days in my society? I have a right to ask this, and it is your duty to give a plain answer unless you want me to think you false."

"Don't let us talk of it now."

"No," he cried angrily. "You play with me as a cat does with a mouse. I will endure it no longer. You can either reveal your own secrets or keep them as you please, but in so far as it touches me, I demand an immediate answer. What is my part in this drama?"

"Do not be angry! I did not keep you back to wound you. But don't talk about it, don't agitate me so that I have another attack like yesterday's. You see that I can hardly stand. I don't want my weakness to be seen at home. Defend me from myself. Come to me at dusk, about six, and I will tell you why I detained you."

"Pardon me, Vera. I am not myself either," he said, struck by her suffering. "I don't know what lies on your heart, and I will not ask. I will come later to fetch you."

"I will tell you if I have the strength," she said.

They went into the shops, where Vera made purchases for herself and Marfinka, she talked eagerly to the acquaintances they met, and even visited a poor godchild, for whom she took gifts. She assented readily to Raisky's suggestion that they should visit Koslov.

When they reached the house, Mark walked out of the door. He was plainly startled, made no answer to Raisky's inquiry after Leonti's health, and walked quickly away. Vera was still more disconcerted but pulled herself together, and followed Raisky into the house.

"What is the matter with him?" asked Raisky. "He did not answer a word, but simply bolted. You were frightened, too, Vera. Is it Mark who signalises his presence at the foot of the precipice by a shot? I have seen him wandering round with a gun," he said joking.

She answered in the same tone: "Of course, Cousin," but she did not look at him.

No, thought Raisky to himself, she could not have taken for her idol a wandering, ragged gipsy like that. Then he wondered whether the possibility could be entirely excluded, since passion wanders where he lists, and not in obedience to the convictions and dictates of man. He is invincible, and master of his own inexplicable moods. But Vera had never had any opportunity of meeting Mark, he concluded, and was merely afraid of him as every one else was.

Leonti's condition was unchanged. He wandered about like a drunken man, silent and listening for the noise of any carriage in the street, when he would rush to the window to look if it bore his fugitive wife.

He would come to them in a few weeks, he said, after Marfinka's wedding, as Vera suggested. Then he became aware of Vera's presence.

"Vera Vassilievna!" he cried in surprise, staring at her as he addressed Raisky. "Do you know, Boris Pavlovich, who else has read your books and helped me to arrange them?"

"Who has been reading my books?" asked Raisky.

But Leonti had been distracted by the sound of a passing carriage and did not hear the question. Vera whispered to Raisky that they should go.

"I wanted to say something, Boris Pavlovich," said Leonti thoughtfully, raising his head, "but I can't remember what."

"You said some one else had been reading my books."

Leonti pointed to Vera, who was looking out of the window, but who now pulled Raisky's sleeve "Come!" she said and they left the house.

When they reached home Vera made over some of her purchases to her aunt, and had others taken to her room. She asked Raisky to go out with her again in the park and down by the Volga.

"Why are you tiring yourself out, Vera?" he asked, as they went. "You are weak."

"Air, I must have air!" she exclaimed, turning her face to the wind.

She is collecting all her strength, he thought, as they entered the room where the family was waiting for them for dinner. In the afternoon he slept for weariness, and only awoke at twilight, when six o'clock had already struck. He went to find Vera, but Marina told him she had gone to vespers, she did not know whether in the village church on the hill or in the church on the outskirts of the town. He went to the town church first, and after studying the faces of all the old women assembled there, he climbed the hill to the village church. Old people stood in the corners and by the door, and by a pillar in a dark corner knelt Vera, with a veil wrapped round her bowed head. He took his stand near her, behind another pillar, and, engrossed in his thoughts of her state of mind, watched her intently as she prayed motionless, with her eyes fixed on the cross. He went sadly into the porch to wait for her, and there she joined him, putting her hand in his arm without a word.

As they crossed the big meadow into the park he thought of nothing but the promised explanation. His own intense desire to be freed from his miserable uncertainty weighed with him less than his duty, as he conceived it, of shielding her, of illuminating her path with his experience, and of lending his undivided strength to keep her from overstepping her moral precipice. Perhaps it was merely a remnant of pride that prevented her from telling him why she had summoned him and detained him.

He could not, and, even if he could, he had not the right to share his apprehensions with anyone else. Even if he might confide in Tatiana Markovna, if he spoke to her of his suspicion and his surmises, he was not clear that it would help matters, for he feared that their aunt's practical, but old-fashioned wisdom would be shattered on Vera's obstinacy. Vera possessed the bolder mind, the quicker will. She was level with contemporary thought, and towered above the society in which she moved. She must have derived her ideas and her knowledge from some source accessible to her alone. Though she took pains to conceal her knowledge, it was betrayed by a chance word, by the mention of a name or an authority in this or that sphere of learning, and it was betrayed also in her speech; in the remarkable aptness of the words in which she clothed her thoughts and feelings. In this matter she held so great an advantage over Tatiana Markovna that the old lady's efforts in argument were more likely to be disastrous than not.

Undoubtedly Tatiana Markovna was a wise woman with a correct judgment of the general phenomena of life. She was a famous housewife, ruling her little tsardom magnificently; she knew the ways, the vices and the virtues of mankind as they are set out in the Ten Commandments and the Gospels, but she knew nothing of the life where the passions rage and steep everything in their colours. And even if she had known such a world in her youth it must have been passion divorced from experience, an unshared passion, or one stifled in its development, not a stormy drama of love, but rather a lyric tenderness which unfolded and perished without leaving a trace on her pure life. How could she lend a rescuing hand to snatch Vera from the precipice, she who had no faith in passion, but had merely sought to understand facts?

The shots in the depths of the precipice, and Vera's expeditions were indeed facts, against which Tatiana Markovna might be able to adopt measures. She might double the watch kept on the property, set men to watch for the lover, while Vera, shut up in the house, endured humiliation and a fresh kind of suffering.

Vera would not endure any such rough constraint, and would make her escape, just as she had fled across the Volga from Raisky. These would be, in fact, no means at all, for she had outgrown Tatiana Markovna's circle of experience and morals. No, authority might serve with Marfinka, but not with the clear-headed, independent Vera.

Such were Raisky's thoughts as he walked silently by Vera's side, no longer desiring full knowledge for his own sake, but for her salvation.

Perhaps, he thought, he would best gain his end by indirect efforts to make her betray herself.

"Leonti said," he began, "that you have been reading books out of my library. Did you read them with him?"

"Sometimes he told me of the contents of certain books; others I read with the priest, Natasha's husband."

"What books did you read with the priest?"

"For the moment I don't remember, but he read the writings of the Fathers, for instance, and explained them to Natasha and me, to my great advantage. We also read with him Voltaire and Spinoza. Why do you laugh?" she asked, looking at Raisky.

"There seems a remarkable gap between the Fathers and Spinoza and Voltaire. The Encyclopædists are also included in my library. Did you read them?"

"Nikolai Ivanovich read some to us, and talked about others."

"Did you also occupy yourselves with Feuerbach, with the Socialists and the Materialists?"

"Yes, Natasha's husband asked us to copy out passages, which he indicated by pencil marks."

"What was his object in this?"

"I think he was preparing to publish a refutation."

"Where did you obtain the newer books that are not in my library? Not the exile," he suggested as she gave no answer, "who lives here under police supervision, the same man about whom you wrote to me? But you are not listening."

"Yes, I am. Who gave me the books? Sometimes one person, sometimes another here in the town."

"Volokov borrowed these books."

"Perhaps so, I had them from professors."

The thought flashed through Raisky's head that there might be other professors of the same kind as Monsieur Charles. But he merely asked what were the views of Nikolai Ivanovich on Spinoza and these other writers.

"He says." replied Vera, "that these writings are the efforts of bold minds to evade the truth; they have beaten out for themselves side paths which must in the end unite with the main road. He says too, that all these attempts serve the cause of truth, in that the truth shines out with greater splendour in the end."

"But he does not tell you where truth lies?"

By way of answer she pointed to the little chapel now in sight.

"And you think he is right?"

"I don't think, I believe. And don't you also believe he is right."

He agreed, and she asked him why, that being so, he had asked her.

"I wanted," he said, "to know your opinion."

"But you have often seen me at prayer," said Vera.

"Yes, but I do not overhear your prayers. Do you pray for the alleviation of the restless sorrow that afflicts your mind?"

They had reached the chapel, and Vera stood still for a moment. She did not appear to have heard his question, and she answered only with a deep sigh. It was growing dark as they retraced their steps, Vera's growing slower and more uncertain as they approached the old house, where she stood still and glanced in the direction of the precipice.

"To still the storm I must not go near the precipice, you say—I beg of you to stand by me, for I am sick and helpless."

"Will not Grandmother know better how to help you, Vera? Confide in her, a woman, who will perhaps understand your pain."

She shook her head. "I will tell you, Grandmother and you, but not now; now I cannot. And yet I beg of you not to leave me, not to allow me out of your sight. If a shot summons me, keep me away from the precipice, and, if necessary, hold me back by force. Things are as bad as that with me. That is all you can do for me. That is why I asked you not to go away, because I felt that my strength is failing, because except you I have no one to help me, for Grandmother would not understand. Forgive me."

"You did right, Vera," he replied, deeply moved. "Depend on me. I am willing to stay here for ever, if that will bring you peace."

"No, in a week's time the shots will cease."

She dried her eyes, and pressed his hand; then with slow, uneven steps, supporting herself by the balustrade she passed up the steps and into the house.

CHAPTER XXII

Two days had passed, and Raisky had had small opportunity of seeing Vera alone, though she came to dinner and to tea, and spoke of ordinary things. Raisky turned once more to his novel, or rather to the plan of it. He visited Leonti, and did not neglect the Governor and other friends. But in order to keep watch on Vera he wandered about the park and the garden. Two days were now gone, he thought, since he sat on the bench by the precipice, but there were still five days of danger. Marfinka's birthday lay two days' ahead, and on that day Vera would hardly leave the family circle. On the next Marfinka was to go with her fiancé and his mother to Kolchino, and Vera would not be likely to leave Tatiana Markovna alone. By that time the week would be over and the threatening clouds dispersed.

After dinner Vera asked him to come over to her in the evening, as she wished him to undertake a commission for her. When he arrived she suggested a walk, and, as she chose the direction of the fields he realised that she wished to go to the chapel, and took the field path accordingly.

As she crossed the threshold, she looked up at the thoughtful face of the Christ.

"You have sought more powerful aid than mine," said Raisky. "Moreover, you will not now go there without me."

She nodded in assent. She seemed to be seeking strength, sympathy and support from the glance of the Crucified, but His eyes kept their expression of quiet thought and detachment.

When she turned her eyes from the picture she reiterated, "I will not go." Raisky read on her face neither prayer nor desire; it wore an expression of weariness, indifference and submission.

He suggested that they should return, and reminded her that she had a commission for him.

"Will you take the bouquet-holder that I chose the other week for Marfinka's birthday to the goldsmith?" she said, handing him her purse. "I gave him some pearls to set in it, and her name should be engraved. And could you be up as early as eight o'clock on her birthday?"

"Of course. If necessary, I can stay up all night!"

"I have already spoken to the gardener, who owns the big orangery. Would you choose me a nice bouquet and send it to me. I have confidence in your taste."

"Your confidence in me makes progress, Vera," he laughed. "You already trust my taste and my honour."

"I would have seen to all this myself," she went on, "but I have not the strength."

Next day Raisky took the bouquet holder, and discussed the arrangement of the flowers with the gardener. He himself bought for Marfinka an elegant watch and chain, with two hundred roubles which he borrowed from Tiet Nikonich, for Tatiana Markovna would not have given him so much money for the purpose, and would have betrayed the secret. In Tiet Nikonich's room he found a dressing table decked with muslin and lace, with a mirror encased in a china frame of flowers and Cupids, a beautiful specimen of Sèvres work.

"Where did you get this treasure?" cried Raisky, who could not take his eyes from the thing. "What a lovely piece!"

"It is my gift for Marfa Vassilievna," said Tiet Nikonich with his kind smile. "I am glad it pleases you, for you are a connoisseur. Your liking for it assures me that the dear birthday child will appreciate it as a wedding gift. She is a lovely girl, just like these roses. The Cupids will smile when they see her charming face in the mirror. Please don't tell Tatiana Markovna of my secret."

"This beautiful piece must have cost over two thousand roubles, and you cannot possibly have bought it here."

"My Grandfather gave five thousand roubles for it, and it was part of my Mother's house-furnishing and until now it stood in her bedroom, left untouched in my birth-place. I had it brought here last month, and to make sure it should not be broken, six men carried it in alternate shifts for the whole hundred and fifty versts. I had a new muslin cover made, but the lace is old; you will notice how yellow it is. Ladies like these things, although they don't matter to us."

"What will Grandmother say?"

"There will be a storm. I do feel rather uneasy about it, but perhaps she will forgive me. I may tell you, Boris Pavlovich, that I love both the girls, as if they were my own daughters. I held them on my knee as babies, and with Tatiana Markovna gave them their first lessons. I tell you in confidence that I have also arranged a wedding present for Vera Vassilievna which I hope she will like when the time comes." He showed Raisky a magnificent antique silver dinner service of fine workmanship for twelve persons. "I may confess to you, as you are her cousin, that in agreement with Tatiana Markovna I have a splendid and a rich marriage in view for her, for whom nothing can be too good. The finest *partie* in this neighbourhood," he said in a confidential tone, "is Ivan Ivanovich Tushin, who is absolutely devoted to her, as he well may be."

Raisky repressed a sigh and went home where he found Vikentev and his mother, who had arrived for Marfinka's birthday, with Paulina Karpovna and other guests from the town, who stayed until nearly seven o'clock. Tatiana Markovna and Marfa Egorovna carried on an interminable conversation about Marfinka's trousseau and house furnishing. The lovers went into the garden, and from there to the village. Vikentev carrying a parcel which he threw in the air and caught again as he walked. Marfinka entered every house, said good-bye to the women, and caressed the children. In two cases she washed the children's faces, she distributed calico for shirts and dresses, and told two elder children to whom she presented shoes that it was time they gave up paddling in the puddles.

"God reward you, our lovely mistress, Angel of God!" cried the women in every yard as she bade them farewell for a fortnight.

CHAPTER XXIII

In the evening the house was aglow with light. Tatiana Markovna could not do enough in honour of her guest and future connexion. She had a great bed put up in the guest-chamber, that nearly reached to the ceiling and resembled a catafalque. Marfinka and Vikentev gave full rein to their gay humour, as they played and sang. Only Raisky's windows were dark. He had gone out immediately after dinner and had not returned to tea.

The moon illuminated the new house but left the old house in shadow. There was bustle in the yard, in the kitchen, and in the servants' rooms, where Marfa Egorovna's coachman and servants were being entertained.

From seven o'clock onwards Vera had sat idle in the dusk by the feeble light of a candle, her head supported on her hand, leaning over the table, while with her other hand she turned over the leaves of a book at which she hardly glanced. She was protected from the cold autumn air from the open window, by a big white woollen shawl thrown round her shoulders. She stood up after a time, laid the book on the table, and went to the window. She looked towards the sky, and then at the gaily-lighted house opposite. She shivered, and was about to shut the window when the report of a gun rolled up from the park through the quiet dusk.

She shuddered, and seemed to have lost the use of her limbs, then sank into a chair and bowed her head. When she rose and looked wildly round, her face had changed. Sheer fright and distress looked from her eyes. Again and again she passed her hand over her forehead, and sat down at the table, only to jump up again. She tore the shawl from her shoulders and threw it on the bed; then with nervous haste she opened and shut the cupboard; she looked on the divan, on the chairs, for something she apparently could not find, and then collapsed wearily on her chair.

On the back of the chair hung a wrap, a gift from Tiet Nikonich. She seized it and threw it over her head, rushed to the wardrobe, hunted in it with feverish haste, taking out first one coat, then another, until she had nearly emptied the cupboard and dresses and cloaks lay in a heap on the floor. At last she found something warm and dark, put out the light, and went noiselessly down the steps into the open. She crossed the yard, hidden in the shadows, and took her way along the dark avenue. She did not walk, she flew; and when she crossed the open light patches her shadow was hardly visible for a moment, as if the moon had not time to catch the flying figure.

When she reached the end of the avenue, by the ditch which divided the garden from the park, she stopped a moment to get her breath. Then she crossed the park, hurried through the bushes, past her favourite bench, and reached the precipice. She picked up her skirts for the descent, when suddenly, as if he had risen out of the ground, Raisky stood between her and her goal.

"Where are you going, Vera?"

There was no answer.

"Go back," he said, offering his hand, but she tried to push past him. "Vera, where are you going?"

"It is for the last time." she said in a pleading, shamed whisper. "I must say good-bye. Make way for me, Cousin! I will return in a moment. Wait for me here, on this bench."

Without replying, he took her firmly by the hand, and she struggled in vain to free herself.

"Let me go! You are hurting me!"

But he did not give way, and the struggle proceeded.

"You will not hold me by force," she cried, and with unnatural strength freed herself, and sought to dash past him.

But he put his arm round her waist, took her to the bench, and sat down beside her.

"How rough and rude!" she cried.

"I cannot hold you back by force, Vera. I may be saving you from ruin."

"Can I be ruined against my own will?"

"It is against your will; yet you go to your ruin."

"There is no question of ruin. We must see one another again in order to separate."

"It is not necessary to see one another in order to separate."

"I must, and will. An hour or a day later, it is all the same. You may call the servants, the whole town, a file of soldiers, but no power will keep me back."

A second shot resounded.

She pulled herself up, but was pressed down on the bench with the weight of Raisky's hands. She shook her head wildly in powerless rage.

"What reward do you hope from me for this virtuous deed?" she hissed.

He said nothing, but kept a watchful eye on her movements. After a time she besought him gently: "Let me go, Cousin," but he refused.

"Cousin," she said, laying her hand gently on his shoulder. "Imagine that you sat upon hot coals, and were dying every minute of terror, and of wild impatience, that happiness rose before you, stretching out enticing arms, only to vanish, that your whole being rose to meet it; imagine that you saw before you a last hope, a last glimmer. That is how it is with me at this moment. The moment will be lost, and with it everything else."

"Think, Vera, if in the hot thirst of fever you ask for ice, it is denied you. In your soberer moments yesterday you pointed out to me the practical means of rescue, you said I was not to let you go, and I will not."

She fell on her knees before him, and wrung her hands.

"I should curse you my whole life long for your violence. Give way. Perhaps it is my destiny that calls me."

"I was a witness yesterday, Vera, of where you seek your fate. You believe in a Providence, and there is no other destiny."

"Yes," she answered submissively. "I do believe. There before the sacred picture I sought for a spark to lighten my path, but in vain. What shall I do?" she said, rising.

"Do not go, Vera."

"Perhaps it is my destiny that sends me there, there where my presence may be needed. Don't try any longer to keep me, for I have made up my mind. My weakness is gone, and I have recovered control of myself and feel I am strong. It is not my destiny alone, but the destiny of another human being that is to be decided down there. Between me and him you are digging an abyss, and the responsibility will rest upon you. I shall never be consoled, and shall accuse you of having destroyed our happiness. Do not hold me back. You can only do it out of egoism, out of jealousy. You lied when you spoke to me of freedom."

"I hear the voice of passion, Vera, with all its sophistry and its deviations. You are practising the arts of a Jesuit. Remember that you yourself bade me, only yesterday, not to leave you. Will you curse me for not yielding to you? On whom does the responsibility rest? Tell me who the man is?"

"If I tell you will you promise not to keep me back?" she said quickly.

"I don't know. Perhaps."

"Give me your word not to keep me any longer, and I give the name."

Another shot rang out.

She sprang to one side, before he had time to take her by the hand.

"Go to Grandmother," he commanded, adding gently, "Tell her your trouble."

"For Christ's sake let me go. I ask for alms like a beggar. I must be free! I take him to whom I prayed yesterday to witness that I am going for the last time. Do you hear? I will not break my oath. Wait here for me. I will return immediately, will only say farewell to the 'Wolf,' will hear a word from him, and perhaps he will yield!" She rushed forward, fell to the ground in her haste, and tried in vain to rise. Tom by an unutterable pity, Raisky took no heed of his own suffering, but raised her in his arms and bore her down the precipice.

"The path is so steep here that you would fall again," he whispered. Presently he set her down on the path, and she stooped to kiss his hand.

"You are generous, Cousin. Vera will not forget."

With that she hurried into the thicket, jubilant as a bird set free from his cage.

Raisky heard the rustle of the bushes as she pushed them aside, and the crackle of the dry twigs.

In the half-ruined arbour waited Mark, with gun and cap laid upon the table. He walked up and down on the shaky floor, and whenever he trod on one end of a board the other rose in the air, and then fell clattering back again.

"The devil's music!" he murmured angrily, sat down on a bench near the table, and pushed his hands through his thick hair. He smoked one cigarette after another, the burning match lighting up his pale, agitated face for a moment. After each shot he listened for a few minutes, went out on the steps, and looked out into the bushes. When he returned he walked up and down, raising the "devil's music" once more, threw himself on the bench, and ran his hands through his hair. After the third shot he listened long and earnestly. As he heard nothing he was on the point of going away. To relieve his gloomy feelings he murmured a curse between his teeth, took the gun and prepared to descend the path. He hesitated a few moments longer, then walked off with decision. Suddenly he met Vera.

She stood still, breathing with difficulty, and laid her hand on her heart. As soon as he took her hand she was calm. Mark could not conceal his joy, but his words of greeting did not betray it.

"You used to be punctual, Vera," he said, "and I used not to have to waste three shots."

"A reproach instead of a welcome!" she said, drawing her hand away.

"It's only by way of beginning a conversation Happiness makes a fool of me, like Raisky."

"If happiness gleamed before us, we should not be meeting in secret by this precipice," she said, drawing a long breath.

"We should be sitting at your Grandmother's tea-table, and waiting till someone arranged our betrothal. Why dream of these impossible things. Your Grandmother would not give you to me."

"She would. She does what I wish. That is not the hindrance."

"You are starting on this endless polemic again, Vera. We are meeting for the last time, as you determined we should. Let us make an end of this torture."

"I took an oath never to come here again."

"Meanwhile, the time is precious. We are parting for ever, if stupidity commands, if your Grandmother's antiquated convictions separate us. I leave here a week from now. As you know the document assuring my freedom has arrived. Let us be together, and not be separated again."

"Never?"

"Never!" he repeated angrily, with a gesture of impatience. "What lying words those are, 'never' and 'always.' Of course 'never.' Does not a year, perhaps two, three years, mean never? You want a never ending tenderness. Does such a thing exist?"

"Enough, Mark! I have heard enough of this temporary affection. Ah! I am very unhappy. The separation from you is not the only cloud over my soul. For a year now I have been hiding myself from my Grandmother, which oppresses me, and her still more. I hoped that in these days my trouble would end; we should put our thoughts, our hopes, our intentions on a clear footing. Then I would go to Grandmother and say: 'This is what I have chosen for my whole life.' But it is not to be, and we are to part?" she asked sadly.

"If I conceived myself to be an angel," said Mark, "I might say 'for our whole lives,' and you would be justified. That gray-headed dreamer, Raisky, also thinks that women are created for a higher purpose."

"They are created above all for the family. They are not angels, neither are they, most certainly, mere animals. I am no wolf's mate, Mark, but a woman."

"For the family, yes. But is that any hindrance for us. You want draperies, for fine feeling, sympathies and the rest of the stuff are nothing but draperies, like those famous leaves with which, it is said, human beings covered themselves in Paradise."

"Yes, Mark, human beings!"

Mark smiled sarcastically, and shrugged his shoulders.

"They may be draperies," continued Vera, "but they also, according to your own teaching, are given by nature. What, I ask, is it that attaches you to me? You say you love me. You have altered, grown thinner. Is it not, by your conception of love, a matter of indifference whether you choose a companion in me, or from the poor quarter of our town, or from a village on the Volga. What has induced you to come down here for a whole year?"

"Examine your own fallacy, Vera," he said, looking at her gloomily. "Love is not a concept merely, but a driving force, a necessity, and therefore is mostly blind. But I am not blindly chained to you. Your extraordinary beauty, your intellect and your free outlook hold me longer in thrall than would be possible with any other woman."

"Very flattering!" she said in a low, pained voice.

"These ideas of yours, Vera, will bring us to disaster. But for them we should for long have been united and happy."

"Happy for a time. And then a new driving force will appear on the scene, the stage will be cleared, and so on."

"The responsibility is not ours. Nature has ordered it so, and rightly. Can we alter Nature, in order to live on concepts?"

"These concepts are essential principles. You have said yourself that Nature has her laws, and human beings their principles."

"That is where the germ of disintegration lies, in that men want to formulate principles from the driving force of Nature, and thus to hamper themselves hand and foot. Love is happiness, which Nature has conferred on man. That is my view."

"The happiness of which you speak," said Vera, rising, "has as its complement, duty. That is my view."

"How fantastic! Forget your duty, Vera, and acquiesce in the fact that love is a driving force of Nature, often an uncontrollable one." Then standing up to her embraced her, saying, "Is that not so, you most obstinate, beautiful and wisest of women?"

"Yes, duty," she said haughtily, disengaging herself. "For the years of happiness retribution will be exacted."

"How? In making soup, nursing one another, looking at one another and pretending, in harping on principles, as we ourselves fade? If one half falls ill and retrogresses, shall the other who is strong, who hears the call of life, allow himself to be held back by duty?"

"Yes. In that case he must not listen to the calls that come to him; he must, to use Grandmother's expression, avoid the voice as he would the brandy bottle. That is how I understand happiness."

"Your case must be a bad one if it has to be bolstered up by quotations from your Grandmother's wisdom. Tell me how firmly your principles are rooted."

"I will go to her to-day direct from here."

"To tell her what?"

"To tell her what there is between us, all that she does not know," she said, sitting down on the bench again.

"Why?"

"You don't understand, because you don't know what duty means. I have been guilty before her for a long time."

"That is the morality which smothers life with mould and dulness. Vera, Vera, you don't love, you do not know how!"

"You ought not to speak like that, unless you wish to drive me to despair. Am I to think that there is deception in your past, that you want to ruin me when you do not love me?"

"No, no, Vera," he said, rising hastily to his feet. "If I had wanted to deceive you I could have done so long ago."

"What a desperate war you wage against yourself, Mark, and how you ruin your own life!" she cried, wringing her hands.

"Let us cease to quarrel, Vera. Your Grandmother speaks through you, but with another voice. That was all very well once, but now we are in the flood of another life where neither authority nor preconceived ideas will help us, where truth alone asserts her power."

"Where is truth?"

"In happiness, in the joy of love. And I love you. Why do you torture me. Why do you fight against me and against yourself, and make two victims?"

"It is a strange reproach. Look at me. It is only a few days since we saw one another, and have I not changed?"

"I see that you suffer, and that makes it the more senseless. Now, I too ask what has induced you to come down here for all this time?"

"Because I had not earlier realised the horror of my position, you will say," she said, with a look that was almost hostile. "We might have asked one another this question, and made this reproach, long ago, and might have ceased to meet here. Better late than never! To-day we must answer the question, What is it that we wanted and expected from one another?"

"Here is my irrefragable opinion—I want your love, and I give you mine. In love I recognise solely the principle of reciprocation, as it obtains in Nature. The law that I acknowledge is to follow unfettered our strong impression, to exchange happiness for happiness. This answers your question of why I came here. Is sacrifice necessary? Call it what you will there is no sacrifice in my scheme of life. I will no longer wander in this morass, and don't understand how I have wasted my strength so long, certainly not for your sake, but essentially for my own. Here I will stay so long as I am happy, so long as I love. If my love grows cold, I shall tell you so, and go wherever Life leads me, without taking any baggage of duties and privileges with me; those I leave here in the depths below the precipice. You see, Vera, I don't deceive you, but speak frankly. Naturally you possess the same rights as I. The mob above there lies to itself and others, and calls these his principles. But in secret and by cunning it acts in the same way, and only lays its ban on the women. Between us there must be equality. Is that fair or not?"

"Sophistry!" she said, shaking her head. "You know my principles, Mark."

"To hang like stones round one another's necks."

"Love imposes duties, just as life demands them. If you had an old, blind mother you would maintain and support her, would remain by her. An honourable man holds it to be his duty and his pleasure too."

"You philosophise, Vera, but you do not love."

"You avoid my argument, Mark. I speak my opinion plainly, for I am a woman, not an animal, or a machine."

"Your love is the fantastic, elaborate type described in novels. Is what you ask of me honourable? Against my convictions I am to go into a church, to submit to a ceremony which has no meaning for me. I don't believe any of it and can't endure the parson. Should I be acting logically or honourably?"

Vera hastily wrapped herself in her mantilla, and stood up to go.

"We met, Mark, to remove all the obstacles that stand in the way of our happiness, but instead of that we are increasing them. You handle roughly things that are sacred to me. Why did you call me here? I thought you had surrendered, that we should take one another's hands for ever. Every time I have taken the path down the cliff it has been in this hope, and in the end I am disappointed. Do you know, Mark, where true life lies?"

"Where?"

"In the heart of a loving woman. To be the friend of such a woman...."

Tears stifled her voice, but through her sobs she whispered: "I cannot, Mark. Neither my intellect nor my strength are sufficient to dispute with you. My weapon is weak, and has no value except that I have drawn it from the armoury of a quiet life, not from books or hearsay. I had thought to conquer you with other weapons. Do you remember how all this began?" she said, sitting down once more. "At first I was sorry for you. You were here alone, with no one to understand you, and everyone fled at the sight of you. I was drawn to you by sympathy, and saw something strange and undisciplined in you. You had no care for propriety, you were incautious in speech, you played rashly with life, cared for no human being, had no faith of your own, and sought to win disciples. From curiosity I followed your steps, allowed you to meet me, took books from you. I recognised in you intellect and strength, but strangely mixed and directed away from life. Then, to my sorrow, I imagined that I could teach you to value life, I wanted you to live so that you should be higher and better than anyone else, I quarrelled with you over your undisciplined way of living. You submitted to my influence, and I submitted to yours, to your intellect, your audacity, and even adopted part of your sophistry."

"But you soon," put in Mark, "retraced your steps, and were seized with fear of your Grandmother. Why did you not leave me when you first became aware of my sophistry? Sophistry!"

"It was too late, for I had already taken your fate too intimately to heart. I believed with all possible ardour that you would for my sake comprehend life, that you would cease to wander about to your own injury and without advantage to anyone else, that you would accept a substantial position of some kind...."

"Vice-governor, Councillor or something of the kind," he mocked.

"What's in the name? Yes, I thought that you would show yourself a man of action in a wide sphere of influence."

"As a well-disposed subject and as jack of all trades, and what else?"

"My lifelong friend. I let my hopes of you take hold on me, and was carried away by them, and what are my gains in the terrible conflict? One only, that you flee from love, from happiness, from life, and from your Vera." She drew closer to him and touched his shoulder. "Don't fly from us, Mark. Look in my eyes, listen to my voice, which speaks with the voice of truth. Let us go to-morrow up the hill into the garden, and to-morrow there will be no happier pair than we are. You love me, Mark. Mark, do you hear? Look at me."

She stooped, and looked into his eyes.

He got sharply to his feet, and shook his mass of hair.

Vera took up her black mantilla once more, but her hands refused to obey her, and the mantilla fell on the floor. She took a step towards the door, but sank down again on the bench. Where could she find strength to hold him, when she had not even strength to leave the arbour, she wondered. And even if she could hold him, what would be the consequences? Not one life, but two separate lives, two prisons, divided by a grating.

"We are both brusque and strong, Vera; that is why we torture one another, why we are separating."

"If I were strong, you would not leave Malinovka; you would ascend the hill with me, not clandestinely, but boldly by my side. Come and share life and happiness with me. It is impossible that you should not trust me, impossible that you are insincere, for that would be a crime. What shall I do? How shall I bring home to you the truth?"

"You would have to be stronger than I, but we are of equal strength. That is why we dispute and are not of one mind. We must separate without bringing our struggle to an issue, one must submit to the other. I could take forcible possession of you as I could of any other woman. But what in another woman is prudery, or petty fear, or stupidity, is in you strength and womanly determination. The mist that divided us is dispersed; we have made our position clear. Nature has endued you with a powerful weapon, Vera. The antiquated ideas, morality, duty, principles, and faiths that do not exist for me are firmly established with you. You are not easily carried away, you put up a desperate fight and will only confess yourself conquered under terms of equality with your opponent. You are wrong, for it is a kind of theft. You ask to be conquered, and to carry off all the spoils! I, Vera, cannot give everything, but I respect you."

Vera gave him a glance in which there was a trace of pride, but her heart beat with the pain of parting. His words were a model of what a farewell should be.

"We have gone to the bottom of the matter," said Mark dully, "and I leave the decision in your hands." He went to the other side of the arbour, keeping his eyes fixed upon her. "I am not deceiving you even now, in this decisive moment, when my head is giddy—I cannot. I do not promise you an unending love, because I do not believe in such a thing. I will not be your betrothed. But I love you more than anything else in the world. If, after all I have told you, you come to my arms, it means that you love me, that you are mine."

She looked across at him with wide open eyes, and felt that her whole body was trembling. A doubt shot through her mind. Was he a Jesuit, or was the man who brought her into this dangerous dilemma in reality of unbending honour?

"Yours for ever?" she said in a low voice. If he said, "yes," it would, she knew, be a bridge for the moment to help her over the abyss that divided them, but that afterwards she would be plunged into the abyss. She was afraid of him.

Mark was painfully agitated, but he answered in a subdued tone, "I do not know. I only know what I am doing now, and do not see even into the near future. Neither can you. Let us give love for love, and I remain here, quieter than the waters of the pool, humbler than grass. I will do what you will, and what do you ask more. Or," he added suddenly, coming nearer, "we will leave this place altogether...."

In a lightning flash the wide world seemed to smile before her, as if the gates of Paradise were open. She threw herself in Mark's arms and laid her hand on his shoulder. If she went away into the far distance with him, she thought, he could not tear himself from her, and once alone with her he must realise that life was only life in her presence.

"Will you decide!" he asked seriously. She said nothing, but bowed her head. "Or do you fear your Grandmother?"

The last words brought her to her senses, and she stepped back.

"If I do not decide," she whispered, "it is only because I fear her."

"The old lady would not let you go."

"She would let me go, and would give me her blessing, but she herself would die of grief. That is what I fear. To go away together," she said dreamily, "and what then?" She looked up at him searchingly.

"And then? How can I know, Vera?"

"You will suddenly be driven from me; you will go and leave me, as if I were merely a log?"

"Why a log? We could separate as friends."

"Separation! Do the ideas of love and separation exist side by side in your mind? They are extremes which should never meet. Separation must only come with death. Farewell, Mark! You can never promise me the happiness that I seek. All is at an end. Farewell!"

"Farewell, Vera!" he said in a voice quite unlike his own.

Both were pale, and avoided one another's eyes. In the white moonlight that gleamed through the trees Vera sought her mantilla, and grasped the gun instead. At last she found the mantilla, but could not put it on her shoulders. Mark helped her mechanically, but left his own belongings behind. They went silently up the path, with slow and hesitating steps, as if each expected something from the other, both of them occupied with the same mental effort to find a pretext for delay. They came at last to the spot where Mark's way lay across a low fence, and hers by the winding path through the bushes up to the park.

Vera stood still. She seemed to see the events of her whole life pass before her in quick succession, but saw none filled with bitterness like the present. Her eyes filled with tears. She felt a violent impulse to look round once more, to see him once more, to measure with her eyes the extent of her loss, and then to hurry on again. But however great her sorrow for her wrecked happiness she dare not look round, for she knew it would be equivalent to saying Yes to destiny. She took a few steps up the path.

Mark strode fiercely away towards the hedge, like a wild beast baulked of his prey. He had not lied when he said that he esteemed Vera, but it was an esteem wrung from him against his will, the esteem of the soldier for a brave enemy. He cursed the old-fashioned ideas which had enchained her free and vivacious spirit. His suffering was the suffering of despair; he was in the mood of a madman who would shatter a treasure of which the possession was denied him, in order that no one else might possess it. He was ready to spring, and could hardly restrain himself from laying violent hands on Vera. By his own confession to her he would have treated any other woman so, but not Vera. Then the conviction gnawed at his heart that for the sake of the woman who was now escaping him he was neglecting his "mission." His pride suffered unspeakably by the confession of his own powerlessness. He admitted that the beautiful statue filled with the breath of life had character; she acted in accordance with her own proud will, not by the influence of outside suggestion. His new conception of truth did not subdue her strong, healthy temperament; it rather induced her to submit it to a minute analysis and to stick closer to her own conception of the truth. And now she was going, and as the traces of her footsteps would vanish, so all that had passed between them would be lost. And with her went all the charm and glory of life, never to return.

He stamped his feet with rage and swung himself on to the fence. He would cast one glance in her direction to see if the haughty creature was really going.

"One more glance," thought Vera. She turned, and shuddered to see Mark sitting on the fence and gazing at her.

"Farewell, Mark," she cried, in a voice trembling with despair.

From his throat there issued a low, wild cry of triumph. In a moment he was by her side, with victory and the conviction of her surrender in his heart.

"Vera!"

"You have come back, for always? You have at last understood. What happiness! God forgive...."

She did not complete her sentence, for she lay wrapt in his embrace, her sobs quenched by his kisses. He raised her in his arms, and like a wild animal carrying off his prey, ran with her back to the arbour.

God forgive her for having turned back.

CHAPTER XXIV

Raisky lay on the grass at the top of the cliff for a long time in gloomy meditation, groaning over the penalty he must pay for his generosity, suffering alike for himself and Vera. "Perhaps she is laughing at my folly, down there with him. Who is there?" he cried aloud, stung with rage. "I will have his name." He saw himself merely as a shield to cover her passion. He sprang up wildly, and hurried down the precipice, tearing his clothes in the bushes and listening in vain for a suspicious rustling. He told himself that it was an evil thing to pry into another's secret; it was robbery. He stood still a moment to wipe the sweat from his brow, but his sufferings overcame his scruples. He felt his way stealthily forward, cursing every broken branch that cracked under his feet, and unconscious of the blows he received on his face from the rebounding branches as he forced his way through. He threw himself on the ground to regain his breath, then in order not to betray his presence crept along, digging his nails into the ground as he went. When he reached the suicide's grave he halted, uncertain which way to follow, and at length made for the arbour, listening and searching the ground as he went.

Meanwhile everything was going on as usual in Tatiana Markovna's household. After supper the company sat yawning in the hall, Tiet Nikonich alone being indefatigable in his attentions, shuffling his foot when he made a polite remark, and looking at each lady as if he were ready to sacrifice everything for her sake.

"Where is Monsieur Boris?" inquired Paulina Karpovna, addressing Tatiana Markovna.

"Probably he is paying a visit in the town. He never says where he spends his time, so that I never know where to send the carriage for him."

Inquiries made of Yakob revealed the fact that he had been in the garden up to a late hour. Vera was not in the house when she was summoned to tea. She had left word that they were not to keep supper for her, and that she would send across for some if she were hungry. No one but Raisky had seen her go.

Tatiana Markovna sighed over their perversity, to be wandering about at such hours, in such cold weather.

"I will go into the garden," said Paulina Karpovna. "Perhaps Monsieur Boris is not far away. He will be delighted to see me. I noticed," she continued confidentially, "that he had something to say to me. He could not have known I was here."

Marfinka whispered to Vikentev that he did know, and had gone out on that account.

"I will go, Marfa Vassilievna, and hide behind a bush, imitate Boris Pavlovich's voice and make her a declaration," suggested Vikentev.

"Stay here, Nikolai Andreevich. Paulina Karpovna might be frightened and faint. Then you would have to reckon with Grandmother."

"I am going into the garden for a moment to fetch the fugitive," said Paulina Karpovna.

"God be with you, Paulina Karpovna," said Tatiana Markovna. "Don't put your nose outside in the darkness, or at any rate take Egorka with you to carry a lantern."

"No, I will go alone. It is not necessary for anyone to disturb us."

"You ought not," intervened Tiet Nikonich politely, "to go out after eight o'clock on these damp nights. I would not have ventured to detain you, but a physician from Düsseldorf on the Rhine, whose book I am now reading and can lend you if you like, and who gives excellent advice, says...."

Paulina Karpovna interrupted him by asking him if he would see her home, and then went into the garden before he could resume his remarks. He agreed to her request and shut the door after her.

Soon after Paulina Karpovna's exit there was a rustling and crackling on the precipice, and Raisky wearing the aspect of a restless, wounded animal, appeared out of the darkness. He sat for several minutes motionless on Vera's favourite bench, covering his eyes with his hands. Was it dream or reality, he asked himself. He must have been mistaken. Such a thing could not be. He stood up, then sat down again to listen. With his hands lying listlessly on his knees, he broke into laughter over his doubts, his questionings, his secret. Again he had an access of terrible laughter. Vera— and *he*. The cloak which he himself had sent to the "exile" lay near the arbour. The rogue had been clever enough to get two hundred and twenty roubles for the settlement of his wager, and the earlier eighty in addition. Sekleteia Burdalakov!

Again he laughed with a laugh very near a groan. Suddenly he stopped, and put his hand to his side, seized with a sudden consciousness of pain. Vera was free, but he told himself she had dared to mock another fellow human being who had been rash enough to love her; she had mocked her friend. His soul cried for revenge.

He sprang up intent on revenge, but was checked by the question of how to avenge himself. To bring Tatiana Markovna, with lanterns, and a crowd of servants and to expose the scandal in a glare of light; to say to her, "Here is the serpent you have carried for two and twenty years in your bosom"—that would be a vulgar revenge of which he knew himself to be incapable. Such a revenge would hit, not Vera, but his aunt, who was to him like his mother. His head drooped for a moment; then he rose and hurried like a madman down the precipice once more.

There in the depths passion was holding her festival, night drew her curtain over the song of love, love ... with Mark. If she had surrendered to another lover, to the tall, handsome Tushin, the owner of land, lake, and forest, and the Olympian tamer of horses....

He could hardly breathe. Against his will there rose before him, from the depths of the precipice, the vision of Vera's figure, glorified with a seductive beauty that he had never yet seen in her, and though he was devoured by agony he could not take his eyes from the vision. At her feet, like a lion at rest, lay Mark, with triumph on his face. Her foot rested on his head. Horror seized him, and drove him onward, to destroy and mar the vision. He seemed to hear in the air the flattering words, the songs and the sighs of passion; the vision became fainter, mist-enshrouded, and finally vanished into air, but the rage for revenge remained.

Everywhere was stillness and darkness, as he climbed the hill once more, but when he reached Vera's bench he saw a human shadow.

"Who is there?" he cried.

"Monsieur Boris, it is I, Paulina."

"You, what are you doing here?"

"I came, because I knew, I knew that you have long had something to say to me, but have hesitated. Du courage. There is no one to see or hear us. *Espérez tout....*"

"What do you want? Speak out."

"*Que vous m'aimez.* I have known it for a long time. *Vous m'avez fui, mais la passion vous a ramené ici....*"

He seized her roughly by the hand, and pushed her to the edge of the precipice.

"Ah, *de grâce. Mais pas si brusquement ... qu'est-ce que vous faites ... mais laissez donc,*" she groaned.

Her anxiety was not altogether groundless, for she stood on the edge of an abrupt fall of the ground, and he grasped her hand more determinedly.

"You want love," he cried to the terrified woman. "Listen, to-night is love's night. Do you hear the sighs, the kisses, the breath of passion?"

"Let me go! Let me go! I shall fall."

"Away from here," he cried, loosening his grasp and drawing a deep breath.

Like a madman he ran across the garden and the flower garden into the yard, where Egorka was washing his hands and face at the spring.

"Bring my trunk," he cried. "I am going to St. Petersburg in the morning." He ran water over his hands and washed his face and eyes before he turned to go to his room.

He could not stay within the four walls of his chamber. He went out again and again, unprotected against the cold, to look at Vera's window. It was hardly possible to see ten paces ahead in the darkness. He went to the acacia arbour to watch for Vera's return, and was furious because he could not conceal himself there, now that the leaves had fallen. He sat there in torture until morning dawned, not from passion, which had been drowned in that night's experiences. What passion would stand such a shock as this? But he had an unconquerable desire to look Vera in the face, this new Vera, and with one glance of scorn to show her the shame, the affront she had put on him, on their aunt, on the whole household, on their society, on womanhood itself. He awaited her return in a fever of impatience. Suddenly he sprang up with an evil look of triumph on his face.

"Fate has given me the idea," he thought. He found the gates still locked, but there was a lamp before the ikon in Savili's room, and he ordered him to let him out and to leave the gates unlocked. He took from his room the bouquet holder and hastened to the orangery to the gardener. He had to wait a long time before it opened. The light grew stronger. When he looked over at the trees in the orangery, an evil smile again crossed his face. The gardener was arranging Marfinka's bouquet.

"I want another bouquet," said Raisky unsteadily.

"One like this?"

"No, only orange blossoms," he whispered, turning paler as he spoke.

"Right, Sir," said the gardener, recalling that one of Tatiana Markovna's young ladies was betrothed.

"I am thirsty," said Raisky. "Give me a glass of water."

He drank the water greedily, and hurried the gardener on. When the second bouquet was ready he paid lavishly.

He returned to the house cautiously, carrying the two bouquets. As he did not know whether Vera had returned in his absence, he had Marina called, and sent her to see if her mistress was at home or had already gone out walking. On hearing she was out he ordered Marfinka's bouquet to be put on Vera's table and the window to be opened. Then he dismissed Marina, and returned to the acacia arbour. Passion and jealousy set loose raged unchecked, and when pity raised her head she was quenched by the torturing, overmastering feeling of outrage. He suppressed the low voice of sympathy, and his better self was silent. He was shuddering, conscious that poison flowed in his veins, the poison of lies and deception.

"I must either shoot this dog Mark, or myself," he thought.

He held the bouquet of orange-blossoms in his two hands, like a sacred thing, and drank in its beauty with a wild delight. Then he fixed his eyes on the dark avenue, but she did not come.

Broad daylight came, a fine rain began to fall and made the paths sodden. At last Vera appeared in the distance. His heart beat faster, and his knees trembled so that he had to steady himself by the bench to keep from falling.

She came slowly nearer, with her bowed head wrapped in a dark mantilla, held in place over her breast by her pale hands, and walked into the porch without seeing him. Raisky sprang from his place of observation, and hid himself under her window.

She entered her room in a dream, without noticing that her clothes which she had flung on the floor when she went out had been put back again, and without observing the bouquet on the table or the opened window. Mechanically she threw aside her mantilla, and changed her muddy shoes for satin slippers; then she sank down on the divan, and closed her eyes. After a brief minute she was awakened from her dream by the thud of something falling on the floor. She opened her eyes and saw on the floor a great sheaf of orange blossoms, which had plainly been thrown through the window.

Pale as death, and without picking up the flowers, she hurried to the window. She saw Raisky, as he went away, and stood transfixed. He looked round, and their eyes met.

She was seized by pain so sharp that she could hardly breathe, and stepped back. Then she saw the bouquet intended for Marfinka on the table. She picked it up, half unconsciously, to press it to her face, but it slipped from her hands, and she herself fell unconscious on the floor.

CHAPTER XXV

At ten o'clock the big bell in the village church began to sound for Mass. Tatiana Markovna's household was full of stir and bustle. The horses were being harnessed to the calèche and to an old fashioned carriage. The coachmen, already drunk, donned their new dark blue caftans, and their hair shone with grease. The women servants made a gay picture in their many coloured cotton dresses, head and neck kerchiefs, and the maids employed in the house diffused a scent of cloves within a ten yards radius. The cooks had donned their white caps in the early morning, and had been incessantly busy in the preparation of the breakfast, dinner and supper to be served to the family and their guests, the kitchen, and the servants the visitors brought with them.

Tatiana Markovna had begun to make her toilet at eight o'clock, as soon as she had given her orders; she descended to the hall to greet her guests with the reserved dignity of a great lady, and the gentle smile of a happy mother and a hospitable hostess. She had set a small simple cap on her grey hair; the light brown silk dress that Raisky had brought from St. Petersburg suited her well, and round her neck she wore beautiful old lace; the Turkish shawl lay on the arm-chair in her room.

Now she was preparing to drive to Mass, and walked slowly up and down the hall with crossed hands, awaiting the assembly of the household. She hardly noticed the bustle around her, as the servants went hither and thither, sweeping the carpets, cleaning the lamps, dusting the mirrors, and taking the covers from the furniture. She went first to one window and then to the other, looking out meditatively on the road, the garden and the courtyards.

Vikentev's mother was dressed in pearl grey with dark lace trimmings. Vikentev himself had been in his dress coat and white gloves from eight o'clock onwards.

Tatiana Markovna's pride and joy knew no bounds when Marfinka appeared, radiating gaiety from her bright eyes. While she slept the walls of her two rooms had been decorated with flowers and garlands. She was going to put on her simple blouse when she woke, but instead there lay on the chair by her bed a morning gown of lace and muslin with pink ribbons. She had not had time to give vent to her admiration when she saw on two other chairs two lovely dresses, one pink and one blue, for her to make her choice for the gala day.

She jumped up, and threw on her new morning gown without waiting to put on her stockings, and when she approached her mirror she found a new surprise in the gifts that lay on her toilet table. She did not know which to look at, or which to take up.

First she opened a lovely rosewood casket which contained a complete dressing set, flasks, combs, brushes and endless trifles in glass and silver, with a card bearing the name of her future Mama. Beside it lay cases of different sizes. She threw a quick glance in the mirror, smoothed back her abundant hair from her eyes, seized all the cases in a heap, and sat down on the bed to look at them. She hesitated to open them, and finally began with the smallest, which contained an emerald ring, which she hastily put on her finger. A larger case held earrings which she inserted in her ears and admired in the glass from the bed. There were massive gold bracelets, set with rubies and diamonds, which she also put on. Last of all she opened the largest case, and looked astonished and dazzled at its splendid contents: a chain of strung diamonds, twenty-one to match her years. The accompanying card said: "With this gift I confide to you another, a costly one, my best of friends—myself. Take care of him. Your lover, Vikentev."

She laughed, looked round, kissed the card, blushed, sprang from the bed and laid the case in her cupboard, in the box where she kept her bonbons. There was still another case on the table, containing Raisky's gift of a watch, whose enamel cover bore her monogram, and its chain.

She looked at it with wide eyes, threw another glance at the other gifts and the garlanded walls, then threw herself on a chair and wept hot tears of joy. "Oh, God!" she sobbed happily. "Why does everyone love me so. I do no good to anyone, and never shall."

And so, undressed, without shoes and stockings, but adorned with rings, bracelets, diamond earrings, she tearfully sought her aunt, who caressed and kissed her darling when she heard the cause of her tears.

"God loves you, Marfinka, because you love others, because all who see you are infected by your happiness."

Marfinka dried her tears.

"Nikolai Andreevich loves me, but he is my fiancé; so does his Mama, but so does my cousin, Boris Pavlovich, and what am I to him?"

"The same as you are to everyone. No one can look at you and not be happy; you are modest, pure and good, obedient to your Grandmother. Spendthrift," she murmured in an aside, to hide her pleasure. "Such a costly gift! You shall hear of this, Borushka!"

"Grandmother! As if Boris Pavlovich could have guessed it. I have wanted a little enamelled watch like this for a long time."

"You haven't asked your Grandmother why she gives you nothing?"

Marfinka shut her mouth with a kiss.

"Grandmother," she said, "love me always, if you want to make me happy."

"With my love I will give you my enduring gift," she said, making the sign of the cross over Marfinka. "So that you shall not forget my blessing," she went on, feeling in her pocket—"You have given me two dresses, Grandmother, but who decorated my room so magnificently?"

"Your fiancé and Paulina Karpovna sent the things yesterday, and kept them out of your sight. Vassilissa and Pashutka hung the garlands up at daybreak. The dresses are part of your trousseau, and there are more to follow." Then taking from its case a gold cross with four large diamonds she hung it round the girl's neck, and gave her a plain, simple bracelet with the inscription: "From Grandmother to her Grandchild," and with the name and the date.

Marfinka kissed her aunt's hand, and nearly wept once more.

"All that Grandmother has, and she has many things, will be divided between you and Veroshka. Now make haste."

"How lovely you are to-day, Grandmother. Cousin is right. Tiet Nikonich will fall in love with you."

"Nonsense, chatterbox. Go to Veroshka, and tell her not to be late for Mass. I would have gone myself, but am afraid of the steps."

"Directly, Grandmother," cried Marfinka, and hastened to change her dress.

Vera lay unconscious for half an hour before she came to herself. The cold wind that streamed through the open window fell on her face, and she sat up to look around her. Then she rose, shut the window, walked unsteadily to the bed, sank down on it, and drawing the cover over herself, lay motionless.

Overpowered with weakness she fell into a deep sleep, with her hair loose over the pillow. She slept heavily for about three hours until she was awakened by the noise in the courtyard, the many voices, the creaking of wheels and the sound of bells. She opened her eyes, looked round, and listened.

There was a light knock at the door, but Vera did not stir. There was a louder knock, but she remained motionless. At the third she got up, glanced in the glass, and was terrified by the sight of her own face. She pushed her hair into order, threw a shawl over her shoulders, picked up Marfinka's bouquet from the floor, and laid it on the table. There was another knock and she opened the door. Marfinka, gay and lovely, gleaming like a rainbow in her pretty clothes, flew into the room. When she saw her sister she stood still in amazement.

"What is the matter with you, Veroshka? Aren't you well?"

"Not quite. I offer you my congratulations."

The sisters kissed one another.

"How lovely you are, and how beautifully dressed!" said Vera, making a faint attempt to smile. Her lips framed one, but her eyes were like the eyes of a corpse that no one has remembered to close. But she felt she must control herself, and hastened to present Marfinka with the bouquet.

"What a lovely bouquet! And what is this?" asked Marfinka as she felt a hard substance, and discovered the holder set with her name and the pearls. "You, too, Veroshka! How is it you all love me so? I love you all, how I love you! But how and when you found out that I did, I cannot think."

Vera was not capable of answering, but she caressed Marfinka's shoulder affectionately.

"I must sit down," she said. "I have slept badly through the night."

"Grandmother calls you to Mass."

"I cannot, darling. Tell her I am unwell, and cannot leave the house to-day."

"What! you are not coming?"

"I shall stay in bed. Perhaps I caught cold yesterday. Tell Grandmother."

"We will come to you."

"You would only disturb me."

"Then we shall send everything over. Ah, Veroshka, people have sent me so many presents, and flowers and bonbons. I must show them to you," and she ran over a list of them.

"Yes, show me everything; perhaps I will come later," said Vera absently.

"Another bouquet?" asked Marfinka, pointing to the one that lay on the floor. "For whom? How lovely!"

"For you too," said Vera, turning paler. She picked a ribbon hastily from a drawer and fastened the bouquet with it. Then she kissed her sister, and sank down on the divan.

"You are really ill. How pale you are! Shall I tell Grandmother, and let her send for the doctor? How sad that it should be on my birthday. The day is spoiled for me!"

"It will pass. Don't say a word to Grandmother. Don't frighten her. Leave me now, for I must rest."

At last Marfinka went. Vera shut the door after her, and lay down on the divan.

CHAPTER XXVI

When Raisky returned to his room at daybreak and looked in the mirror, he hardly recognised himself. He felt chilly, and sent Marina for a glass of wine which he drank before he threw himself on his bed. Overcome by moral and physical exhaustion he slept as if he had thrown himself into the arms of a friend and had confided his trouble to him. Sleep did him the service of a friend, for it carried him far from Vera, from Malinovka, from the precipice, from the fantastic vision of last night. When the ringing of many bells awoke him he lay for several minutes under the soothing influence of the physical rest, which built a rampart between him and yesterday. There was no agony in his awakening moments. But soon memory revived, and his face wore an expression more terrible than in the worst moments of yesterday. A pain different from yesterday's, a new devil had hurled itself upon him. He seized one piece of clothing after another and dressed as hastily and nervously as Vera had done as she prepared to go to the precipice.

He rang for Egorka, from whom he learnt that everybody except Vera, who was not well, had driven to Mass. In wild agitation he dashed across to the old house. There was no response when he knocked at Vera's door. He opened it cautiously, and stole in like a man with murderous intent, with horror imprinted on his features, and advanced on tiptoe, trembling, deadly pale, with swaying steps as if he might fall at any minute.

Vera lay on the divan, with her face turned away, her hair falling down almost to the floor, and her slipper-clad feet hardly covered by her grey skirt. She tried to turn round when she heard the noise of the opening door, but could not.

He approached, knelt at her feet, and pressed his lips to the slipper she wore. Suddenly she turned, and stared at him in astonishment. "Is it comedy or romance, Boris Pavlovich," she asked brusquely, turned in annoyance, and hid her foot under the skirt which she straightened quickly.

"No, Vera, tragedy," he whispered in a lifeless voice, and sat down on the chair near the divan.

The tone of his voice moved her to turn and look keenly at him, and her eyes opened wide with astonishment. She threw aside her shawl, and rose, she had divined in Raisky's face the presence of the same deadly suffering that she herself endured.

"What is your trouble? Are *you* unhappy?" she said, laying her hand on his shoulder. In the simple word and in the tone of her voice there were revealed the generous qualities of a woman, sympathy, selflessness, and love.

Keenly touched by the kindness and tenderness in her voice he looked at her with the same rapturous gratitude which she had worn on her face yesterday when in self-forgetfulness he had helped her down the precipice. She returned generosity with generosity, just as yesterday there had streamed from him a gleam of one of the highest qualities of the human mind. He was all the more in despair over what he had done, and wept hot tears. He hid his face in his hands like a man for whom all is lost.

"What have I done? I have insulted you, woman and sister."

"Do not make us both suffer," she said in a gentle, friendly tone. "Spare me; you see how I am."

He tried not to meet her eyes, and she again lay down on the divan.

"What a blow I dealt you," he whispered in horror. "You see my punishment, Vera!"

"Your blow gave me a minute's pain, and then I understood that it was not delivered with an indifferent hand, that you loved me. And it became clear to me how you must have suffered ... yesterday."

"Don't justify my crime, Vera. A knife is a knife, and I aimed a knife at you."

"You brought me to myself. I was as if I slept, and you, Grandmother, Marfinka and the whole house I saw as if in a dream."

"What am I to do, Vera? Fly from here? In what a state of mind I should leave! Let me endure my penance here, and be reconciled, as far as is possible, with myself, with all that has happened here."

"Your imagination paints what was only a fault as a crime. Remember your condition when you did it, your agitation!" She gave him her hand, and continued, "I know now what one is capable of doing in the fever of emotion."

She set herself to calm him in spite of her own weariness.

"You are good, Vera, and, womanlike, judge not with your brain, but with your heart."

"You are too severe with yourself. Another would have thought himself justified after all the jesting.... You remember those letters. With whatever good intention of calming your agitation, of answering your jest with jests, it was malicious mockery. You suffered more from those letters than I did yesterday."

"Oh, dear, no! I have often laughed over them, especially when you asked for a cloak, a rug, and money for the exile."

"What money? what cloak? what exile?" she exclaimed in astonishment. "I don't understand."

"I myself had suspicions," he said, his face clearing a little. "I could not believe that that was your idea." And in a few words he told her the contents of the two letters.

Her lips turned white.

"Natasha and I wrote to you turn and turn about in the same handwriting, amusing little letters in which we tried to imitate yours; that is all. I didn't know anything about the other letters," she whispered, turning her face to the wall.

Raisky strode up and down in thought, while Vera appeared to be resting, exhausted by the conversation.

"Cousin," she said suddenly, "I ask your help in a very important matter, and I know you will not refuse me." A glance at his face told her that there was nothing she could not ask of him. "While I still have strength, I want to tell you the whole history of this year."

"Why should you do that? I will not and I ought not to know."

"Do not disturb me, Boris. I can hardly breathe and time is precious. I will tell you the whole story, and you must repeat it to our Grandmother. I could not do it," she said. "My tongue would not say the words—I would rather die."

He looked at her with an expression of blank terror. "But why should Grandmother be told? Think of the consequences. Would it not be better to keep her in ignorance?"

"No, the burden must be borne. It is possible that Grandmother and I will both die of it, or we shall lose our senses, but I will not deceive her. She ought to have known it long ago, but I hoped to be able to tell her another story, and therefore was silent."

"To tell her everything, even of yesterday evening," he asked in a low tone. "And the name also?"

She nodded almost imperceptibly in assent. Then she made him sit down on the divan beside her, and in low, broken sentences told the story of her relations with Mark. When she had finished she wrapped herself, shivering with cold, in her shawl. He rose from his seat. Both were silent, each of them in terror, she as she thought of her grandmother, he as he thought of them both. Before him lay the prospect of having to deal Tatiana Markovna one thrust after another, and that not in the heat of passion, or in an access of blind revenge, but in the consciousness of a most painful duty. It might be as she said an important service, but it was certainly a terrible commission.

"When shall I tell her?" he asked.

"As soon as possible, for I shall suffer so long as I know she is in ignorance, and now, give me the eau-de-Cologne from the dressing-table, and leave me alone."

"It would not do to tell Grandmother to-day when the house is full of guests, but to-morrow...." said Raisky.

"How shall I survive it? But till to-morrow, calm her by some means or other, so that she has no suspicion and sends no one here."

She closed her eyes in a longing for impenetrable night, for rest without an awakening; she would like to have been turned into a thing of stone so that she could neither think nor feel.

When he left her he was weighed down with a greater weight of fear than that which he had brought to the interview. Vera rose as soon as he left her, closed the door, and lay down again. She had found consolation and help in Raisky's friendship, his sympathy and devotion, as a drowning man rises to the surface for a moment, but as soon as he was gone she fell back deeper into the depths. She told herself in despair that life was over. Before her there stretched the bare steppe; there was no longer for her a family, nor anything on which a woman's life depends. She would have to stand before her aunt, to look her in the eyes, and to tell her how she had recompensed her love and care. Suddenly she heard steps and her aunt's voice. Pale and motionless, as if she had lost the use of hands and feet, she listened to the light tap at the door. I will not get up, I cannot, she thought. But when the knock was repeated, she sprang up with a strength which astonished herself, dried her eyes and went smiling to meet her aunt.

When Tatiana Markovna had heard from Marfinka that Vera was ill, and would remain in her room all day, she had come herself to inquire; she glanced at Vera and sat down on the divan.

"The service has tired me so that I could hardly walk up the steps. What's the matter with you, Vera?" she continued, looking keenly at her.

"I congratulate Marfinka on her birthday," said Vera, in the voice of a little girl who has learnt her speech by heart. She kissed her grandmother's hand and wondered how she had managed to bring the words over her lips. "I got wet feet yesterday, and have a headache." She tried to smile, but there was no smile on her lips.

"You must rub your feet with spirit," remarked Tatiana Markovna, who had noticed the strained voice and the unnatural smile, and guessed a lack of frankness. "Are you coming to be with us, Vera? Don't force yourself to do so, and so make yourself worse," she continued, seeing that Vera was incapable of answering.

Vera was all the more frightened by her aunt's consideration for her. Her conscience stirred, and she felt that Tatiana Markovna must already know all, and that her confession would come too late. She was on the point of falling on her breast, and making her confession there and then, but her strength failed her.

"Excuse me, Grandmother, from dinner; perhaps I will come over in the afternoon."

"As you like. I will send your dinner across."

"Thank you, I am already quite hungry," said Vera quickly, without knowing what she said.

Tatiana Markovna kissed her, and stroked her hair, remarking casually that one of the maids should come and do her room, as she might have a visitor.

Tatiana Markovna returned sadly to the house. She was, indeed, politely attentive to her guests as she always was, but Raisky noticed immediately that something was wrong with her after her visit to Vera. She found it hard to restrain her emotion, hardly touched the food, did not even look round when Petrushka smashed a pile of plates, and more than once broke off in the middle of a sentence. In the afternoon as the guests took coffee on the broad terrace in the mild September sunshine, Tatiana Markovna moved among her guests as if she were hardly aware of them. Raisky wore a gloomy air and had eyes for no one but his aunt. "Something is wrong with Vera," she whispered to him. "She is in trouble. Have you seen her?"

"No," he said. But his aunt looked at him as if she doubted what he said.

Paulina Karpovna had not come. She had sent word that she was ill, and the messenger brought flowers and plants for Marfinka. In order to explain the scene of the day before, and to find out whether she had guessed anything, Raisky had paid a visit in the morning to Paulina Karpovna. She received him with a pretence of being offended, but with hardly disguised satisfaction. His excuse was that he had dined with friends that night and had had a glass too much. He begged for forgiveness which was accorded with a smile, all which did not prevent Paulina Karpovna from recounting to all her acquaintance her love scene.

Tushin came to dinner, and brought Marfinka a lovely pony to ride. He asked for Vera, and was plainly disturbed when he heard of the indisposition which prevented her from coming to dinner. Tatiana Markovna observed him, wondering why Vera's absence had such a remarkable effect on him, though this had often been the case before without exciting any surprise on her part. She could not keep out of her head anxiety as to what change had come over Vera since yesterday evening. She had had a little quarrel with Tiet Nikonich, and had scolded him for having brought Marfinka the Sèvres mirror. Afterwards she was closeted with him for a quarter of an hour in her sitting-room, and he emerged from the interview looking serious. He shifted his foot less, and even when he was talking to ladies his serous inquiring glance would wander to Raisky or Tushin.

Up till this time Tatiana Markovna had been so gay. Her one anxiety, and at the moment the only one perhaps, had been the celebration of Vera's nameday a fortnight ahead, she would have liked to have celebrated it with the same magnificence as Marfinka's birthday, although Vera had roundly declared that on that day she meant to go on a visit to Anna Ivanovna Tushin, or to her friend Natasha. But how Tatiana Markovna had changed since Mass. As she talked with her guests she was thinking only of Vera, and gave absent-minded answers. The excuse of a cold had not deceived her, and as she had touched Vera's brow on leaving her, she had realised that a cold could be nothing but a pretext. She remembered that Vera and Raisky had vanished in the afternoon and that neither had appeared at supper. She was constantly watching Raisky, who sought to avoid her glance, thereby only arousing her suspicions the more. Then Vera herself unexpectedly appeared amongst the guests, wearing a warm mantilla over her light dress and a wrap round her throat. Raisky was so astonished that he looked at her as if she were an apparition. A few hours ago she had been almost too exhausted to speak, and now here she was in person. He wondered where women found their strength. Vera went round speaking to the guests, looked at Marfinka's presents, and ate, to quench her thirst, as she said, a slice of water melon. Tatiana Markovna was to some extent relieved to see Vera, but it disturbed her to notice that Raisky's face had changed. For the first time in her life she cursed her guests; they were just sitting down to cards, then there would be tea, and then supper, and Vikentev was not going until to-morrow morning.

CHAPTER XXVII

Raisky found himself between two fires. On the one hand, Tatiana Markovna looked at him as much as to say that he probably knew what was the matter with Vera, while Vera's despairing glance betrayed her anxiety for the moment of her confession. He himself would have liked to have sunk into the earth. Tushin looked in an extraordinary manner at Vera, as both Tatiana Markovna and Raisky, but most of all Vera herself, noticed. She was terrified, and asked herself whether he had heard any rumour. He esteemed her so highly, thought her the noblest woman in the world, and, if she were silent, she would be accepting his esteem on false premisses. He, too, would have to be told, she thought. She exchanged greetings with him without meeting his eyes; and he looked strangely at her, timidly and sympathetically. Vera told herself that she must know what was in his mind, that if he looked at her again like that she would collapse. He did look at her again, and she could endure no more and left the company. Before she went she signed secretly to Tushin to follow her.

"I cannot receive you in the old house," she said, "Come into the avenue."

"Is it not too damp, as you are not well?"

"That does not matter," she said.

He looked at his watch and said that he would be going in an hour. After giving orders to have his horses taken out of the stable and brought into the yard, he picked up his silver-handled whip and with his cloak on his arm followed Vera into the avenue. "I will not beat about the bush," he said. "What is the matter with you to-day? You have something on your mind."

She wrapped her face in her mantilla as she spoke, and her shoulders shivered as if with cold. She dare not raise her eyes to him as he strode silently beside her.

"But you are ill, Vera Vassilievna. I had better talk to you another time. You were not wrong in thinking I had something to say to you."

"No, Ivan Ivanovich, let it be to-day. I want to know what you have to say to me. I myself wanted to talk to you, but perhaps it is too late for what I have to say. Do you speak," she said, wondering painfully how and where he could have learnt her secret.

"I came here to-day...." he said as they sat down on the bench.

"What have you to say to me? Speak!" she interrupted.

"How can I say it to you now, Vera Vassilievna?" said Tushin springing to his feet.

"Do not make me suffer," she murmured.

"I love you...."

"Yes, I know it," she interrupted. "But what have you heard?"

"I have heard nothing," he said, looking round in amazement. He was now for the first time aware of her agitation, and his heart stood still with delight. She has guessed my secret and shares my feelings, he thought, and what she is asking, is for a frank, brief avowal. "You are so noble, so beautiful, Vera Vassilievna, so pure...." An exclamation was wrung from her, and she would have risen, but could not.

"You mock me, you mock me," she said, raising her hands beseechingly.

"You are ill, Vera Vassilievna," he said, looking at her in terror. "Forgive me for having spoken to you at such a time."

"A day earlier or later makes no difference. Say what you have to say, for I also desire to tell you why I have brought you here."

"Is it really true?" he cried, hardly knowing how to contain his delight.

"What is true? You want to say something else, not what I expected," she said. "Speak, and do not prolong my sufferings."

"I love you," he repeated. "If you can grant what I have confessed to you (and I am not worthy of it), if your love is not given elsewhere, then be my forest queen, my wife, and there will be no happier man on earth than I. That is what I have long wished to say to you and have not dared. I should have done it on your nameday but I could no longer endure the suspense, and have come to-day, on the family festival, on your sister's birthday."

"Ivan Ivanovich," she moaned. The thought flashed through his head like lightning that this was no expression of joy, and he felt his hair was beginning to stand on end. He sat down beside her and said, "What is wrong with you, Vera Vassilievna? You are either ill, or are bearing a great sorrow."

"Yes, Ivan Ivanovich! I feel that I shall die."

"What is your trouble? For God's sake, tell me. You said that you had something to confide in me, which means that I must be necessary to you; there is nothing I would not do for you. You have only to command me. Forgive me my too hasty speech."

"You, too, my poor Ivan Ivanovich! I can find neither prayers nor tears, nor is there any guidance or help for me anywhere."

"What words of despair are these, Vera Vassilievna?"

"Do you know *whom* you love?"

He threw his cloak on the bench, and wiped the sweat from his brow. Her words told him that his hopes were ruined, that her love was given elsewhere. He drew a deep breath, and sat motionless, awaiting her further explanations.

"My poor friend," she said, taking his hand. The simple words filled him with new sorrow; he knew that he was in fact to be pitied.

"Thank you," he whispered. "Forgive me ... I did not know, Vera Vassilievna ... I am a fool.... Please forget my declaration. But I should like to help you, since you say yourself you rely on me for a service. I thank you for holding me worthy of that. You stand so high above me; I always feel that you stand so high, Vera Vassilievna."

"My poor Ivan Ivanovich, I have fallen from those heights, and no human power can reinstate me," she said, as she led him to the edge of the precipice.

"Do you know this place?" she asked.

"Yes, a suicide is buried there."

"There, in the depths below the precipice, your 'pure' Vera also lies buried," she said with the decision of despair.

"What are you saying? I don't understand. Enlighten me, Vera Vassilievna."

Summoning all her strength she bent her head and whispered a few words to him, then returned, and sank down on the bench. Tushin turned pale, swayed, lost his balance, and sat down beside her. Even in the dim light Vera noticed his pallor.

"And I thought," he said, with a strange smile, as if he were ashamed of his weakness, rising to his feet with difficulty, "that only a bear was strong enough to knock me over." Then he stooped to her and whispered, "Who?"

The question sent a shudder through her, but she answered quickly:

"Mark Volokov."

His face twitched ominously. Then he pressed his whip over his knee so that it split in pieces, which he hurled away from him.

"So it will end with him too," he shouted. As he stood trembling before her, stooping forward, with wild eyes, he was like an animal ready to spring on the enemy. "Is he there now?" he cried, pointing with a violent gesture in the direction of the precipice.

She looked at him as if he were a dangerous animal, as he stood there, breathing heavily; then she rose and took refuge behind the bench.

"I am afraid, Ivan Ivanovich! Spare me! Go!" she exclaimed, warding him off with her arms.

"First I will kill him, and then I will go."

"Are you going to do this for my sake, for my peace of mind or for your own sake?"

He kept silence, his eyes fixed on the ground, and then began to walk about in great strides. "What should I do?" he said, still trembling with agitation. "Tell me, Vera Vassilievna."

"First of all, calm yourself, and explain to me why you wish to kill him and whether I desire it."

"He is your enemy, consequently also mine."

"Does one kill one's enemies?"

He bent his head and seeing the pieces of the whip lying on the ground he picked them up as if he were ashamed, and put them in his pocket.

"I do not accuse him. I alone bear the blame, and he has justification," she said with such bitter misery that Tushin took her hand.

"Vera Vassilievna," he said, "you are suffering horribly. I do not understand," he went on, looking at her with sympathy and admiration, "what you mean by saying that he has justification, and that you bring no accusation against him. If that's the case, why did you wish to speak to me and call me here into the avenue?"

"Because I wanted you to know the whole truth."

"Don't leave me in the dark, Vera Vassilievna. You must have had some reason for confiding your secret to me."

"You looked at me so strangely to-day that I could not understand your meaning, and thought you must already be informed of all that had happened and could not rest until I knew what was in your mind. I was too hasty, but it comes to the same thing, for sooner or later I should have told you. Sit down, and hear what I have to say, and then have done with me." She explained the situation to him in a few words.

"So you forgive him," he asked, after a moment's thought.

"Forgive him, of course. I tell you that I alone am guilty."

"Have you separated from him, or do you hope for his return?"

"There is nothing whatever in common between us, and we shall never see one another again."

"Now, I understand a little, for the first time, but still not everything," said Tushin, sighing bitterly. "I thought you had been vulgarly betrayed, and, since you called me to your help, I imagined that the time had come for the Bear to do his duty. I was on the point of rendering you the service of a Bear, and it was for that reason that I permitted myself to ask boldly for the man's name. Forgive me, and now tell me why you have revealed the story to me."

"Because I was not willing that you should think better of me than I deserve, and esteem me...."

"But how would you accomplish that? I shall not cease to think of you as I have always thought of you, and I cannot do otherwise than respect you."

A gleam of pleasure lighted her eyes, only to be immediately extinguished. "You want to restore my self-esteem," she said, "because you are good and generous. You are sorry for a poor unfortunate girl and want to raise her up again. I understand your generosity, Ivan Ivanovich, but I will have none of it."

"Vera Vassilievna," he said, kissing her hand. "I could not esteem anybody under compulsion. If I give anyone a greeting in the street, he has my esteem; if he has not my esteem, I pass him by. I greet you as before, and because you are unhappy my love for you is greater than before. You are enduring a great sorrow, as I am. You have lost your hopes of happiness," he added in a low, melancholy tone. "If you had kept your secret from me and I had heard it by chance, even so my esteem for you could not have been diminished. For there is no duty laid on you to reveal a secret which belongs to you alone. No one has the right to judge you." The last words were spoken in a trembling voice which made it clear that he also was oppressed by the secret, the weight of which he desired to lighten for Vera.

"I had to tell you to-day when you made your declaration to me. I felt it was impossible to leave you in ignorance."

"You might very well have answered me with a categorical 'No.' But since you do me the honour, Vera Vassilievna, of bestowing your particular friendship on me, you might have gilded your 'No' by saying that you loved another. That would have been sufficient for me, for I should never have asked you who, and your secret would, without doubt, have remained your own." He pointed to the precipice, and collecting his whole strength whispered, "A misfortune...." Although he tried with all his might not to let her see how disturbed he was, he was hardly able to speak clearly. "A misfortune," he repeated. "You say that he has justification, that the guilt is yours; if that is so, where does justice lie?"

"I told you, Ivan Ivanovich, that my confession was not necessary for your sake, but for mine. You know how I esteem your friendship, and it would have caused me unspeakable pain to deceive you. Even now, when I have hidden nothing from you, I cannot look you in the eyes." Tears stifled her voice, and it was with difficulty that Tushin held back his own tears; he stooped and kissed her hand once more.

"Thanks, a thousand thanks, Vera Vassilievna. I see that an affection for another has no power to lessen your friendship for me, and that is a wonderful consolation."

"Ivan Ivanovich, if I could only cut this year out of my life."

"A speedy forgetfulness," he said, "comes to the same thing."

"How can I forget, and where can I find the strength to endure its memory?"

"You will find strength in friendship, and I am one of your friends."

She breathed another air for the moment, conscious that there was beside her a tower of strength, under whose shadow her passion and her pain were alleviated. "I believe in your friendship, Ivan Ivanovich, and thank you for it," she said, drying her tears. "I already feel calmer, and should feel still calmer if Grandmother...."

"She does not yet know anything of this?" he asked, but broke off immediately in the consciousness that his question involved a reproach.

"She has guests to-day and could not possibly be told, but to-morrow she shall learn all. Farewell, Ivan Ivanovich, my head aches, and I am going back to the house to lie down." Tushin looked at Vera, asking himself how any man could be such a blind fool as Volokov. Or is he merely a beast, he thought to himself in impotent rage. He pulled himself together, however, and asked her if she had any instructions for him.

"Please ask Natasha," she said, "to come over to me to-morrow or the next day."

"And may I come one day next week to inquire whether you are better?"

"Do not be anxious, Ivan Ivanovich. And now good-bye, for I can hardly stand."

When he left her, he drove his horses so wildly down the steep hill that he himself was in danger of being hurled to the bottom of the precipice. When he put his hand out as usual for his whip, it was not there, and he remembered that he had broken it, and threw away the useless pieces on the road. In spite of his mad haste he reached the Volga too late for the ferry. He had to stay in the town with a friend, and drove next morning to his home in the forest.

CHAPTER XXVIII

In Tatiana Markovna's house, servants, cooks and coachmen were all astir, and at a very early hour in the morning were already drunk. The mistress of the house herself was unusually silent and sad when she let Marfinka go with her future mother-in-law. She had no instructions or advice to give, and hardly listened to Marfinka's questions about what she ought to take with her. "What you like," she said absently, and gave orders to Vassilissa and the maid who was going with Marfinka to Kolchino to put everything in order and pack up what was necessary. She handed over her dear child to Marfa Egorovna's charge, at the same time pointing out to Marfinka's fiancé that he must take the greatest care of her, and that in order not to give strangers a wrong impression, he must be more dignified and must not chase about the garden and the woods with her as he did in Malinovka.

When she saw that Vikentev coloured at this advice, which indicated doubt of his tactfulness, and that Marfa Egorovna bit her underlip, Tatiana Markovna changed her tone; she laid her hand on his shoulder calling him "Dear Nikolinka," and telling him that she knew herself how unnecessary her words were, but that old women liked to preach. Then she sighed, and said not another word to her guests before their departure.

Vera too came to breakfast; she looked pale, and it was clear that she had had a sleepless night. She said she still had a headache, but felt better than she did yesterday. There was no change in Tatiana Markovna's affectionate manner to her. Now and then Marfa Egorovna cast questioning glances in Vera's direction. What was the meaning of pain without any definite illness? Why did she not appear yesterday until after dinner, and then only for a moment, to go out followed by Tushin. What had they found to say to one another for an hour in the twilight? Being a sensible woman she did not pursue these inquiries, though they flashed for a moment in her eyes; nevertheless Vera saw them, although they were quickly exchanged for looks of sympathy. Neither did Marfa Egorovna's questioning glances escape Tatiana Markovna, who kept her eyes on the ground, while Vera maintained her indifferent manner. Already people are wondering what had happened, thought Tatiana Markovna sadly; on my arms she came into the world, she is my child and yet I do not know what her trouble is.

Raisky had been out for a walk before breakfast, and wore on his face a look as if he had just come to a decision on a momentous question. He looked at Vera as calmly as at the others, and did not avoid Tatiana

Markovna's eyes. He promised Vikentev to come over to see him in a day or two, and listened attentively to his guest's conversation about hunting and fishing.

At last everything was ready for their departure. Tatiana Markovna and Raisky went with their guests as far as the Volga, leaving Vera at home.

Vera's world had always been a small one, and its boundaries were now drawn more narrowly than ever. She had been contented during the long years with the observation and experience which were accessible to her in her immediate environment. Her small circle represented to her the crowd; she made her own in a short time what it took others many years in many places to learn. Unlike Marfinka she was cautious in her sympathies, granting her friendship only to the priest's wife and to Tushin, whom she openly called her friend. The simple things and the simple people who surrounded her did not serve only trivial purposes. She understood how to embroider on this ordinary canvas the bold pattern of a richer life with other needs, thoughts and feelings; she guessed at these by reading between the lines of everyday life other lines which expressed the desires of her mind and heart. If she was cautious in her sympathies she was excessively so in the sphere of thought and knowledge. She read books from the library in the old house, taking from the shelves at first without choice or system as a pastime whatever came into her hands; then she began to experience curiosity, and finally a definite desire for knowledge. She was keen-sighted enough to understand how aimless and unfruitful it was to wander among these other minds without any guiding thread. Without making direct inquiries she procured some explanations from Koslov, and although she understood many things at a bound, she never let it be seen that she had any knowledge of things beyond her immediate circle. Without losing sight of Koslov's instructions she read the books once more, to find that they meant much more to her and that her interest in them was steadily increasing. At the request of the young priest, Natasha's husband, she brought him books too, and listened when he expressed his views on this or that author, without herself adopting the seminarist view.

Later on she came into contact with Mark, who brought a new light to bear on all that she had read and heard and known; his attitude was one of blank denial. No authority in heaven or earth weighed with him, he despised science as it had hitherto developed, and made no distinction between virtue and crime. If he thought that he would soon be able to triumph over Vera's convictions he was mistaken. She regarded these bold and often alluring ideas with shy admiration, without giving herself up blindly to their influence; she listened cautiously to the preaching of the apostle, but found in it neither a new life, nor happiness, nor truth, and, though she followed attentively what he had to say, it was only because she was drawn on by the ardent desire to find the reality that lay behind Mark's extraordinary and audacious personality. Mark displayed his unsparing negation, enmity and scorn against all that men believe, love and hope for; Vera did not agree with all she heard, because she observed the malady that lay concealed behind the teaching, even if she could not discover where it lay. Her Columbus could show her nothing but a row of open graves standing ready to receive all that by which society had hitherto existed. Vera remembered the story of Pharaoh's lean kine, which without themselves becoming fatter devoured the fat kine.

Mark would have despoiled mankind of his crown in the name of wisdom; he would acknowledge in him nothing but an animal organism. And while he denied man in man, denied him the possession of a soul and the right to immortality, he yet spoke of his strivings to introduce a better order of things, neglecting to observe that in accordance with his own theory of the chance arrangement of existence, by which men herd together like flies in the hot weather; such efforts were useless.

Granting the correctness of his ideas as a premiss, thought Vera, there can be no sense in striving to be better, kinder, truer and purer, if this life enduring only for a few decades is the end of all things. When she looked deeper into the matter and examined the new truth taught by the young apostle, the new conception of good and the new revelation, she saw with astonishment that what in his talk was good and incontrovertible was not new, that it was derived from sources from which others also drew, who certainly did not belong to the new society; she recognised that the seed of the new civilisation which he preached with so much boastfulness and such a parade of mystery lay in the old-fashioned doctrine, and for this reason she believed more firmly than ever in the older philosophy of life. She looked on Mark's personality with such suspicion that she gradually withdrew herself from his influence. Hideously disturbed by his audacity of thought, she had even gone so far as to tell Tatiana Markovna of this accidental acquaintance, with the result that the old lady told the servants to keep a watch on the garden, but Volokov came from the direction of the precipice, from which the watchmen were effectually kept away by their superstitious fears. Mark himself had noted Vera's distrust, and he set himself to overcome it.

He was the more easily able to accomplish this because, when her interest was once awakened, she met him halfway, imperceptibly to herself. She meditated carefully on the facts that made up her life; her mind was occupied by new questionings, and for that reason she listened more attentively to his words when she met him in the fields. Often they went out walking on the banks of the Volga, and eventually found a meeting-place in the arbour at the bottom of the precipice. Gradually Vera adopted a more active role in their intercourse. She wanted to convert him, to lead him back to the acceptance of proved truth, the truth of love, of human as opposed to animal happiness, of faith and hope. Mark gave way in some things, though only gradually; his manners became less eccentric, he was less provocative in his behaviour to the police than before, he lived in a more orderly fashion, and ceased to stud his conversation with cynical remarks.

The change pleased Vera, and this was the cause of the happy excitement that Tatiana Markovna and Raisky had remarked in her. Since her influence was effective even if only in what affected his external life, she hoped by incessant effort and sacrifice gradually to produce a miracle; her reward was to be the happiness of being loved by the man of her heart's choice. She flattered herself that she would be introducing a new strong man into society. If he were to show himself in wisdom and strength of will, simply and reliable, as Tushin was, her life was mapped out for her. While she was engaged in these efforts she allowed her passionate nature to be carried away by his personality; she fell in love, not with his doctrine, which she refused to accept, but with himself. He called to new activity, but she saw in his appeal nothing more than the lending of forbidden books. She agreed with him that work was necessary, and herself avoided idleness; she drew up for herself a picture of simple genuine activity for the future, and envied Marfinka because she understood how to make herself useful in the house and the village. She intended to share these labours with her sister when once the stiff battle with Mark had been brought to a conclusion; but the struggle was not to end with a victory for either one or the other, but with mutual overthrow and a permanent separation.

These were the thoughts that passed through Vera's mind while Tatiana Markovna and Raisky were accompanying their guests and Marfinka as far as the Volga. What was the Wolf doing now? was he enjoying his triumph? She took from her letter case a sealed letter on blue paper which she had received early that morning and looked at it thoughtfully for a minute before she threw it down with its seals unbroken on the table. All her troubles were submerged in the painful question, what would become of her Grandmother. Raisky had already whispered to Vera that he would speak to Tatiana Markovna that evening if she were alone, and that he would take care that none of the servants should have the opportunity of seeing the impression which the news was bound to make on her. Vera shivered with foreboding when he spoke of these precautions; she would have liked to have died before evening came. After her talk of past events with Raisky and Tushin she recovered something of her usual calmness; a part of her burden was gone now that, like a sailor in a storm, she had lightened the ship of some of its ballast, but she felt that the heaviest load of all still lay on her conscience. It is impossible to go on living like this, she told herself, as she made her way to the chapel. There, on her knees, she looked anxiously up at the holy picture as if she expected a sign, but the sign she longed for was not granted, and she passed out of the chapel in despair as one who lay under the ban of God.

CHAPTER XXIX

When Tatiana Markovna returned from the ferry she sat down to work at her accounts, but soon laid them aside, and dismissed the servants. She asked for Raisky, who had gone over to see Koslov because he did not want to be left alone with his aunt. She sent across to ask Vera whether she was coming to dinner. Vera said that she would rather stay in her room and go to bed early.

In the courtyard a scene by no means unusual was being enacted. Savili had nearly broken Marina's back with a severe beating because he had seen her slipping out at dawn from the room in which Vikentev's servant was quartered. She hid herself in the fields and the vegetable garden, but at last she emerged, thinking that he would have forgotten. He struck her with the whip while she sought refuge in one corner after another, swearing by all that was sacred that the devil had taken on her figure and had made a fool of him. But when he exchanged the whip for the stick she cried out aloud at the first blow and fell at his feet. "I am guilty," she cried, begging for mercy. She promised not to transgress again, calling God to witness of her sincerity. Thereupon Savili threw away the stick and wiped his face with his sleeve.

"You may go this time," he said, "since you have confessed, and since you call God to witness."

Tatiana Markovna was informed of this proceeding, but she only wrinkled her forehead, and made a sign to Vassilissa not to be too severe with Marina.

There were visitors to dinner who had heard of Vera's indisposition and had come to inquire. Tatiana Markovna spoke of a chill, suffering all the time from her insincerity, since she did not know what was the truth that lay behind this feigned illness. She had not dared to send for the doctor, who would have immediately seen that it was a moral, not a physical malady.

She ate no supper; Tiet Nikonich politely said that he had no appetite either. Then came Raisky, who also wanted no supper, but sat silently at table pretending not to notice the glances which Tatiana Markovna directed towards him from time to time.

When Tiet Nikonich had made his bow and departed, Tatiana Markovna prepared to retire. She hardly looked at Raisky when she bade him goodnight, because her affections and her self-esteem were both too deeply wounded. A secret and serious misfortune had befallen the family, but she was left on one side like a stranger, as if she were a useless, incapable woman. Raisky said in a low voice that he must speak with her.

"Bad news?" she whispered, shivering and looking fixedly at him before she passed with him into her own room. She dropped into her old chair and pushed the lamp farther away, first covering it with a shade, so that the room was dimly lighted. Raisky began his tale as cautiously as possible, but his lips trembled and now and again his tongue refused its office, but he collected all his strength and went on, although towards the end of his story his voice was hardly audible.

Dawn had come, but throughout the long hours Tatiana Markovna had sat motionless and speechless with bowed head, giving vent now and then to a low moan. Raisky fell on his knees before her and implored her, "Go to Vera's help."

"She has sent too late for Grandmother. God will go to her help. Spare her and console her as you know how to do. She no longer has a Grandmother," she said, going towards the door.

"Grandmother, what is the matter with you?" cried Raisky barring her way.

"You have no longer a Grandmother," she said absently. "Go, go." As he did not obey, she cried angrily, "Don't come here. I will see no one. You must all of you leave me in peace." He would have replied, but she made an impatient gesture with her hand. "Go to her," she continued. "Help her as far as you can. Grandmother can do nothing: you have no longer a Grandmother."

She made another gesture with her hand, so imperious this time that he went without further parley, but he concealed himself in the yard and watched her window. Tatiana Markovna sank back in her chair and closed her eyes, and for a long time she remained there, cold and stiff as if she were a dead woman. Raisky, who had not gone to bed, and Vassilissa and Yakob as well, saw Tatiana Markovna with her head uncovered and her Turkish shawl thrown round her shoulders leave the house in the early morning and go out into the garden. It was as if a bronze figure had descended from its pedestal and had begun to walk.

She passed through the flower garden and then through the avenue to the precipice; then, striding slowly along, with her head held high and without looking round, she went down the face of the cliff, and disappeared. Concealing his presence in the trees, Raisky hurried after her, following her as she passed deeper and deeper down the precipice and until she reached the arbour, where she paused. Raisky came closer, and held his breath as he listened to Tatiana Markovna's heavy sighs, and then heard her whisper, "My sin." With her hands above her head she walked hastily on, until she came to the bank of the river and stood still. The wind wound her dress round her ankles, disordered her hair, and tugged at her shawl, but she noticed nothing. A terrible idea dawned on Raisky that she intended to drown herself. But his aunt turned back as she had come, with slow strides which left deep prints in the damp sand. Raisky breathed more freely; but when, following her track in a parallel direction, he caught sight of her face, he held his breath in horror at the agony he saw written there. She had spoken truly, their grandmother existed no longer. This was not grandmother, not Tatiana Markovna, the warm-hearted mistress of Malinovka, where the life and prosperity of the whole place depended on her, the wise and happy ruler of her little kingdom. It was as if she were not walking of her own accord but was driven on by an impulse exterior to herself, as unconscious of her movements she climbed the steep hill through the brushwood, with her shawl hanging down from her shoulders dragging its corners in the dust; her eyes, from which stony horror looked forth, were unwinking; her manner was that of a moonstruck woman. Raisky found it difficult to follow her. She paused once, leaning both hands on a tree. "My sin," she exclaimed again. "How heavy is the burden! If it is not lightened, I can bear it no longer." She began again to climb quickly up the hill, surmounting the difficulties of the steep path with unnatural strength and leaving tags of her dress and her shawl behind her in the bushes.

Overcome with amazement and horror, Raisky watched this new strange woman. He knew that only great souls conquer heavy trouble with strength like hers. They have wings like eagles to soar into the clouds and eagle eyes to gaze into the abyss. This was not his grandmother; she seemed to him to be one of those feminine figures which emerge from the family circle in the supreme moments of life under the heavy blows of fate, who bear great misfortunes majestically and are not overwhelmed. He saw in her a Jewess of the olden days, a noble woman of Jerusalem, who scorns the prophecy that her people will lose their fame and their honour to the Romans, but when the hour of fate has arrived, when the men of Jerusalem are watering its walls with their tears and beating their heads against the stones, then she takes the ornaments from her hair, puts on mourning garments, and goes on her pilgrimage wherever the hand of Jehovah leads. His mind went back to another queen of misfortune, to the Russian Marfa, the enemy of the city of Moscow, who maintained her defiance even in her chains, and, dying, directed the destiny of free Novgorod. Before his imagination there passed a procession of other suffering women, Russian Tsaritsas, who, at the wish of their husbands, had adopted the dress of the nun and had maintained their intellect and their strength of character in the cloister....

Raisky diverted his attention from these unsummoned apparitions, and looked attentively at the suffering woman before him. Tatiana Markovna's kingdom was perishing. Her house was left desolate; her dearest treasure, her pride, her pearl, had been taken from her, and she wandered lonely among the ruins. When she paused in her walk in order to collect her strength, she tottered and would have fallen but for an inner whisper which assured her she would yet reach her goal. She pulled herself together, and wandered on until evening. Half asleep, terrified by her crowding fancies, she spent the night on the sofa. At dawn she rose, and went once more to the precipice. With her head resting on the bare boards she sat for a long time on the crumbling threshold of the arbour, then she went through the fields, and was lost in the thicket on the bank of the river. By chance her steps led her to the chapel, where new terror seized her at the sight of the picture of the Christ. She fell on her knees like a wounded animal, covered her face with her shawl, and moaned, "My sin! my sin!"

Tatiana Markovna's servants had lost their heads in terror. Vassilissa and Yakob hardly stirred from the church. She intended, if her mistress recovered, to make her pilgrimage on foot to Kiev in order to venerate the miracle worker; he promised to the patron saint of the village a thick wax candle ornamented with gold. The rest of the servants hid themselves, and only looked shyly out after their mistress as she wandered distraught through the fields and the woods.

For two days already Tatiana Markovna had eaten nothing. Raisky indeed tried to restrain her from leaving the house again, but she waved him imperiously away. Then with decision he took a jug of water, came up to her, and took her hand. She looked at him as if she did not know who he was, then mechanically seized the jug in her trembling hand, and drank greedily in big mouthfuls.

"Grandmother, come home again, and do not make both yourself and us wretched," he begged. "You will kill yourself."

"It is God's will; I shall not lose my reason, for I am upheld by His strength. I must endure to the end. Do you raise me if I fall. My sin!" she murmured and went on her way. After she had gone a few steps, she turned round and he ran to her.

"If I do not survive," she began, signing to him to bow his head. Raisky knelt down, and she pressed his head to her breast, laid her hands on it and kissed him. "Accept my blessing, deliver it to Marfinka, and to her, to my poor Vera. Do you understand, to her also."

"Grandmother!" he cried, kissing her hand.

She tore her hand away, and set out to wander once more through the thicket, by the river bank, and in the fields. A devout soul obeys its own laws, thought Raisky, as he dried his tears; only a saint could suffer like this for the object of her love.

Things were not going any better with Vera. Raisky made haste to tell her of his conversation with their aunt; when she sent for him early next morning, in her anxiety to have news of Tatiana Markovna, he pointed out of the window, and Vera saw how Tatiana Markovna was drifting, urged on by the heavy hand of misfortune. For a moment she caught sight of her expression, and sank horrified on the floor, but she pulled herself up again, ran from one window to the other, and stretched her hands out towards her grandmother. Then she rushed through the wide empty hall of the old house in a wild desire to follow Tatiana Markovna, but she realised in time that it would have killed her aunt if she approached her just now. Vera was conscious now how deeply she had wounded another life so close to her own, as she saw the tragic figure of her aunt, so happy until recently and now bearing the punishment of another's sin. Raisky brought her Tatiana Markovna's blessing, and Vera fell on his neck and wept for a long time.

On the evening of the second day, Vera was found sitting in a corner of the great hall, half dressed. Raisky and the priest's wife, who had just arrived, led her almost by force into her room and laid her down on the bed. Raisky sent for the doctor, to whom he tried to explain her indisposition. The doctor prescribed a sedative, which Vera drank without being any calmer for it; she often waked in her sleep to ask after her grandmother.

"Give me something to drink ... don't say a word. Do not let anyone come to see me. Find out what Grandmother is doing." It was just the same in the night. When she awoke, she would whisper, "Grandmother doesn't come, Grandmother doesn't love me any more. She has not forgiven me."

On the third day Tatiana Markovna left the house without being observed. After two sleepless nights, Raisky had lain down and had given instructions to wake him if she left the house, but Yakob and Vassilissa had gone to early Mass, and the other servants had paid no attention. Later on Savili saw that his mistress, catching hold of the trees as she went, was making her way from the precipice to the fields. Raisky hurried after her and watched her slow return to the house; she stood still, looked round as if she were saying goodbye to the group of houses, groped with her hands, and swayed violently. Then he rushed up to her, brought her back to the house with Vassilissa's help, put her in her armchair and sent for the doctor. Vassilissa fell on her knees before her mistress.

"Little mother! Tatiana Markovna," she begged, "come back to us. Make the sign of the Cross."

Tatiana Markovna crossed herself, sighed, and signed that she could not speak and wanted something to drink. Vassilissa undressed her, wrapped her in warm sheets, rubbed her hands and feet with spirit, and then gave her some warm wine to drink. The doctor prescribed for her, but said that it was most important of all that she should not be disturbed, but should be allowed to sleep.

An incautious word that Tatiana Markovna was ill reached Vera's ears. She pushed past Natalie Ivanovna, and wanted to go over to the new house; Raisky had great difficulty in persuading her to abandon her intention as Tatiana Markovna lay in a deep sleep. In the evening Vera was worse, she had fever and was delirious, and during the night she flung herself from one side to another, calling on her grandmother in her sleep, and weeping. Raisky wanted to call the old doctor; he waited impatiently till the morning and spent his time in going from Vera to Tatiana Markovna, and from Tatiana Markovna back to Vera.

As Vera's condition had not improved next morning, Raisky went with Vassilissa into Tatiana Markovna's bedroom, where they found the old lady in the same state as she had been in the whole of the day before.

"I am afraid of going near her in case I alarm her," he whispered.

"Should I awaken the mistress?"

"She must be awakened. Vera Vassilievna is ill, and I don't know whether I ought to send for the old doctor."

The words were hardly out of his mouth when Tatiana Markovna sat up. "Is Vera ill?" she said in a low voice.

Raisky breathed more freely, for his aunt, in her present anxiety, had lost the stony expression of yesterday. She signed to him to leave the room. Half an hour later she was walking across the courtyard to the old house with trouble plainly depicted on her face, but apparently without a trace of weariness. She entered Vera's room cautiously, and when she saw the pale sleeping face, whispered to Raisky, "Send for the old doctor." She now noticed for the first time the priest's wife and her weary eyes; she embraced Natalie Ivanovna, and advised her kindly to go and get a whole day's rest.

When the doctor arrived, Tatiana Markovna gave him an ingenious explanation of Vera's indisposition. He discovered symptoms of a nervous fever and prescribed medicine; but on the whole he did not think that serious consequences need be expected if the patient could be kept quiet. Vera was half asleep when she took the medicine and towards evening fell fast asleep. Tatiana Markovna sat down at the head of the bed, watching her movements and listening to her breathing. Presently Vera woke up and asked, "Are you asleep, Natasha?"

As she received no answer she closed her eyes, but she could not go to sleep again, and the darkness seemed to her to be a dark and terrible prison. After a time she asked for something to drink. Someone handed her a cup.

"How is Grandmother?" asked Vera, opening her eyes only to close them again immediately. "Natasha, where are you? Come here. Why are you hiding?" she sighed and fell asleep again. Presently she woke again and whispered pitifully, "Grandmother doesn't come. Grandmother loves me no longer, and has not forgiven me."

"Grandmother is here. She loves you and has forgiven you."

Vera sprang from the bed and rushed up to Tatiana Markovna. "Grandmother," she cried, half fainting and hiding her head on her breast.

Tatiana Markovna put her to bed again, leaned her grey head by Vera's white suffering face, while the girl in a low voice, with sighs and tears, made her confession on her breast. Her aunt listened without speaking, and presently wiped away Vera's tears with her handkerchief, and kissed her warmly and affectionately.

"Do not waste your caresses on me, Grandmother; only do not leave me. I do not deserve your caresses. Keep your kisses for my sister."

"Your sister is no longer in need of my caresses. But I need your love. If you forsake me, Vera, I shall be a desolate old woman." Tatiana Markovna wept.

"Mother, forgive me," whispered Vera, embracing her with her whole strength. "I have not been obedient to you, and God has punished me," she went on, but Tatiana Markovna shut her mouth with a kiss.

"Do not talk like that, Vera," interrupted her grandmother, who had turned pale with horror and once more wore the aspect of the old woman who had been wandering about in the thicket by the precipice.

"Yes, I thought that my own brain and will were self-sufficing, that I was wiser than you all."

"You are wiser than I and have more learning," said Tatiana Markovna, breathing more freely. "God has given you a clear understanding, but you have not my experience."

Vera thought that she had more experience also, but she merely said, "Take me away from here. There is no Vera any longer. I want to be your Marfinka. Take me away from this old house over there to you."

The two heads rested side by side on the pillow. They lay in a close embrace and fell asleep.

CHAPTER XXX

Vera rose the next morning pale and exhausted, but without any fever. She had wept out her malady on her grandmother's breast. The doctor professed himself satisfied, and said she should stay in her room for a few days. Everything in the house went on as before. There were no festivities in honour of Vera's name day, as she had expressed a wish that there should be none. Neither Marfinka nor the Vikentevs came; a messenger was sent to Kolchino with the announcement that Vera Vassilievna was unwell and was keeping her room. Tushin sent his congratulations in a respectful note, asking for permission to come and see her. Her reply was that he should wait a little until she was better. Under the pretext of Vera's illness, callers who came from the town to present their congratulations were not admitted. Only the servants celebrated the occasion in their own way; the maids appeared in their gay dresses, and the coachmen and the lackeys got drunk.

Vera and her aunt developed a new relationship. Tatiana Markovna's consideration for Vera was by no means assumed, but her kindness did not make Vera's heart lighter. What she had expected and wished was severe judgment, a penance, perhaps exile for half a year or a year to Tatiana Markovna's distant estate, where she would gradually win back her peace of mind or at any rate forget, if it was true, as Raisky said, that time extinguishes all impressions. "I see," thought Vera, "that Grandmother suffers inexpressibly. Grief has changed her altogether; her figure is bowed and her face more deeply furrowed. Perhaps she is only sparing me now because her heart has opened itself to pity. She cannot bear to punish me, now that I am ill and repentant." Vera had lost her pride, her self-respect and her dignity, and if once these flowers are taken out of the crown which adorns the head of man, his doom is at hand. She tried to pray and could not, for she had nothing to pray for, and could only bow her head in humility.

Raisky came into much closer relation with his aunt and Vera. His naturalness and genuine affection, the friendly intimacy of his conversation, his straightforwardness, his talkative humour, and the gleaming play of his fancy were a distraction and a consolation to both of them. He often drew a laugh from them, but he tried in vain to distract them from the grief which hung like a cloud over them both and over the whole house. He himself was sad when he saw that neither his esteem nor Tatiana Markovna's kindness could give back to poor Vera her courage, her pride, her confidence and her strength of will.

Tatiana Markovna spent the nights in the old house on the divan opposite Vera's bed and watched her sleep. But it nearly always happened that they were both observing one another, so that neither of them found refreshing sleep. On the morning after a sleepless night of this kind, Tatiana Markovna sent for Tiet Nikonich. He came gladly, plainly delighted that the illness which threatened Vera Vassilievna had blown over, and bringing with him a water melon of extraordinary size and a pineapple for a present. But a glance at his old friend was enough to make him change colour. Tatiana Markovna hastily put on her fur-trimmed cloak, threw a scarf over her head, and signed to him to follow her as she led the way into the garden. They sat for two hours on Vera's bench. Then she went back to the house with bowed head, while he drove home, overcome with grief, ordered his servants to pack, sent for post horses, and drove to his estate, to which he had not been for many years.

Raisky, who had gone to see him, heard the news with astonishment. He questioned his aunt, who told him that some disturbance had broken out on Tiet Nikonich's estate. Vera was sadder than ever. Lines began to appear on her forehead, which would one day become furrows. Sometimes she would approach the table on which the unopened blue letter lay and then turn away. Where should she flee, where conceal herself from the world? When night fell, she lay down, put out the light, and stared wide-eyed in front of her. She wanted to forget, to sleep, but sleep would not come. Dark spots, blacker than night, danced before her eyes, shadows moved up and down with a wave-like motion in the glimmer of light that lay around the window. But she felt no fear, she would not have died of terror if there had risen suddenly out of the corner a ghost, a thief or a murderer; she would not have felt any fear if she had been told that her last hour was come. She looked out unceasingly into the darkness, at the waving shadows, at the flitting specks which stood out the more clearly in the blackness of the night, at the rings of changing colour which whirled shimmering round her.

Slowly and quietly the door opened. Vera propped herself on her elbow and saw a hand carrying a lamp carefully shaded. Tatiana Markovna dropped her cloak from her shoulder on to a chair and approached the bed, looking not unlike a ghost in her white dressing-gown. Vera had laid her head back on the pillow and pretended to sleep. Tatiana Markovna put the lamp on the table behind the bed-head, and sat down carefully and quietly on the divan with her head leaning on her hand. She did not take her eyes from Vera, and when Vera opened her own an hour later Tatiana Markovna was still looking fixedly at her. "Can't you sleep, Vera?"

"No."

"Why?"

"Why do you punish me in the night too, Grandmother?" asked Vera in a low tone. The two women looked at one another and both seemed to understand the speech in their eyes. "You are killing me with sympathy, Grandmother," Vera went on. "It would be better to drive me from your sight. But it is very hard for me to bear when you measure out your scorn drop by drop. Either forgive me or, if that is impossible, bury me alive. Why are you silent? What is in your mind? Your silence tortures me; it seems to say something, and yet never says it."

"It is so hard, Vera, to speak. Pray, and understand your Grandmother even when she is silent."

"I have tried to pray, and cannot. What have I to pray for, except that I should die the sooner. I shall die I know; only let it come quickly, for like this it is impossible to live."

"It is possible," said Tatiana Markovna, drawing a deep sigh.

"After ... that?"

"After *that*," replied her grandmother.

"You don't know, Grandmother," said Vera with a hopeless sigh. "You have not been a woman like me."

Tatiana Markovna stooped down to Vera, and whispered in a hardy audible voice, "A woman like you."

Vera looked at her in amazement, then let her head fall back on the pillow and said wearily, "You were never in my position. You are a saint."

"A sinner," rejoined Tatiana Markovna.

"We are all sinners, but not a sinner of that kind."

"Of that kind."

Vera seized Tatiana Markovna's dress with both hands, and pressed her face to hers. The words that came from her troubled breast sounded like hisses. "Why do you slander yourself? Is it in order to calm and help me? Grandmother, do not lie!"

"I never lie and you know it, and how should I begin to do so now. I am a sinner, and myself need forgiveness," she said, throwing herself on her knees and bowing her grey head.

"Why do you say these things to me?" said Vera, staring at the kneeling woman, and pressing her head to her breast. "Take your words back again. I have not heard them or will forget them; will regard them as the product of a dream. Do not torture yourself for my sake. Rise, Grandmother." Tatiana Markovna lay on her breast, sobbing like a child. "Why did you tell me this?" said Vera.

"It was God's wish that I should humble myself to ask you, my child, for forgiveness. If you grant me your forgiveness, Vera, I, too, can forgive you. I had hoped to keep my secret until I died, and now my sin has plunged you into ruin."

"You rescue me, Grandmother, from despair."

"And myself, Vera. God forgives, but he demands cleansing. I thought my sin was forgotten and forgiven. Because of my silence I seemed to men to be virtuous, but my virtue was a lie. God has punished my sin. Forgive me from your heart."

"Does one forgive one's Mother? You are a saint, a Mother without a peer in the whole wide world. If I had known you, as you really are, how could I have acted contrary to your will?"

"That is my second terrible sin. I was silent, and did not tell you to beware of the precipice. Your dead Mother will call me to account for my failure, I know. She comes to me in my dreams, and is now here between us. Do you also forgive me, Departed One," she cried wildly, stretching out her arms in supplication.

Vera shuddered.

"Forgive me, Vera. I ask forgiveness of you both. We will pray."

Vera tried to raise her to her feet, and Tatiana Markovna raised herself with difficulty, and sat down on the divan.

Vera bathed her temples with eau de Cologne, and gave her a sedative; then she kneeled down before her and covered her hand with kisses.

"What is hidden must be revealed," began Tatiana Markovna, when she had recovered a little. "For forty-five years only two human beings beside myself have known it, *he* and Vassilissa, and I thought the secret would die with me. And now it is made public. My God!" she cried, wildly, stretching her folded arms to the picture of the Christ. "Had I known that this stroke would ever fall on another, on *my* child, I would have confessed my sin there and then to the all world in the Cathedral square."

Vera still hesitated to believe what she heard. Was it a heroic measure, a generous invention to rescue and restore her own self-respect? But her aunt's prayers, her tears, her appeal to Vera's dead mother, no actress would have dared to use such devices, and her aunt was the soul of truth and honour.

Warm life pulsed in Vera's heart, and her heart was lightened. She felt as if life was streaming through her veins after an evil dream. Peace tapped at the door of her soul, the dark forsaken temple, which was now gaily lighted once more and a home of prayer. She felt that Tatiana Markovna and she were inseparable sisters, and she even began involuntarily to address her as "thou," as she had done Raisky when her heart responded to his kindness. As these thoughts whirled in her head, she had a sensation of lightness and freedom, like a prisoner whose fetters have been removed.

"Grandmother," she said, rising, "you have forgiven me, and you love me more than you do any of the others, more than Marfinka, that I realise. But do you know and understand my love for you? I should not have suffered as I did, but for my love for you. How long we have been strangers!"

"I will tell you all, Vera, and you must hear my confession. Judge me severely, but pardon me, and God will pardon us both."

"I will not, I ought not, I may not," cried Vera. "To what end should I hear it?"

"So that I may suffer once more, as I suffered five-and-forty years ago. You know my sin, and Boris shall know it. He may laugh at the grey hairs of old Kunigunde."

As she strode up and down, shaking her head in her fanatical seriousness, with sorrow and triumphant dignity in her face, her resemblance to the old family portrait in the gallery was very marked.

Beside her Vera felt like a small and pitiful child as she gazed timidly into her aunt's eyes; she measured her own young strength by the strength of this old woman who had ripened and remained unbroken in the long struggle of life.

"My whole life can never repay what you have done for me, Grandmother. Let this be the end of your penance, and tell me no more. If you are determined that Boris shall know, I will whisper a word about your past to him. Since I have seen your anguish, why should you suffer a longer martyrdom? I will not listen. It is not my place to sit in judgment on you. Let me hold your grey hairs sacred."

Tatiana Markovna sighed, and embraced Vera.

"As you will. Your will is like God's forgiveness to me, and I am grateful to you for sparing my grey hairs."

"Now," said Vera, "let us go across to your house, where we can both rest."

Tatiana Markovna almost carried her across to the new house, laid her on her own bed, and lay down beside her.

When Vera had fallen peacefully asleep, her aunt rose cautiously, and, in the light of the lamp, watched the marble beauty of her forehead, her closed eyes, all sculptured pure and delicate as if by a master hand, and at the expression of deep peace that lay on her face. She made the sign of the cross over Vera as she slept, touched her forehead with her lips, and sank on her knees in prayer.

"Have mercy on her!" she breathed. "If Thy anger is not yet appeased, turn it from her and strike my grey head."

Presently she lay down beside Vera, with her arm around her neck. Vera woke occasionally, opened her eyes, and closed them again. She pressed closer and closer to Tatiana Markovna as if no harm could befall her within the circle of those faithful arms.

CHAPTER XXXI

As the days went by Malinovka assumed its wonted calm. The quiet life which had been brought to a pause by the catastrophe, flowed evenly on. The peaceful atmosphere was not undisturbed by anxiety. Autumn had laid her hand on men as well as on nature. The household was thoughtful, silent, and cold; smiles, laughter, and joy had vanished like the falling leaves, and even though the worst crisis was passed, it had left behind it an atmosphere of gloom.

Tatiana Markovna ruled her little kingdom once more. Vera was busily engaged in the house, and devoted much care and taste to the choice of Marfinka's trousseau. She had determined not to avoid any task, however simple and trivial it might be, while she awaited the opportunity of some serious work that life might offer her; she recognised that with most people avoidance of the trivial and the hope of something extraordinary and unprecedented were dictated either by idleness and incompetence, or by morbid self-love and vanity.

She was paler than before, her eyes were less sparkling, and she had lost some of her vivacity of gesture; but these changes were put down by everyone to her narrow escape from nervous fever.

In fulfilment of Tatiana Markovna's insistently expressed wish, Vera had spoken to Raisky of their aunt's passion, of which Tiet Nikonich had been the object, but she said nothing of the sin. Even this partial confidence explained to Raisky the riddle, how Tatiana Markovna, who in his eyes was an old maid, could find the strength, not only to bear the brunt of Vera's misfortune, but to soothe her, and to rescue her from moral collapse and despair.

He showed in his intercourse with her, more clearly than before, a deep and affectionate esteem, and an unbounded devotion. He now no longer contradicted her, so that an end was put to the earlier semi-comic warfare he had waged against her; even in his gestures there was a certain reserve. She inspired him with the astonishment and admiration which are called forth by women of exceptional moral strength.

The servants, too, were different, even though the cloud had passed. There was no sound of quarrelling, abuse or laughter. Vassilissa found herself in an exceptionally difficult position, since, now that her mistress was restored to health, she was called on to fulfil her vow.

One morning Yakob vanished from the yard. He had taken money from the box where the cash was kept for buying the oil for the lamps kept burning in front of the ikons, which were in his charge, and had bought the promised candle, which he set up before the sacred picture in the village church at early Mass. As there was a small surplus he crossed himself piously, then betook himself to the poorer quarter of the town, where he spent his riches, and then reeled home again on his unsteady legs, displaying a slight redness on his nose and his cheeks. Tatiana Markovna happened to meet him. She immediately smelt the brandy, and asked in surprise what he had been doing. He replied that he had been to church, bowed his head devoutly, and folded his arms on his breast.

He explained to Vassilissa that he had done his duty in fulfilling his vow. She looked at him in perturbation, for in her anxieties about her mistress and in the preparations for the wedding she had not thought of her own vow. Here was Yakob who had fulfilled his and was going about with a pious jubilant air, and reminding her of her promised pilgrimage to Kiev.

"I don't feel strong enough," she complained. "I have hardly any bones in me, only flesh. Lord, have mercy on me!"

For thirty years she had been steadily putting on flesh; she lived on coffee, tea, bread, potatoes and gherkins, and often fish, even at those times of the year when meat was permitted. In her distress she went to Father Vassili, to ask him to set her doubts at rest. She had heard that kind priests were willing to release people from their vows or to allow substituted vows, where weakness of body hindered the performance of the original.

"As you agreed to go, you must go," said Father Vassili.

"I agreed because I was frightened, Little Father. I thought that Mistress would die, but she was well again in three days; why then should I make the long journey?"

"Yes, there is no short road to Kiev. If you had no inclination to go you should not have registered the vow."

"The inclination is there, but strength fails me. I suffer from want of breath even when I go to church. I am already in my seventh decade, Father. It would be different if Mistress had been three months in bed, if she had received the sacraments and the last unction, and then had been restored to health by God in answer to my prayer; then I would have gone to Kiev on my hands and knees."

"Well, what is to be done?" asked Father Vassili, smiling.

"Now I should like to promise something different. I will lay a fast on myself, never to eat another bit of meat until I die."

"Do you like meat?"

"I can't bear the sight of it, and have weaned myself from eating it."

"A difficult vow," said Father Vassili with another smile, "must be replaced by something as difficult or more difficult, but you have chosen the easiest. Isn't there anything that it would be hard for you to carry out? Think again!"

Vassilissa thought, and said there was nothing.

"Very well then, you must go to Kiev."

"I would gladly go, if I were not so stout."

"How can your vow be eased?" said Father Vassili, thinking aloud. "What do you live on?"

"On tea, coffee, mushroom soup, potatoes...."

"Do you like coffee?"

"Yes, Little Father."

"Abstain from coffee."

"That is nearly as bad," she sighed, "as going to Kiev. What am I to live on?"

"On meat."

It seemed to her that he was laughing, and indeed he did laugh when he saw her face.

"You don't like it," he said. "But make the sacrifice."

"What good does it do me, and to eat meat is not fasting, Father."

"Eat it on the days when it may be eaten. The good it will do is that you will lay on less fat. In six months you are absolved of your vow."

She went away in some distress, and began to execute the priest's instructions the next day, turning her nose sadly away from the steaming coffee that she brought her mistress in the morning.

In about ten days Marfinka returned in company with her fiancé and his mother. Vikentev and she brought their laughter, their gaiety and their merry talk into the quiet house. But within a couple of hours after their arrival they had become quiet and timid, for their gaiety had aroused a melancholy echo, as in an empty house. A mist lay on everything. Even the birds had ceased to fly to the spot where Marfinka fed them; swallows, starlings and all the feathered inhabitants of the park were gone, and not a stork was to be seen flying over the Volga. The gardener had thrown away the withered flowers; the space in front of the house, usually radiant and sweet with flowers, now showed black rings of newly-dug earth framed in yellowish grass. The branches of some of the trees had been enveloped in bast, and the trees in the park became barer with every day. The Volga grew darker and darker, as if the river were preparing for its icy winter sleep.

Nature does not create, but it does emphasise human melancholy. Marfinka asked herself what had happened to everybody in the house, as she looked doubtfully round her. Even her own pretty little room did not look so gay; it was as if Vera's nervous silence had invaded it.

Her eyes filled with tears. Why was everything so different? Why had Veroshka come over from the other house, and why did she walk no more in the field or in the thicket? Where was Tiet Nikonich?

They all looked worried, and hardly spoke to one another; they did not even tease Marfinka and her fiancé. Vera and grandmother were silent. What had happened to the whole house? It was the first trouble that Marfinka had encountered in her happy life, and she fell in unconsciously with the serious, dull tone that obtained in Malinovka.

Silence, reserve and melancholy were equally foreign to Vikentev's nature. He urged his mother to persuade Tatiana Markovna to allow Marfinka to go back with them to Kolchino until the wedding at the end of October. To his surprise permission was given easily and quickly, and the young people flew like swallows from autumn to the warmth, light, and brightness of their future home.

Raisky drove over to fetch Tiet Nikonich. He was haggard and yellow, and hardly stirred from his place, and he only gradually recovered, like a child whose toys have been restored to him, when he saw Tatiana Markovna in her usual surroundings and found himself in the middle of the picture, either at table with his serviette tucked in his collar, or in the window on the stool near her chair, with a cup of tea before him poured out by her hands.

Another member was added to the family circle at Malinovka, for Raisky brought Koslov to dinner one day, to receive the heartiest of welcomes. Tatiana Markovna had the tact not to let the poor forsaken man see that she was aware of his trouble. She greeted him with a jest.

"Why have you not been near us for so long, Leonti Ivanovich? Borushka says that I don't know how to entertain you, and that you don't like my table. Did you tell him so?"

"How should I not like it? When did I say such a thing?" he asked Raisky severely. "You are joking!" he went on, as everybody laughed, and he himself had to smile.

He had had time to find his own bearings, and had begun to realise the necessity of hiding his grief from others.

"Yes, it is a long time since I was here. My wife has gone to Moscow to visit her relations, so that I could not...."

"You ought to have come straight to us," observed Tatiana Markovna, "when it was so dull by yourself at home."

"I expect her, and am always afraid she may come when I am not at home."

"You would soon hear of her arrival, and she must pass our house. From the windows of the old house we can see who comes along the road, and we will stop her."

"It is true that the road to Moscow can be seen from there," said Koslov, looking quickly, and almost happily, at his hostess.

"Come and stay with us," she said.

"I simply will not let you go to-day," said Raisky. "I am bored by myself, and we will move over into the old house. After Marfinka's wedding I am going away, and you will be Grandmother's and Vera's first minister, friend and protector."

"Thank you. If I am not in the way...."

"How can you talk like that. You ought to be ashamed of yourself."

"Forgive me, Tatiana Markovna."

"Better eat your dinner; the soup is getting cold."

"I am hungry too," he said suddenly, seizing his spoon. He ate his soup silently, looking round him as if he were seeking the road to Moscow, and he preserved the same demeanour all through the meal.

"It is so quiet here," he said after dinner, as he looked out of the window. "There is still some green left, and the air is so fresh. Listen, Boris Pavlovich, I should like to bring the library here."

"As you like. To-morrow, as far as I am concerned. It is your possession to do as you please with."

"What should I do with it now? I will have it brought over, so that I can take care of it; else in the end that man Mark will...."

Raisky strode about the room, Vera's eyes were fixed on her needlework, and Tatiana Markovna went to the window. Shortly after this Raisky took Leonti to the old house, to show him the room that Tatiana Markovna had arranged for him. Leonti went from one window to another to see which of them commanded a view of the Moscow road.

CHAPTER XXXII

On a misty autumn day, as Vera sat at work in her room, Yakob brought her a letter written on blue paper, which had been brought by a lad who had instructions to wait for an answer. When she had recovered from the first shock at the sight of the letter, she took it, laid it on the table, and dismissed Yakob. She tried to go on with her work but her hands fell helplessly on her lap.

"When will there be an end of this torture?" she whispered, nervously. Then she took from her bureau the earlier unopened blue letter, laid it by the side of the other, and covered her face with her hands. What answer could he expect from her, she asked herself, when they had parted for ever? Surely he dare not call her once more. If so, an answer must be given, for the messenger was waiting. She opened the letters and read the earlier one:—

"Are we really not to meet again, Vera? That would be incredible. A few days ago there would have been reason in our separation, now it is a useless sacrifice, hard for both of us. We have striven obstinately with one another for a whole year for the prize of happiness; and now that the goal is attained you run away. Yet it is you who spoke of an eternal love. Is that logical?"

"Logical!" she repeated, but she collected her courage and read on.

"I am now permitted to choose another place of residence. But now I cannot leave you, for it would be dishonourable. You cannot think that I am proud of my victory, and that it is easy for me to go away. I cannot allow you to harbour such an idea. I cannot leave you, because you love me."

Once more she interrupted her reading, but resumed it with an effort—

"And because my whole being is in a fever. Let us be happy, Vera. Be convinced that our conflict, our quarrelling was nothing but the mask of passion. The mask has fallen, and we have no other ground of dispute. In reality we have long been one. You ask for a love which shall be eternal; many desire that, but it is an impossibility."

She stopped her reading to tell herself with a pitying smile that his conception of love was of a perpetual fever.

"My mistake was in openly asserting this truth, which life itself would have revealed in due course. From this time onwards, I will not assail your convictions, for it is not they, but passion, which is the essential factor in our situation. Let us enjoy our happiness in silence. I hope that you will agree to this logical solution."

Vera smiled bitterly as she continued to read.

"They would hardly allow you to go away with me, and indeed that is hardly possible. Nothing but a wild passion could lead you to do such a thing, and I do not expect it. Other convictions, indifferent to me, would be needed to impel you to this course; you would be faced with a future which fulfils neither your own wishes nor the demands of your relations, for mine is an uncertain existence, without home, hearth or possessions. But if you think you can persuade your Grandmother, we will be betrothed, and I will remain here until—for an indefinite time. A separation now would be like a bad comedy, in which the unprofitable role is yours, at which Raisky, when he hears of it, will be the first to laugh. I warn you again now, as I did before. Send your reply to the address of my landlady, Sekletaia Burdalakov."

In spite of her exhaustion after reading this epistle Vera took up the one which Yakob had just brought. It was hastily written in pencil.

"Every day I have been wandering about by the precipice, hoping to see you in answer to my earlier letter. I have only just heard by chance of your indisposition. Come, Vera. If you are ill, write two words, and I will come myself to the old house. If I receive no answer to-day, I will expect you to-morrow at five o'clock in the arbour. I must know quickly whether I should go or stay. But I do not think we shall part. In any case, I expect either you or an answer. If you are ill, I will make my way into your house."

Terrified by his threat of coming, she seized pen and paper, but her hands trembled too much to allow her to write.

"I cannot," she exclaimed. "I have no strength, I am stifled! How shall I begin, and what can I write? I have forgotten how I used to write to him, to speak to him."

She sent for Yakob, and told him to dismiss the messenger and to say that an answer would follow later. She wondered as she walked slowly back to her room, when she would find strength that day to write to him; what she should say. She could only repeat that she could not, and would not, and to-morrow she told herself, he would wait for her in the arbour, he would be wild with disappointment, and if he repeats his signals with the rifle he will come into conflict with the servants, and eventually with grandmother herself. She tried to write, but threw the pen aside; then she thought she would go to him herself, tell him all she had to say, and then leave him. As once before her hands sought in vain her mantilla, her scarf, and without knowing what she did, she sank helplessly down on the divan.

If she told her grandmother the necessary steps would be taken, but otherwise the letters would begin again. Or should she send her cousin, who was after all her natural and nearest friend and protector, to convince Mark that there was no hope for him? But she considered that he also was in the toils of passion, and that it would be hard for him to execute the mission, that he might be involved in a heated dispute, which might develop into a dangerous situation. She turned to Tushin, whom she could trust to accomplish the errand effectively without blundering. But it seemed impossible to set Tushin face to face with the rival who had robbed him of his desires. Yet she saw no alternative. No delay was possible; to-morrow would bring another letter, and then, failing an answer, Mark himself.

After brief consideration, she wrote a note to Tushin, and this time the same pen covered easily and quickly the same paper that had been so impracticable half an hour before. She asked him to come and see her the next morning.

Until now Vera had been accustomed to guard her own secrets, and to exercise an undivided rule in the world of her thoughts. If she had given her confidence to the priest's wife, it was out of charity. She had confided to her the calendar of her everyday life, its events, its emotions and impressions; she had told her of her secret meetings with Mark, but concealed from her the catastrophe, telling her simply that all was over between them. As the priest's wife was ignorant of the dénouement of the story at the foot of the precipice, she put down Vera's illness to grief at their parting.

Vera loved Marfinka as she loved Natalie Ivanovna, not as a comrade, but as a child. In more peaceful times she would again confide the details of her life to Natalie Ivanovna as before; but in a crisis she went to Tatiana Markovna, sent for Tushin, or sought help from her cousin Boris.

Now she put the letters in her pocket, found her aunt, and sat down beside her.

"What has happened, Vera? You are upset."

"Not upset, but worried. I have received letters, from *there*."

"From *there*!" repeated Tatiana Markovna, turning pale.

"The first was written some time ago, but I have only just opened it, and the second was brought to me to-day," she said, laying them both on the table.

"You want me to know what is in them?"

"Read them, Grandmother."

Tatiana Markovna put on her glasses, and tried to read them, but she found that she could not decipher them, and eventually Vera had to read them. She read in a whisper, suppressing a phrase here and there; then she crumpled them up and put them back in her pocket.

"What do you think, Veroshka?" asked Tatiana Markovna, uncertainly. "He is willing to be betrothed and to remain here. Perhaps if he is prepared to live like other people, if he loves you, and if you think you could be happy—"

"He calls betrothal a comedy, and yet suggests it. He thinks that only that is needed to make me happy. Grandmother, you know my frame of mind; so why do you ask me?"

"You came to me to ask me what you should decide," began Tatiana Markovna with some hesitation, as she did not yet understand why Vera had read her the letters. She was incensed at Mark's audacity, and feared that Vera herself might be seized with a return of her passion. For these reasons she concealed her anxiety.

"It was not for that that I came to you, Grandmother. You know that my mind has long been made up. I will have no more to do with him. And if I am to breathe freely again, and to hope to be able to live once more, it is under the condition that I hear nothing of him, that I can forget everything. He reminds me of what has happened, calls me down there, seeks to allure me with talk of happiness, will marry me.... Gracious Heaven! Understand, Grandmother," she went on, as Tatiana Markovna's anxiety could no longer be concealed, "that if by a miracle he now became the man I hoped he would be, if he now were to believe all that I believe, and loved me as I desired to love him, even if all this happened I would not turn aside from my path at his call." No song could have been sweeter to the ears of Tatiana Markovna. "I should not be happy with him," Vera continued. "I could never forget what he had been, or believe in the new Mark. I have endured more than enough to kill any passion. There is nothing left in my heart but a cold emptiness, and but for you, Grandmother, I should despair."

She wept convulsively, her head pressed against her aunt's shoulder.

"Do not recall your sufferings, Veroshka, and do not distress yourself unnecessarily. We agreed never to speak of it again."

"But for the letters I should not have spoken, for I need peace. Take me away, Grandmother, hide me, or I shall die. He calls me—to that place."

Tatiana Markovna rose and drew Vera into the armchair, while she drew herself to her full height.

"If that is so," she said, "if he thinks he can continue to annoy you, he will have to reckon with me. I will shield and protect you. Console yourself, child, you will hear no more of him."

"What will you do?" she asked in amazement, springing from her chair.

"He summons you. Well, I will go to the rendezvous in your place, and we will see if he calls you any more, or comes here, or writes to you." She strode up and down the room trembling with anger. "At what time does he go to the arbour to-morrow. At five, I think?" she asked sharply.

"Grandmother, you don't understand," said Vera gently, taking her hand. "Calm yourself. I make no accusation against him. Never forget that I alone am guilty. He does not know what has happened to me during these days, and therefore he writes. Now it is necessary to explain to him how ill and spiritless I am, and you want to fight. I don't wish that. I would have written to him, but could not; and I have not the strength to see him. I would have asked Ivan Ivanovich, but you know how he cares for me and what hopes he cherishes. To bring him into contact with a man who has destroyed those hopes is impossible."

"Impossible," agreed Tatiana Markovna. "God knows what might happen between them. You have a near relation, who knows all and loves you like a sister, Borushka."

"If that were how he loved me," thought Vera. She did not mean to reveal Raisky's passion for her, which remained her secret.

"Perhaps I will ask my cousin," she said. "Or I will collect my strength, and answer the letter myself, so as to make him understand my position and renounce all hope. But in the mean time, I must let him know so that he does not come to the arbour to wait in vain for me."

"I will do that," struck in Tatiana Markovna.

"But you will not go yourself?" asked Vera, looking direct into her eyes. "Remember that I make no complaint against him, and wish him no evil."

"Nor do I," returned her aunt, looking away. "You may be assured I will not go myself, but I will arrange it so that he does not await you in the arbour."

"Forgive me, Grandmother, for this fresh disturbance."

Tatiana Markovna sighed, and kissed her niece. Vera left the room in a calmer frame of mind, wondering what means her aunt proposed to take to prevent Mark from coming next day to the arbour.

Next day at noon Vera heard horse's hoofs at the gate. When she looked out of the window her eyes shone with pleasure for a moment, as she saw Tushin ride into the courtyard. She went to meet him.

"I saw you from the window," she said, adding, as she looked at him, "Are you well?"

"What else should I be?" he answered with embarrassment, turning his head away so that she should not notice the signs of suffering on his face. "And you?"

"I fell ill, and my illness might have taken an ill turn, but now it is over. Where is Grandmother?" she asked, turning to Vassilissa.

"The Mistress went out after tea, and took Savili with her."

Vera invited Tushin to her room, but for the moment both were embarrassed.

"Have you forgiven me?" asked Vera after a pause, without looking at him.

"Forgiven you?"

"For all you have endured. Ivan Ivanovich, you have changed. I can see that you carry a heavy heart. Your suffering and Grandmother's is a hard penance for me. But for you three, Grandmother, you, and Cousin Boris, I could not survive."

"And yet you say that you give us pain. Look at me; I think I am better already. If you would only recover your own peace of mind it will all be over and forgotten."

"I had begun to recover, and to forget. Marfinka's marriage is close at hand, there was a great deal to do and my attention was distracted, but yesterday I was violently excited, and am not quite calm now."

"What has happened? Can I serve you, Vera Vassilievna?"

"I cannot accept your service."

"Because you do not think me able...."

"Not that. You know all that has happened; read what I have received," she said, taking the letters from a box, and handing them to him.

Tushin read, and turned as pale as he had been when he arrived.

"You are right. In this matter my assistance is superfluous. You alone can...."

"I cannot, Ivan Ivanovich," she said, while he looked at her interrogatively. "I can neither write a word to him, nor see him; yet I must give him an answer. He will wait there in the arbour, or if I leave him without an answer he will come here, and I can do nothing."

"What kind of answer?"

"You ask the same question as Grandmother. Yet you have read the letter! He promises me happiness, will submit to a betrothal. Yesterday I tried to write to him to tell him that I was not happy, and should not be happy after betrothal, and to bid him farewell. But I cannot put these lines on paper, and I cannot commission anyone to deliver my answer. Grandmother flared up when she read the letter, and I fear she would not be able to restrain her feelings. So I...."

"You thought of me," said Tushin, standing up. "Tushin, you thought, would do you this service, and then you sent for me." Pride, joy, and affection shone in his eyes.

"No, Ivan Ivanovich. I sent for you, so that you might be at my side in these difficult hours. I am calmer when you are here. But I will not send you—down there, I will not inflict on you this last insult, will not set you face to face with a man, who cannot be an object of indifference to you—no, no."

Tushin was about to speak, but instead he stretched out his hands in silence, and Vera looked at him with mixed feelings of gratitude and sorrow, as she realised with what small things he was made happy.

"Insult!" he said. "It would have been hard to bear if you were to send me to him with an olive branch, to bring him up here from the depths of the precipice. But even though that dove-like errand would not suit me, I would still undertake it to give you peace, if I thought it would make you happy."

"Ivan Ivanovich," replied Vera, hardly restraining her tears, "I believe you would have done it, but I would never send you."

"But now I am not asked to go outside my rôle of Bear; to tell him what you cannot write to him, Vera Vassilievna, would give me happiness."

She reflected that this was all the happiness with which she had to reward him, and dropped her eyes. His mood changed when he noticed her thoughtful, melancholy air; his proud bearing, the gleam in his eyes, and the colour in his face disappeared. He regretted his incautious display of pleasure. It seemed to him that his delight and his mention of the word "happiness!" had been tantamount to a renewal of his profession of love and the offer of his hand, and had betrayed to her the fact that he rejoiced selfishly at her breach with Mark.

Vera guessed that he was deceiving himself once more. Her heart, her feminine instinct, her friendship, these things prevented Tushin from abandoning his hope; she gave what she could, an unconditional trust and a boundless esteem.

"Yes, Ivan Ivanovich, I see now that I have placed my hopes on you, though I did not confess it to myself, and no one would have persuaded me to ask this service of you. But since you make the generous offer yourself, I am delighted, and thank you with all my heart. No one can help me as you do, because no one else loves me as you do."

"You spoil me, Vera Vassilievna, when you talk like that. But it is true; you read my very soul."

"Will it not be hard for you to see him."

"No, I shan't faint," he smiled.

"Go at five o'clock to the arbour and tell him....." She considered a moment, then scribbled with a pencil what she had said she wished to say without adding a word. "Here is my answer," she said, handing him the open envelope. "You may add anything you think necessary, for you know all. And don't forget, Ivan Ivanovich, that I blame him for nothing, and consequently," she added, looking away, "you may leave your whip behind."

"Very well," he said between his teeth.

"Forgive me," said Vera, offering her hand. "I do not say it as a reproach. I breathe more freely now that I have told you what I wish, and what I don't wish in your interview."

"And you thought I needed the hint?"

"Pardon a sick woman," she said, and he pressed her hand again.

CHAPTER XXXIII

A little later Tatiana Markovna and Raisky returned to the house. Raisky and Tushin were embarrassed in one another's presence, and found it difficult to talk naturally about the simplest things. But at the dinner-table the real sympathy between them conquered the awkwardness of the situation. They looked one another straight in the eyes and read there a mutual confidence. After dinner Raisky went to his room, and Tushin excused himself on the ground of business. Vera's thoughts followed him.

It was nearly five o'clock when he was trying to find his direction in the thicket. Although he was no stranger there he seemed not to be able to find what he sought; he looked from side to side where the bushes grew more thickly, certain that he must be in the neighbourhood of the arbour. He stood still and looked impatiently at his watch. It was nearly five o'clock, and neither the arbour nor Mark were visible.

Suddenly he heard a rustle in the distance, and among the young pines a figure appeared and disappeared alternately. Mark was approaching, and reached the place where Tushin was standing. They looked at one another a full minute when they met.

"Where is the arbour?" said Mark at last.

"I don't exactly know in which direction...."

"In which direction? We are standing on the spot where it was still standing yesterday morning."

The arbour had vanished to allow of the literal carrying out of Tatiana Markovna's promise that Mark should not wait for Vera in the arbour. An hour after her conversation with Vera she had descended the precipice, accompanied by Savili and five peasants with axes, and within two hours the arbour had been carried away, the peasant women and children helping to remove beams and boards. Next day the site of the arbour was levelled, covered with turf, and planted with young fir trees. "If I had had the arbour removed before," thought Tatiana Markovna regretfully, "the rascal would have noticed it, and would not have written her the letters."

The situation was clear enough to the "rascal" now. "That is the old lady's handiwork," he thought, when he saw the young fir trees. "Her Vera, like a well-bred young woman, has told her the whole story." He nodded to Tushin, and was turning away, when he saw his rival's eyes were fixed on him.

"Are you out for a stroll?" said Mark. "Why do you look at me in that extraordinary fashion? I suppose you are visiting at Malinovka."

Tushin replied drily and politely that he was a visitor at the house, and had come down especially to see Mark.

"To see me?" asked Mark quickly with a look of inquiry. Has he heard too? he wondered. He remembered that Tushin admired Vera and wondered whether the "Forest Othello" was meditating tragedy and murder on the green.

"I have a commission for you," said Tushin, handing him the letter.

Without betraying any sense of discomfort, or any sign of pain or rage Mark read it rapidly.

"Do you know the whole story?" he asked.

"Allow me to leave that question unanswered, and instead to ask you whether you have any answer to give," said Tushin.

Mark shook his head.

"I take it for granted, that, in accordance with her wish, you will leave her in peace in the future, that you will not remind her of your existence in any way, will not write to her, nor visit this place...."

"What business is it of yours?" asked Mark. "Are you her declared lover, that you make these demands?"

"One does not need to be her fiancé to execute a commission; it is sufficient to be a friend."

"And if I do write, or do come here, what then?" cried Mark angrily.

"I cannot say how Vera Vassilievna would take it, but if she gives me another commission, I will undertake it," said Tushin.

"You are an obedient friend," observed Mark maliciously.

"Yes, I am her friend," replied Tushin seriously. "I thought her wish would be law to you too. She is just beginning to recover from a serious illness."

"What is the matter with her?" said Mark, gently for him. As he received no answer he went on, "Excuse my outburst, but you see my agitation."

"Calmness is desirable for you too. Is there any answer to this letter?"

"I do not need your assistance for that. I will write."

"She will not receive your letter. Her state of health necessitates quiet, which she cannot have if you force yourself on her. I tell you what was told me, and what I have seen for myself."

"Do you wish her well?" asked Mark.

"I do."

"You see that she loves me. She has told you so."

"She has not said so to me; indeed she never spoke of love. She gave me the letter I handed you, and asked me to make it clear that she did not wish, and was not indeed in a condition to see you or to receive any letter from you."

"How ridiculous to make herself and other people suffer. If you are her friend you can relieve her of her misery, her illness, and her collapse of strength. The old lady has broken down the arbour, but she has not destroyed passion, and passion will break Vera. You say yourself she is ill."

"I did not say that passion was the cause of her illness."

"What can have made her ill?" asked Mark.

"Your letters. You expect her in the arbour, and threaten to come to her yourself. That she cannot endure, and has asked me to tell you so."

"She says that, but in reality...."

"She always speaks the truth."

"Why did she give you this commission?" Receiving no answer, Mark continued: "You have her confidence, and can therefore tell her how strange it is to refuse happiness. Advise her to put an end to the wretched situation, to renounce her Grandmother's morality, and then I propose...."

"If you understood Vera Vassilievna, you would know that hers is one of those natures that declines explanations and advice."

"You execute your errands most brilliantly and diplomatically," said Mark angrily.

Tushin looked at him without replying, and his calm silence enraged Mark. He saw in the disappearance of the arbour and the appearance on the scene of Tushin as a mediator, the certain end of his hopes. Vera's hesitation was over, and she was now firmly determined on separation.

He was enraged by his consciousness that Vera's illness was really not the result of her infatuation for him, which she would not have confessed to her aunt, much less to Tushin. Mark knew her obstinacy, which resisted even the flame of passion, and on that very account he had, almost in despair, resigned himself to submit to a formal betrothal, and had communicated his decision to her, had consented to remain in the town indefinitely, that is, so long as the tie between them held. Convinced of the truth of his conception of love, he foresaw that in the course of time passion would grow cool and disappear, that they would not for ever be held by it, and then.... Then, he was convinced, Vera would herself recognise the situation, and acquiesce in the consequences.

And now his offer had become superfluous; no one was prepared to accept it, and he was simply to be dismissed.

"I do not know what to do," he said proudly. "I cannot find any answer to your diplomatic mission. Naturally, I shall not again visit the arbour, as it has ceased to exist."

"And you will write no more letters either," added Tushin, "as they would not in any case reach her. Neither will you come to the house, where you would not be admitted."

"Are you her guardian?"

"That would depend on Vera Vassilievna's wishes. There is a mistress of the house who commands her servants. I take it that you accept the facts."

"The devil knows," cried Mark, "how ridiculous all this is. Mankind have forged chains for themselves, and make martyrs of themselves." Although he still justified himself in making no reply, he felt that his position was untenable. "I am leaving the place shortly," he said, "in about a week's time. Can I not see Vera—Vassilievna for a minute?"

"That cannot be arranged, because she is ill."

"Is any pressure being put upon her?"

"She requires only one medicine—not to be reminded of you."

"I do not place entire confidence in you, because you do not appear to me to be an indifferent party."

Tushin did not answer in the same tone. He understood Mark's feeling of bitter disillusion, and made another attempt at conciliation. "If you do not trust me," he said, "you hold the evidence in your hand."

"A dismissal. Yes, but that proves nothing. Passion is a sea, where storm reigns to-day, and tomorrow dead calm. Perhaps she already repents having sent this."

"I think not. She takes counsel with herself before acting. It is plain from your last words that you don't understand Vera Vassilievna. You will, of course, act in accordance with her wishes. I will not insist any more on an answer."

"There is no answer to give. I am going away."

"That is an answer."

"It is not she who needs an answer, but you, the romantic Raisky, and the old lady."

"Why not include the whole town! But I will take on myself to assure Vera Vassilievna that your answer will be literally carried out. Farewell."

"Farewell ... Sir Knight."

Tushin frowned slightly, touched his cap, and was gone.

Mark's face was very pale. He recognised bitterly that he was beaten, that his romance ended here at the foot of the precipice, which he must leave without once turning round, with no pity, no word of farewell to speed him; he was bidden to go as if he were a contemptible enemy. Why had all this come about? He was not conscious of any fault. Why should he part from her like this. She could not pretend that he had been the cause of what old-fashioned people would call her "fall." He had gone so far as to belie his own convictions, to neglect his mission, and was even prepared to contemplate marriage. Yet he received a laconic note instead of a friendly letter, a go-between instead of herself. It was as if he had been struck with a knife, and a cold shiver ran through his body. It was not the old lady who had invented these measures, for Vera did not allow others to dictate to her. It must have been she herself. What had he done, and why should she act with such severity? He went slowly away. When he reached the fence he swung himself on to the top and sat there, asking himself again where his fault lay. He remembered that at their last meeting he had fairly warned her. He had said in effect: "Remember that I have warned you. If you stretch out your hand to me you are mine, and the responsibility for the consequences rests with you; I am innocent." That was surely logical, he thought. Suddenly he sprang down on to the road, and went without looking back. He remembered how at this very spot he had prepared to leave her. But he heard her nervous, despairing cry of farewell, and had then looked round and rushed to her. As he answered these questions his blood hammered in his veins. He strode up the hill. The knife had done its work; it bored deeper and deeper. Memory pitilessly revived a series of fleeting pictures. The inner voice told him that he had not acted honourably, and spared her when her strength had failed.

She used to call you a "Wolf" in jest, but the name will be no jest in her memory, for you joined to the fierceness of a wolf a fox's cunning and the malice of a yapping dog; there was nothing human about you. She took with her from the depths of the precipice nothing but a bitter memory and a lifelong sorrow. How could she be so blind as to be led astray, to let herself be dazzled, to forget herself? You may triumph, for she will never forget you.

He understood now the laconic note, her illness and the appearance of Tushin instead of herself at the foot of the precipice.

Leonti told Raisky that Mark had informed him that he was going to spend some time with his old aunt in the government of Novgorod; he intended to enter the army once more as an ensign, in the hope of being sent to the Caucasus.

CHAPTER XXXIV

Raisky and Tushin had been talking all the evening, and for the first time in their lives observed one another closely, with the result that both felt a desire for a closer acquaintance. Tushin asked Raisky to be his guest for a week, to have a look at the forest, the steam-saw, and the timber industry. Raisky accepted, and the next day they crossed the river together in Tushin's boat.

Vera's name did not cross their lips. Each was conscious that the other knew his secret. Raisky in any case had learned of Tushin's offer, of his behaviour on that occasion, and of his part in the whole drama from Vera herself. His jealous prejudices had instantly vanished, and he felt nothing but esteem and sympathy for Tushin. As he studied the personality of Vera's friend, as his fancy did him its usual service of putting the object, not in itself a romantic one, in the best light, he admired Tushin's simplicity and frankness.

After a week spent at "Smoke," after seeing him at home, in the factory, in field and forest, after talking through the night with him by the flickering light of the fire, he understood how Vera's eye and heart should have recognised the simple completeness of the man and placed Tushin side by side with Tatiana Markovna and her sister in her affections. Raisky himself was attracted to this simple, gentle and yet strong personality, and would like to have stayed longer at "Smoke," but Tatiana Markovna wrote asking him to return without delay as his presence was necessary at Malinovka.

Tushin offered to drive with him, for company's sake, as he said; in reality he wanted to know why Tatiana Markovna had sent for Raisky, whether there was a new turn in Vera's affairs, or any service to be rendered her. He remembered uncomfortably his meeting with Mark, and how unwillingly he had said that he was going away. Tushin wondered anxiously whether he had kept his promise, whether he was annoying Vera in any way.

When Raisky reached Malinovka he hurried straight to Vera. While his impressions were still fresh, he drew in vivid colours a full length portrait of Tushin, describing his surroundings and his activities with sympathetic appreciation.

Vera sighed, perhaps for sorrow that she did not love Tushin more and differently.

Raisky would have gone on talking about his visit if he had not had a message from his aunt that she would like to see him immediately. He asked Vera if she knew why he had been sent for.

"I know something is wrong, but she has not told me, and I don't like to ask. Indeed, I fear...."

She broke off, and at that moment Tushin sent in word to know if she would receive him. She assented.

When Raisky entered her room, Tatiana Markovna dismissed Pashutka and locked the door. She looked worried and old, and her appearance terrified Raisky.

"Has something disagreeable happened?" he asked, sitting down opposite her.

"What is done is done," she said sadly.

"I am sitting on needles, Grandmother. Tell me quickly."

"That old thief Tychkov has had his revenge on us both. He wormed out a tale about me from a crazy old woman, but this has had no special results, for people are indifferent to the past, and in any case I stand with one foot in the grave, and don't care about myself, but Vera—"

"What about Vera, Grandmother?"

"Her secret has ceased to be a secret. Rumours are going about the town. At first I did not understand why on Sunday at church, the Vice-governor's wife asked me twice after Vera's health, and why two other ladies listened curiously for my answers. I looked round, and read on every face the same question, what was the matter with Vera? I said she had been ill, but was better again. Then there were further questions, and I extricated myself with difficulty. The real misfortune, thank God, is concealed. I learned from Tiet Nikonich yesterday, that the gossip is on the wrong track. Ivan Ivanovich is suspected. Do you remember that on Marfinka's birthday he said not a word, but sat there like a mute, until Vera came in, when he suddenly woke up. The guests, of course, noticed it. In any case it has long been no secret that he loves Vera, and he has no arts of concealment. People said that they vanished into the garden, that Vera went later to the old house and Tushin drove away. Do you know what he came for?"

Raisky nodded.

"Vera and Tushin are coupled together in everybody's mouth."

"You said that Tychkov had dragged me in too."

"Paulina Karpovna did that. She went out to find you in the evening when you were out late with Vera. You said something to her, apparently in jest, which she understood in her own way, and she has involved you. They say she had alienated you from Vera, with whom you were supposed to be in love, and she keeps on repeating that she dragged you from the precipice. What had you to do with her, and what is the tale about Vera? Perhaps you had been in her confidence for a long time, and you both kept silence with me—this is what your freedom has brought you to." She sighed.

"That silly old bird got off too easily," said Raisky, clenching his fists. "To-morrow I will have it out with her."

"You have found someone whom you can call to account. What is the use of reproaching her? She is ridiculous, and no one cares what she says. But the old chatterbox Tychkov has established that on Marfinka's birthday, Vera and Tushin had a long conversation in the avenue, that the day before she stayed out far into the night, and was subsequently ill, and he has put his own construction on Paulina Karpovna's tale. He is trumpeting it in the town that it was not with you, but with Tushin that she was walking about at night. Then to crown all a drunken old woman made revelations about me. Tychkov has extracted everything...."

Tatiana's eyes dropped, and her face flushed for a moment.

"That is another story," said Raisky seriously, striding up and down the room. "The lesson you gave him was not sufficient. I will try a repetition of it."

"What do you mean? God forbid that you should. You will try to prove that the tale is not true, which is not difficult; it is only necessary to know where Ivan Ivanovich spent the evening before Marfinka's birthday. Supposing he was in his forest, then people will ask who was with Vera in the park. The Kritzki woman saw you at the top of the precipice, and Vera was—"

"What is to be done?" asked Raisky in fear for Vera.

"God's judgments are put in the mouths of men," whispered Tatiana Markovna sadly, "and they must not be despised. We must humble ourselves, and our cup is apparently not yet full."

Conscious of the difficulties of their position, both were silent. Vera's retired way of life, Tushin's devotion to her, her independence of her aunt's authority, were familiar and accustomed facts. But Raisky's attentions to her wrapped this simple situation in an uncertainty, which Paulina Karpovna had noticed, and had naturally not kept to herself. It was not only Tatiana

Markovna who had marked out Tushin as Vera's probable husband. The town expected two great events, Marfinka's marriage with Vikentev which was about to take place, and, in no distant future, Tushin's marriage with Vera. Then suddenly there were these incomprehensible, unexpected happenings. On her sister's birthday Vera appeared among the guests only for a moment, hardly spoke to anyone, then vanished into the garden with Tushin, and afterwards to the old house, while Tushin left without even saying good-bye to his hostess.

Paulina Markovna had related how Raisky, on the eve of the family festival, had gone out for a walk with Vera.

Following on this Vera had fallen ill, then Tatiana Markovna, no one was admitted to the house, Raisky wandered about like one possessed, and the doctors gave no definite report.

There was no word or sign of a wedding. Why had Tushin not made his offer, and if he made it, why was it not accepted? People surmised that Raisky had entrapped Vera; if so, why did he not marry her. They were determined to know who was wrong and who was right, and to give judgment accordingly. Both Tatiana Markovna and Raisky were conscious of all this, and feared the verdict for Vera's sake.

"Grandmother," said Raisky at last, "you must tell Ivan Ivanovich this yourself, and be guided by what he says. I know his character now, and am confident that he will decide on the right course. He loves Vera, and cares more for what happens to her than to himself. He came over the Volga with me because your letter to me made him anxious about Vera. When you have talked this over with him, I will go to Paulina Karpovna, and perhaps see Tychkov as well."

"I am determined you shall not meet Tychkov."

"I must," replied Raisky.

"I will not have it, Boris. No good can come of it. I will follow your advice and speak to Ivan Ivanovich; then we will see whether you need go to Paulina Karpovna. Ask Ivan Ivanovich to come here, but say not a word to Vera. She has heard nothing so far, and God grant that she never will."

Raisky went to Vera, and his place with Tatiana Markovna was taken by Tushin.

Tatiana Markovna could not disguise her agitation when Ivan Ivanovich entered her room. He made his bow in silence.

"How did you find Vera?" she asked, after a pause.

"She seemed to be well and calm."

"God grant that she is! But how much trouble all this has caused you," she added in a low voice, trying to avoid his eyes.

"What does that matter, if Vera Vassilievna has peace."

"She was beginning to recover, and I too felt happier, so long as our distress was concealed." Tushin started as if he had been shot. "Ivan Ivanovich," continued Tatiana Markovna, "there is all sorts of gossip in the town. Borushka and I in a moment of anger tore the mask from that hypocrite Tychkov—you have no doubt heard the story. Such an outburst ill fitted my years, but he had been blowing his own trumpet so abominably that it was unendurable. Now he, in his turn, is tearing the mask from us."

"From you? I don't understand."

"When he gossipped about me, no one took any heed, for I am already counted with my fathers. But with Vera it is different, and they have dragged your name into the affair."

"Mine? with Vera Vassilievna's? Please tell me what the talk is."

When Tatiana Markovna had told the story he asked what she wished him to do.

"You must clear yourself," she said. "You have been beyond reproach all your life, and must be again. As soon as Marfinka's wedding is over I shall settle on my estate at Novosselovo for good. You should make haste to inform Tychkov that you were not in the town on the day before Marfinka's fête-day, and consequently could not have been at the precipice."

"It ought to be done differently."

"Do just as you like, Ivan Ivanovich. But what else can you say?"

"I would rather not meet Tychkov. He may have heard through others that I certainly was in the town; I was spending a couple of days with a friend. I shall spread it about that I did visit the precipice on that evening with Vera Vassilievna, although that is not the case. I might add that I had offered her my hand and had met with a refusal, by which you, Tatiana Markovna, who gave me your approval, were aggrieved; that Vera Vassilievna felt bitterly the breach of our friendship. One might even speak of a distant hope ... of a promise...."

"People will not be kept quiet by that, for a promise cannot always remain a promise."

"It will be forgotten, Tatiana Markovna, especially if you, as you say, leave the neighbourhood. If it is not forgotten, and you and Vera

Vassilievna are further disturbed, it is still possible," he added in a low tone, "to accept my proposal."

"Ivan Ivanovich," said Tatiana Markovna reproachfully, "do you think Vera and I are capable of such a thing? Are we to avail ourselves of your past affection and your generosity merely to still malicious gossip, to stifle talk for which there is a basis of truth. Neither you nor Vera would find happiness in that way."

"There is no question of generosity, Tatiana Markovna. If a forest stands in one's way, it must be hewn down; bold men see no barrier in the sea, and hew their way through the rock itself. Here there is no obstacle of forest, sea, or rock. I am bridging the precipice, and my feet will not tremble when I cross the bridge. Give me Vera Vassilievna. No devil should disturb my happiness or her peace of mind, if she lived to be a hundred. She will be my Tsaritsa, and in the peace that reigns in my forest will forget all that now oppresses her. You don't yet understand me!"

"I do," whispered Tatiana Markovna tearfully, "but the decision does not lie with me."

He passed his hands across his eyes and through his thick hair, then seized her hands.

"Forgive me, I forgot the important point. It is not mountain, forest or sea, but an insurmountable obstacle that confronts me—Vera Vassilievna is not willing. She looks forward to a happier future than I can offer her. You sent for me to let me know of the gossip there is going about, in the view that it must be painful, didn't you? Do not let it disturb either yourself or Vera Vassilievna, but take her away, so that no word of it penetrates to her ears. In the meantime I will spread in the town the account we have discussed. That man," he could not bring Mark's name over his lips, "leaves the town to-morrow or the day after, and all will be forgotten. As for me, since it is decided that Vera Vassilievna is not to be my wife, it does not matter whether I die or live."

Tatiana Markovna, pale and trembling, interrupted him.

"She will be your wife," she said, "when she has learnt to forget. I understand for the first time how you love Vera."

"Do not lure me on with false hopes, for I am not a boy. Who can give me security that Vera Vassilievna will ever...."

"I give you that security."

His eyes shone with gratitude as he took her hand. Tatiana Markovna felt that she had gone too far, and had promised more than she could perform. She withdrew her hand, and said soothingly: "She is still very unhappy, and would not understand at present. First of all she must be left alone."

"I will wait and hope," he said in a low tone. "If only I might, like Vikentev, call you Grandmother."

She signed to him to leave her. When he had gone she dropped on to her chair, and covered her face with her handkerchief.

CHAPTER XXXV

Raisky had written to Paulina Karpovna asking her if he might call the next day about one o'clock. Her answer ran: "*Charmée, j'attends....*" and so on.

He found her in her boudoir in a stifling atmosphere of burning incense, with curtains drawn to produce a mysterious twilight. She wore a white muslin frock with wide lace sleeves, with a yellow dahlia at her breast. Near the divan was placed a sumptuously spread table with covers for two.

Raisky explained that he had come to make a farewell call.

"A farewell call! I won't hear of such a thing. You are joking, it is a bad joke! No, no! Smile and take back the hated word," she protested, slipping her arm in his and leading him to the table. "Don't think of going away. *Vive l'amour et la joie.*"

She invited him with a coquettish gesture to be seated, and hung a table napkin over his coat, as she might to a child. He devoted an excellent morning appetite to the food before him. She poured out champagne for him and watched him with tender admiration.

After a longish pause when she had filled his glass for the third or fourth time she said: "Well, what have you to say about it?" Then as Raisky looked at her in amazement she continued: "I see, I see! Take off the mask, and have done with concealment."

"Ah!" sighed Raisky, putting his lips to his glass. They drank to one another's health.

"Do you remember that night," she murmured, "the night of love as you called it."

"How should it fade from my memory," he whispered darkly. "That night was the decisive hour."

"I knew it. A mere girl could not hold you ... *une nullité, cette pauvre petite fille, qui n'a que sa figure* ... shy, inexperienced, devoid of elegance."

"She could not. I have torn myself free."

"And have found what you have long been seeking, have you not? What happened in the park to excite you so?"

After a little fencing, Raisky proceeded with his story. "When I thought my happiness was within my grasp, I heard...."

"Tushin was there?" whispered Paulina Karpovna, holding her breath.

He nodded silently, and raised his glass once more.

"*Dites tout*," she said with a malicious smile.

"She was walking alone, lost in thought," he said in a confidential tone, while Paulina Karpovna played with her watch chain, and listened with strained attention. "I was at her heels, determined to have an answer from her. She took one or two steps down the face of the precipice, when someone suddenly came towards her."

"He?"

"He."

"What did he do?"

"'Good evening, Vera Vassilievna,' he said. 'How do you do?' She shuddered."

"Hypocrisy!"

"Not at all. I hid myself and listened. 'What are you doing here?' she said. 'I am spending two days in town,' he said, 'to be present at your sister's fête, and I have chosen that day…. Decide, Vera Vassilievna, whether I am to love or not.'"

"*Où le sentiment va-t-il se nicher?*" exclaimed Paulina Karpovna. "Even in that clod."

"'Ivan Ivanovich!' pleaded Vera," continued Raisky. "He interrupted her with 'Vera Vassilievna, decide whether to-morrow I should ask Tatiana Markovna for your hand, or throw myself into the Volga!'"

"Those were his words?"

"His very words."

"*Mais, il est ridicule.* What did she do? She moaned, cried yes and no?"

"She answered, 'No, Ivan Ivanovich, give me time to consider whether I can respond with the same deep affection that you feel for me. Give me six months, a year, and then I will answer "yes" or "no."' Your room is so hot, Paulina Karpovna, could we have a little air?"

Raisky thought he had invented enough, and glanced up at his hostess, who wore an expression of disappointment.

"*C'est tout?*" she asked.

"*Oui*," he said. "In any case Tushin did not abandon hope. On the next day, Marfinka's birthday, he appeared again to hear her last word. From the precipice he went through the park, and she accompanied him. It seems that next day his hopes revived. Mine are for ever gone."

"And that is all? People have been spreading God knows what tales about your cousin—and you. They have not even spared that saint Tatiana Markovna with their poisonous tongues. That unendurable Tychkov!"

Raisky pricked up his ears. "They talk about Grandmother?" he asked waveringly.

He remembered the hint Vera had given him of Tatiana Markovna's love story, and he had heard something from Vassilissa, but what woman has not her romance? They must have dug up some lie or some gossip out of the dust of forty years. He must know what it was in order to stop Tychkov's mouth.

"What do they say about Grandmother?" he asked in a low, intimate voice. "*Ah, c'est degôutant.* No one believes it, and everybody is jeering at Tychkov for having debased himself to interrogate a drink-maddened old beggar-woman. I will not repeat it."

"If you please," he whispered tenderly.

"You wish to know?" she whispered, bending towards him. "Then you shall hear everything. This woman, who stands regularly in the porch of the Church of the Ascension, has been saying that Tiet Nikonich loved Tatiana Markovna, and she him."

"I know that," he interrupted impatiently. "That is no crime."

"And she was sought in marriage by the late Count Sergei Ivanovich—"

"I have heard that, too. She did not agree, and the Count married somebody else, but she was forbidden to marry Tiet Nikonich. I have been told all that by Vassilissa. What did the drunken woman say?"

"The Count is said to have surprised a rendezvous between Tatiana Markovna and Tiet Nikonich, and such a rendezvous.

"No, no!" she cried, shaking with laughter. "Tatiana Markovna! Who would believe such a thing?"

Raisky listened seriously, and surmises flitted across his mind.

"The Count gave Tiet Nikonich a box on the ears."

"That is a lie," cried Raisky, jumping up. "Tiet Nikonich would not have endured it."

"A lie naturally—he did not endure it. He seized a garden knife that he found among the flowers, struck the Count to the ground, seized him by the throat, and would have killed him."

Raisky's face changed. "Well?" he urged.

"Tatiana Markovna restrained his hand. 'You are' she said, 'a nobleman, not a bandit, your weapon is a sword.' She succeeded in separating them, and a duel was not possible, for it would have compromised her. The opponents gave their word; the Count to keep silence over what had happened, and Tiet Nikonich not to marry Tatiana Markovna. That is why she remains unmarried. Is it not a shame to spread such calumnies?"

Raisky could no longer contain his agitation, but he said, "You see it is a lie. Who could possibly have seen and heard what passed."

"The gardener, who was asleep in a corner, is said to have witnessed the whole scene. He was a serf, and fear ensured his silence, but he told his wife, the drunken widow who is now chattering about it. Of course it is nonsense, incredible nonsense. I am the first to cry that it is a lie, a lie. Our respected and saintly Tatiana Markovna!" Paulina Karpovna burst out laughing, but checked herself when she looked at Raisky.

"What is the matter? *Allons donc, oubliez tout. Vive la joie!* Do not frown. We will send for more wine," she said, looking at him with her ridiculous, languishing air.

"No, no, I am afraid—" He broke off, fearing to betray himself, and concluded lamely, "It would not agree with me—I am not accustomed to wine."

He rose from his seat, and his hostess followed his example.

"Good-bye, for ever," he said.

"No, no," she cried.

"I must escape from these dangerous places, from your precipices and abysses. Farewell, farewell!"

He picked up his hat, and hurried away. Paulina Karpovna stood as if turned to stone, then rang the bell, and called for her carriage and for her maid to dress her, saying she had calls to pay.

Raisky perceived that there was truth in the drunken woman's story, and that he held in his hand the key to his aunt's past. He realised now how she had grown to be the woman she was, and where she had won her strength, her practical wisdom, her knowledge of life and of men's hearts; he understood why she had won Vera's confidence, and had been able to calm her niece in spite of her own distress. Perhaps Vera, too, knew the story. While he had been manoeuvring to give another turn to the gossip about Vera's relations to himself and Tushin, he had lighted by chance on a forgotten but vivid page of his family history, on another drama no less dangerous to those who took part in it, and found that his whole soul was moved by this record of what had happened forty years ago.

"Borushka!" cried Tatiana Markovna in horror, when he entered her room. "What has come to you, my friend? You have been drinking!" She looked keenly at him for a long minute, then turned away when she read in his tell-tale face that he, too, had heard the talk about her past self.

CHAPTER XXXVI

Against universal expectation, Marfinka's wedding was a quiet one, no one being invited except a few neighbouring landowners and the important personages in the town, about fifty guests in all. The young people were married in the village church on Sunday, after morning service, and afterwards in the hall, which had been transformed for the occasion, a formal breakfast was served without any of the gaiety and excitement usual to such occasions. The servants were most disappointed, for their mistress had taken precautions against their drinking to excess, which made the whole affair seem dull to them.

Marfinka's trousseau and her contributions to the household had already been taken across the Volga, the process having occupied a full week. She herself shone with the charm of a rose grown to perfection; in her face a new emotion was visible which found expression now in a musing smile, now in a stray tear. Her face was shadowed with the consciousness of a new life, of a far stretching future with unknown duties, a new dignity and a new happiness. Vikentev wore an expression of modesty, almost of timidity, and was visibly affected.

Raisky looked at the pretty bride with the emotions of a brother, but he had an impulse of terror when he noticed in her sheaf of orange blossom some faded blooms.

"They are from the bouquet that Vera gave me for my birthday," she explained naively.

Raisky pretended that withered flowers were a bad omen, and helped her to pick them out.

When the time for their departure came, the bride had to be literally dragged sobbing from her aunt's breast, but her tears were tears of joy. Tatiana Markovna was pale, only maintaining her self-restraint with difficulty, and it was plain that she could only just stand as she looked out on the Volga after her departing child. Once at home again, she gave way to her tears. She knew that she possessed the almost undivided love of her other child, the passionate Vera, whose character had been ripened by bitter experience.

Tushin stayed with a friend in the town for the wedding. Next day he came to Tatiana Markovna, accompanied by an architect, and they spent nearly a week over plans, going over the two houses, the gardens and the servants' quarters, making sketches and talking of radical alterations in the spring. Everything of value—furniture, pictures, even the parquet flooring—had been taken out of the old house and stored, partly in the new house, partly in outhouses and on the ground.

Tatiana Markovna and Vera intended to go to Novosselovo, and later on to visit the Vikentevs; for the summer they were invited to be the guests of Anna Ivanovna, Tushin's sister, at "Smoke." Tatiana Markovna had given no definite answer to the suggestion, saying that it must be "as God wills." In any case Tushin was making the necessary arrangements with the architect, and intended to make extensive alterations in his house for the reception of the honoured visitors.

Raisky stayed in his rooms in the new house, but Leonti had returned to his own home for the time being, to return to Malinovka after the departure of Tatiana Markovna and Vera. He, too, had been invited by Tushin to "Smoke," but Leonti had answered with a sigh, "Later in the winter. Just now I am expecting...." and had broken off to look out on to the road from Moscow. He was in fact expecting a letter from his wife in answer to one he had just written. Not long before, Juliana Andreevna had written to their housekeeper and had asked her to send her winter cloak. She indicated the address, but said not a word about her husband. Leonti dispatched the cloak himself with a glowing letter in which he asked her to come, and spoke of his love and friendship.

The poor man received no reply. Gradually he resumed his teaching, though he still betrayed his melancholy now and again during the lessons, and was apt to be absentminded and unconscious of the behaviour of his scholars, who took pitiless advantage of his helplessness.

Tushin had offered to look after Malinovka during Tatiana Markovna's absence. He called it his winter quarters and made a point of crossing the Volga every week to give an eye to the house, the farm yard and the servants, of whom only Vassilissa, Egor, the cook and the coachman accompanied their mistress to Novosselovo. Yakob and Savili were put especially at Tushin's disposition.

Raisky proposed to leave a week after the wedding.

Tiet Nikonich was in the most melancholy plight of all. At any other time he would have followed Tatiana Markovna to the end of the world, but after the outbreak of gossip it would have been unsuitable to follow her for the moment, because it might have given colour to the talk about them which was half-believed and already partly forgotten. Tatiana Markovna, however, said he might come at Christmas, and by that time perhaps circumstances would permit him to stay. In the meantime, he accepted Tushin's invitation to be his guest at "Smoke."

The gossip about Vera had given ground to the universal expectation of her marriage with Tushin. Tatiana Markovna hoped that time would heal all her wounds, but she recognised that Vera's case stood in a category by itself, and that ordinary rules did not apply to it. No rumour reached Vera, who continued to see in Tushin the friend of long standing, who was all the dearer to her since he had stretched out to her his helping hand.

In the last days before his departure Raisky had gone through and sorted his sketches and notebooks, and had selected from his novel those pages which bore reference to Vera. In the last night that he spent under the roof of home he decided to begin his plot then and there, and sat down to his writing-table. He determined that one chapter at least should be written. "When my passion is past," he told himself, "when I no longer stand in the presence of these men, with their comedy and their tragedy, the picture will be clearer and in perspective. I already see the splendid form emerge fresh from the hand of its creator, I see my statue, whose majesty is undefiled by the common and the mean." He rose, walked up and down the room, and thought over the first chapter. After half an hour's meditation he sat down and rested his head on his hands. Weariness invaded him, and as it was uncomfortable to doze in a sitting posture he lay down on the sofa. Very soon he fell asleep, and there was a sound of regular breathing.

When he woke it was beginning to get light. He sprang up hastily and looked round in astonishment, as if he had seen something new and unexpected in his dreams.

"In my dream, even, I saw a statue," he said to himself. "What does it mean? Is it an omen?"

He went to the table, read the introduction he had written, and sighed. "What use do I make of my powers?" he cried. "Another year is gone." He angrily thrust the manuscript aside to look for a letter he had received a month ago from the sculptor Kirilov, and sat down at the table to answer it.

"In my sound and clear mind, dear Kirilov, I hasten to give you the first intimation of the new and unexpected perspective of my art and my activity. I write in answer to the letter in which you tell me that you are going to visit Italy and Rome. I am coming to St. Petersburg; so for God's sake wait for me and I will travel with you. Take me with you, and have pity on a blind, insane individual, who has only to-day had his eyes opened to his real calling. I have groped about in the darkness for a long time, and have very nearly committed suicide, that is, let my talent perish. You discovered talent in my pictures, but instead of devoting myself solely to my brush I have dabbled in music, in literature—have dissipated my energies. I meant to write a novel, and neither you nor anybody else prevented me and told me that I am a sculptor, a classical artist. A Venus of living marble is born of my imagination. Is it then my cue to introduce psychology into my pictures, to describe manners and customs? Surely not, my art is concerned with form and beauty.

"For the novelist quite other qualities are required, and years of labour are necessary. I would spare neither time nor endeavour if I thought that my talent lay in my pen. In any case, I will keep my notes—or perhaps no!—I must not deceive myself by harbouring an uncertain hope. I cannot accomplish what I have in mind with the pen. The analysis of the complicated mechanism of human nature is contrary to my nature. My gift is to comprehend beauty, to model it in clear and lovely forms.... I shall keep those notes to remind me of what I have seen, experienced, and suffered.

"If the art of sculpture fails me I will humiliate myself, and seek out, wherever he may be, the man (his name is Mark Volokov) who first doubted the completion of my novel and will confess to him, 'You are right, right, I am only half a man!' But until that time comes, I will live and hope.

"Let us go to Rome, Rome. There dwells Art, not snobbishness and empty pastime; there is work, enjoyment, life itself. To our early meeting!"

The house was early astir to bid Raisky Godspeed. Tushin and the young Vikentevs had come, Marfinka, a marvel of beauty, amiability and shyness. Tatiana Markovna looked sad, but she pulled herself together and avoided sentiment.

"Stay with us," she said reproachfully. "You do not even know, yourself, where you are going."

"To Rome, Grandmother."

"What for? To see the Pope?"

"To be a sculptor."

"Wha-at?"

Marfinka also begged him to stay. Vera did not add her voice to the request, because she knew he would not stay; she thought sorrowfully that his manifold talents had not developed so far to give the pleasure they should do to himself and others.

"Cousin," she said, "if ever you grow weary of your existence abroad, will you come back to glance at this place where you are now at last understood and loved?"

"Certainly I will, Vera. My heart has found a real home here. Grandmother, Marfinka and you are my dear family; I shall never form new domestic ties. You will always be present with me wherever I go, but now do not seek to detain me. My imagination drives me away, and my head is whirling with ideas, but in less than a year I shall have completed a statue of you in marble."

"What about the novel?" she asked, laughing.

"When I am dead anyone who has a fancy for them may examine my papers, and will find material enough. But my immediate intention is to represent your head and shoulders in marble."

"Before the year is out you will fall in love with somebody else, and will not know which to choose as your model."

"I may fall in love, but I shall never love anyone as I do you. I will carve your statue in marble, for you always stand vividly before my eyes. That is certain," he concluded emphatically, as he caught her smiling glance.

"Certain again!" interrupted Tatiana Markovna. "I don't know what you are discussing there, but I know that when you say 'certain,' Boris, it is safe to say that nothing will come of it."

Raisky went up to Tushin, who was sitting in a corner silently watching the scene.

"I hope, Ivan Ivanovich, that what we all wish will be accomplished," he said.

"All of us, Boris Pavlovich? Do you think it will be accomplished?"

"I think so; it could hardly be otherwise. Promise to let me know wherever I am, because I wish to hold the marriage crown over Vera's head at the ceremony."

"I promise."

"And I promise to come."

Leonti took Raisky on one side, gave him a letter for Juliana Andreevna, and begged him to seek her out.

"Speak to her conscience," he said. "If she agrees to return, telegraph to me, and I will travel to Moscow to meet her."

Raisky promised, but advised him, in the meantime, to rest and to spend the winter with Tushin.

The whole party surrounded the travelling carriage. Marfinka wept copiously, and Vikentev had already provided her with no less than five handkerchiefs. When Raisky had taken his seat he looked out once more, and exchanged glances with Tatiana Markovna, with Vera and with Tushin. The common experience and suffering of the six months, which had drawn them so closely together, passed before his vision with the rapidity, the varying tone and colour, and the vagueness of a dream.

CHAPTER XXXVII

As soon as Raisky reached St. Petersburg he hurried off to find Kirilov. He felt an impulse to touch his friend to assure himself that Kirilov really stood before him, and that he had not started on the journey without him. He repeated to him his ardent confidence that his artistic future lay in sculpture.

"What new fancy is this?" asked Kirilov, frowning and plainly expressing his mistrust. "When I got your letter I thought you were mad. You have one talent already; why do you want to follow a sidetrack. Take your pencil, go to the Academy, and buy this," he said, showing him a thick book of lithographed anatomical drawings. "What do you want with sculpture? It is too late."

"I feel I have the right touch here," he said, rubbing his fingers one against the other.

"Whether you have the right touch or not, it is too late."

"Why too late? There is an ensign I know who wields the chisel with great success."

"An ensign, yes! But you, with your grey hair...." Kirilov emphasised his remarks with a vigorous shake of the head.

Raisky would wrangle with him no longer. He spent three weeks in the studio of a sculptor, and made acquaintance with the students there. At home he worked zealously; visited with the sculptor and his students the Isaac Cathedral, where he stood in admiration before the work of Vitali; and he spent many hours in the galleries of the Hermitage. Overwhelmed with enthusiasm he urged Kirilov to start at once for Italy and Rome.

He had not forgotten Leonti's commission, and sought out Juliana Andreevna in her lodgings. When he entered the corridor he heard the strains of a waltz and, he thought, the voice of Koslov's wife. He sent in his name and with it Leonti's letter. After a time the servant, with an air of embarrassment, came to tell him that Juliana Andreevna had gone with a party of friends to Zarskoe-Selo, and would travel direct from there to Moscow. Raisky did not think it necessary to mention this incident to Leonti.

His former guardian had sent him a considerable sum raised by the mortgage of his estate, and with this in hand he set out with Kirilov at the beginning of January for Dresden. He spent many hours of every day in the gallery, and paid an occasional visit to the theatre. Raisky pressed his fellow-traveller to go farther afield; he wanted to go to Holland, to England, to Paris.

"What should I do in England?" asked Kirilov. "There, all the art-treasures are in private galleries to which we have no access, and the public museums are not rich in great works of art. If you are determined to go, you must go by yourself from Holland. I will wait for you in Paris."

Raisky agreed to this proposition. He only stayed a fortnight in England, however, and was very much impressed by the mighty sea of social life. Then he hastened back to his eager study of the rich art treasures of Paris; but he could not possess his soul in the confusion and noisy merriment, in the incessant entertainments of Paris.

In the early spring the friends crossed the Alps. Even while he abandoned himself to the new impressions which nature, art, and a different race made on his mind, Raisky found that the dearest and nearest ties still connected him with Tatiana Markovna, Vera and Marfinka. When he watched the towering crests of the waves at sea or the snow-clad mountain tops his imagination brought before him his aunt's noble grey head; her eyes looked at him from the portraits of Velasquez and Gerard Dow, just as Murillo's women reminded him of Vera, and he recalled Marfinka's charming face as he looked at the masterpieces of Greuze, or even at the women of Raphael. Vera's form flitted before him on the mountain side; he saw once more before him the precipice overlooking the narrow plain of the Volga, and fought over again the despairing struggle from which he had emerged. In the flowery valleys Vera beckoned to him under another aspect, offering her hand with her affectionate smile. So his memories followed him even as he contemplated the mighty figures of Nature, Art and History as they were revealed in the mountains and the plains of Italy.

He gave himself up to these varied emotions with a passionate absorption which shook the foundations of his physical strength. In Rome he established himself in a studio which he shared with Kirilov, and spent much of his time in visiting the museums and the monuments of antiquity. Sometimes he felt he had suddenly lost his appreciation of natural beauty, and then he would shut himself up and work for days together. Another time he was absorbed in the crowded life of the city, which appeared to him as a great, crude, moving picture in which the life of bygone centuries was reflected as in a mirror.

Through all the manifestations of this rich and glowing existence he remained faithful to his own family, and he was never more than a guest on the foreign soil. In his leisure hours his thoughts were turned homewards;

he would have liked to absorb the eternal beauty of nature and art, to saturate himself with the history revealed in the monuments of Rome in order that he might take his spiritual and artistic gains back to Malinovka.

The three figures of Vera, Marfinka, and his "little mother" Tatiana Markovna, stretched out beckoning hands to him; and calling him to herself with even greater insistence than these, was another, mightier figure, the "great mother," Russia herself.

THE END

Milton Keynes UK
Ingram Content Group UK Ltd.
UKHW050034220624
444555UK00004B/385